First Episodes

For Sue and Dunc

who managed to keep their own educational
careers moving on while all this was happening

First Episodes:
Pupil Careers in the Early Years of School

Stephen R. Waterhouse

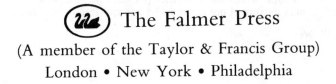 The Falmer Press

(A member of the Taylor & Francis Group)
London • New York • Philadelphia

UK   The Falmer Press, 4 John St, London WC1N 2ET
USA   The Falmer Press, Taylor & Francis Inc., 1900 Frost Road, Suite 101, Bristol, PA 19007

© Stephen R. Waterhouse 1991

First published 1991

British Library Cataloguing in Publication Data

A record of this book is kept by the British Library

**Library of Congress Cataloging-in-Publication Data
available on request**

ISBN 1-85000-976-7 (cased)
ISBN 1-85000-977-5 (pbk)

Set in 9.5/11pt Bembo
by Graphicraft Typesetters Ltd, Hong Kong

Printed in Great Britain by Burgess Science Press, Basingstoke
on paper which has a specified pH value on final paper
manufacture of not less than 7.5 and is therefore 'acid free'.

Contents

Contents

Acknowledgments

I am most grateful to all the teachers and children who made me welcome in their classrooms during the fieldwork of this investigation. The teachers were especially generous with their time in making themselves available for interview to provide continuing data on the cohort of children in this study. Special thanks are owed to the two headteachers whose support during the four years of fieldwork made the continuing investigation possible. The assurance of confidentiality and anonymity prevents them being named.

The encouragement and support of colleagues, past and present, helped to keep up the enthusiasm during a lengthy period of fieldwork.

David Hargreaves was particularly encouraging during the planning of the research. His sound advice was much appreciated. I am grateful to Mike Beveridge for help in developing classroom research strategies.

I should like to thank the following authors and publishers for permission to quote from their work:

McHugh, Peter, *Defining the Situation*. Copyright © 1968 by Bobbs-Merrill Company.

Rist, Ray C., 'Student Social Class and Teacher Expectations: The Self-Fulfilling Prophecy in Ghetto Education', *Harvard Educational Review*, **40**, 3, pp. 411–51. Copyright © 1970 by the President and Fellows of Harvard College. All rights reserved.

Rose, Arnold (Ed.) Human Behaviour and Social Processes. Copyright © 1962 by Houghton Mifflin Company. Used with permission.

Part I

Person Formulation in Early Schooling

Chapter 1

Introduction: Social Interaction in Schools and Classrooms

This book sets out to discover how the early classroom experiences of children in their initial encounters with teachers during the first weeks, months and years of their life in school lead to the emergence and maintenance of distinct identities as pupils begin their educational careers. It continues an established tradition of the exploration of social processes in schooling. Within the sociology of education it has become unquestionably recognized that the structures and processes of schooling are critical features which significantly influence the course of events for children as they pass through the school 'system'.

Sociology of education has over many years shown how the structural elements of society may influence the course of a child's school career (Halsey, Floud and Anderson, 1961; Halsey, Heath and Ridge, 1980; Douglas, 1964; Davie, Butler and Goldstein, 1972). There have been a number of studies of the processes within schools (Hargreaves, 1967; Lacey, 1970; Keddie, 1971) as social scientists have attempted to locate those significant features of the process of schooling which may account for some of the inequalities and inconsistencies in the social distribution of 'successful' school careers (Sharp and Green, 1975; Willis, 1977; Woods, 1979; Ball, 1981). Although there have been attempts to uncover some of the more significant structures and processes contributing to patterns of 'success' and 'failure' in schools, it seems that the enigmatic nature of some aspects of classroom life continues to present resistance to social scientists, researchers and educationists in their attempts to provide convincing and complete accounts of the nature and outcomes of schooling. This study was begun with a recognition of the major contributions made by social scientists in documenting the impact on schooling of certain social structures and processes. In particular, such phenomena as 'social class' at a societal level and the 'self-fulfilling prophecy' at school or classroom level had become recognized as providing powerful explanations for many of the events and outcomes in the process of schooling. While these studies offered quite convincing accounts at a generalized level of many aspects of school life and of the inequalities and inconsistencies in pupil careers within and beyond school, there was much left to explain, particularly at the micro-level, to understand how such processes may actually take effect and especially how they may continue to operate in the day-to-day dealings of classroom life as teachers and pupils interact. More especially it seemed important to know how these processes may proceed as ongoing features of school and classroom life as pupils continue to negotiate, accomplish and maintain their 'identities' over the course of their educational careers. Like Sharp and Green, (1975) this book takes an interest in 'the construction of pupil identities ... within the context of social structure in the classroom, school and the wider society'.

The construction of pupil identities is a substantial task for the sociology of education and a particularly broad and all-encompassing focus of interest for a writer. For a researcher it is a field of almost impossibly wide scope for empirical investigation involving simultaneously the examination of many 'levels' and contexts of the social world. Where, then, can the search for understanding begin? For many reasons it was decided in this case to begin with a sample of pupils as they were about to embark on their school careers and to follow them through the first few years of their school life. Perhaps the most important reason was that the school careers of children are visible phenomena and consequently would be accessible to close scrutiny by a researcher. A conscious decision was taken to begin in the empirical world rather than in the world of existing sociological and educational theory; the exploration began as an attempt to contribute to an analysis of schooling in the spirit of 'grounded theory' (Glaser and Strauss, 1968).

It has been repeatedly recognized that teachers are a powerful and significant 'variable' in the classroom (Jackson, 1968; Mortimore, 1988; Sharp and Green, 1975). As key participants in the events of classroom life their 'definition of the situation' (Hargreaves, 1972; Stebbins, 1969) is demonstrably of consequence both to the other key participants — the pupils — and also to the researcher in allowing access to the 'realities' of the social world of classroom and school. The social construction of pupil careers (Hughes, 1937) is quite obviously a process in which teachers are actively and centrally involved. Clearly, they can be seen to influence significantly both the course of events in schools and classrooms and even how these are perceived or interpreted by others. Perhaps for pupils, the major source of information about how they are really getting on, or what the possibilities and prospects are for them in school and in life, is the key figure of the teacher.

This book is not an attempt to document the varieties and patterns of pupil career within the primary school in order to theorize about these as a post hoc enterprise from the vantage point of a researcher who is external to the context. Instead, it recognizes the importance of seeing the social world of the classroom through the eyes of insiders. The constructs and meanings used in uncovering the realities necessary to understanding what is going on are those of the authentic participants to it. Indeed, following Schutz (1963), an 'adequate' social science can only be built upon these participants' accounts as the raw material for generating theories of society and social relations. This book examines closely the emergence of pupil identities as these are seen, interpreted and constructed, by their teachers who are the 'natural' participant observers of the classroom lives of children. In addition, it sets out to provide a *dynamic* account of some of the processes in the emergence of identities and careers. In recent years it has seemed to become something of a cliché in social science, and in common parlance too, to use this adjective as a highly favoured and self-promoting indicator of the worth of an issue under discussion. The use here of course is more deliberate and measured, in keeping with the interactionist tradition of social science which recognizes that events in everyday life, and the interpretations of them by participants are not to be treated as lifeless static phenomena but as having properties of continuity, progression and process. Many have argued the case for respecting the dynamic elements of social interaction in relation to any social scientific theorizing. In this book it is of vital importance to do so since a temporal dimension is clearly built in to the phenomenon being investigated. It is noticeable in the early days of school life that teachers' attempts to get to know children is indeed a very fast-moving process. Teachers process information rapidly as they attempt to get to know their new children at the beginning of a new term or school year. When teachers 'know' children there is a noticeably dynamic dimension to the way in which that knowledge may be used in constructing the social reality of their life in classrooms. It may even involve making rapid shifts across different 'time zones' as the role-identity of an individual pupil's career is constructed, interpreted and maintained. The knowledge of Other may be used in predicting childrens' actions in *future* events and in extracting properties from *present* events by linking them back in time to *past* situations or encounters which are seen to illuminate the reality of current events.

This book takes a particular interest in the construction of reality within a temporal perspective. It places 'time' at the centre of the investigation as it is derived from a longitudinal study of a cohort of children over the first four years of schooling. In doing so it allows for the possibility that the construction of reality may not be constant over an extended period of time. Because children's relationships with the same set of teachers may last for several years in early schooling, it is recognized that the categories employed by teachers to interpret them may experience a continuous process of modification and redefinition. A dynamic perspective is vital for permitting the *continuing* construction of reality to be investigated. A second dynamic perspective is included in allowing for, and focusing upon, the phenomenology of teachers' construction of episodes.[1] As teachers begin the interpretation of identities in their first encounters with children, the various fragments of these identities are pieced together as they become indicated in certain episodes of classroom life. Once an identity has emerged it may not always apply constantly. As children behave 'out-of-character' for the duration of an episode then the construction of reality can be seen to have two temporal dimensions. A construction of the child's identity with its *continuing* and ongoing properties and a short-term construction which may define the child's current actions as quite separate from this identity for a limited period of time. There will later be an attempt to understand the dynamics of this process.

As a basis for attempting to offer an account of how identities emerge as pupils proceed through school, it seems natural to make use of the theoretical tradition in social science which has made some contribution to the analysis of both the dynamics of social interaction and the processes by which individuals interpret each other as well as themselves. This tradition originated in the work of G.H. Mead (1934) and was developed by his followers as a 'theory' of symbolic interactionism (SI). It has become well exemplified and also much popularized in the accounts of educational process by such writers as Sara Delamont (1976), David Hargreaves (1972), and Peter Woods (1986).

The Construction of Other

The symbolic interactionist tradition within sociology and social psychology has long concerned itself with understanding the nature of interpersonal interaction (Blumer, 1962; Rose, 1962; Manis and Meltzer, 1972). Within this tradition is a basic assumption that the process of social interaction proceeds through the fundamental actions of interpretation and definition by participants in their construction of Self and Others. It assumes that in the course of interaction participants are engaged in interpretive work in which they attempt to make sense of each other by 'taking the role of the other' actor in the situation (Mead, 1934) and 'fitting' a constructed social performance to the perceived role of 'the Other'. In so doing they attempt to engage in, or bring about, 'joint action', the springboard of social interaction in everyday life.

If the symbolic interactionist account of everyday life has relevance for understanding schools and classrooms it can be assumed that teachers, in their everyday encounters with children, will be engaged in 'taking the role' of each pupil as an 'Other'. Everyday interaction in schools will involve an interpretive process by teachers in the social construction of pupils as 'Others' with whom they interact. It is this construction of 'Others' that prompts the present interest in providing an empirically based account of:

a)   the *nature* of Other construction
b)   the *process* by which it occurs

This book illustrates the process by which pupils as 'Others' are constructed by teachers and considers how these constructions of Others appear in the ongoing processes of social interaction within schools.

Note

1   An episode is used here to refer to constructions of reality which relate to a particular sequence or temporal unit of behaviour. Following Ryle (1949), Warr and Knapper (1968) it corresponds with the notion of an 'episodic judgement' which has 'to do with a temporary state of the person'. It might be distinguished from a 'dispositional judgement', a more enduring construction of reality, which may be said to refer to the perception of 'permanent characteristics ... which are relatively independent of a particular episode.' A dispositional judgment is a construction of reality which asserts that a perceived characteristic in a person may apply 'without limiting the situations in which he is alleged to possess it'.

Chapter 2

The Process of Formulation in Early Schooling

If this research were merely another school case study in the ethnographic tradition, there might be some doubt about the justification for presenting yet another one to the educational world — but it is not. It is a case study of children in two schools followed through the first four years of their life in school. Its modest claim might be that it provides an ethnographic complement to some of the major large-scale longitudinal investigations of the early years of school which have become established landmarks in the educational world (Douglas, 1964; Davie, Butler and Goldstein, 1972). If it were only a longitudinal study, there might be enough justification for it to be offered. This study tries to do more, however. It sets out to provide insights into the less accessible processes of how teachers interpret children at a critical time in their lives: when children begin, establish and maintain their educational careers in the early years of schooling.

The ethnographic tradition of research into schooling has come a long way in recent years. From the early work of Jackson (1968), Hargreaves (1967), and Lacey (1970), which had a major impact on establishing the tradition, there has developed a string of imitators and followers. In order to document the full range of types of educational institution and to represent the complete span of the ages and stages of schooling there will perhaps always be room for more case studies. When we have a large enough collection it will be possible to piece together a more complete and nomothetic (Woods, 1985) account of schooling.

It has often seemed that the sociology of education has neglected the study of primary schools. This, of course, is only an impression and probably not borne out by a close scrutiny of reality. After all, some of the works of greatest impact in the sociology of education (Jackson, 1968; Sharp and Green, 1975) were investigations of primary schools. These accounts of the social world of early schooling provided a backcloth, and justification, for later writers to explore and illustrate the ideas and themes which they generated. Yet in the main, the sociology of education has, as perhaps in educational planning generally, seemed to become somewhat dominated by those whose interests have settled predominantly upon the secondary sector as represented in the work of Hargreaves (1967), Keddie (1971), Lacey (1970), Willis (1977), Reynolds and Sullivan (1979), Woods (1979), Hammersley (1980), Ball (1981), Bird (1980), Burgess (1983), Evans (1985).

In the study of deviance particularly it has seemed that a 'top down' model has been too readily handed down to the study of schools, first from the study of 'nuts and sluts' in the USA (more usually derived from an analysis of the adult world), transposed to secondary schools, and finally primary schools have had to try to make sense as best they could of implications of accounts of the marijuana user, the suicide and coroner's court verdicts, the check forgers, the delinquent gang, the deviant subculture, etc. The ideas of Glaser and Strauss on the generation of grounded theory had an impact on my own approach to research because of the convincing arguments in phenomenological sociology for showing respect for the 'postulate of adequacy' (Schutz, 1963). The arguments for 'adequacy' seem to have additional force when trying to relate mainstream sociological ideas to the social world of the primary school. More usually the central ideas of mainstream sociology have been imported or imposed onto the analysis of primary schooling. Although even the more prominent primary school studies have not easily accommodated the ideas of mainstream sociology of deviance within their analysis and have seemed to treat it as a peripheral phenomenon (Sharp and Green, 1975; King, 1979) to be incorporated within a more general account of typification or social control.

The particular character of primary schools sometimes seems enigmatic to the observer. On the one hand, a primary school is quite a simple and straight-forward social setting in which the knowledge, the language, the conversation and everyday dealings are relatively accessible to the outsider (a recognized problem for the maintenance of a professional 'mystique', Geer, 1971). Yet at the same time, it is somewhat mysterious to the outsider or 'stranger' (Schutz, 1971) when those professionals working in it are impressively able to engage naturally as participants in the events of this unique and complex social world, keeping close scrutiny over what is going on within the fast-moving, open-structured, negotiated world of individualized activities for a large group of children, making sense of the diverse activities and also of the many individuals involved. The capacity shown by teachers to construct the social reality of their classroom and, in particular, to 'know' about their individual pupils within this fast-moving world both fascinated and impressed me and provided the rationale for beginning of this investigation.

Primary school researchers have continually reminded us of the peculiar nature of the flow of classroom events. Life in classrooms proceeds at such a complex and rapid pace that it is difficult for the teacher or the observer to monitor teacher and pupil behaviour accurately (Good and Brophy, 1978). Jackson (1968) too has recognized that classrooms are busy places in spite of sometimes appearing placid to the casual observer. How teachers begin to make sense of this fast-moving world and manage to sustain a construction of reality encompassing the classroom lives of twenty or thirty children simultaneously is only partially understood by researchers.

The starting point for this investigation was to leave aside questions about how accurately teachers knew their pupils. After all, in the social construction of reality, there may be many views about the 'objective facts'. Instead, it seemed to demand that more important questions be addressed. In seeking to understand the processes of schooling, it is perhaps not the 'facts' but the beliefs about the factual world which are important. 'If men (sic) define situations as real then they are real in their consequences' (Thomas, 1928). This 'definition of reality' has always been a powerful idea in social science. The 'effects' or 'consequences' in schooling, then, are likely to be as much the products of people's ideas about the real world as a consequence of its 'objective' properties. This construction of reality is not only a strong plank of the symbolic interactionist (SI) and phenomenological perspectives within sociology but has been given empirical strength by those studies which have shown the potential of the school, and especially the teacher to interpret the 'facts' of the social world somewhat idiosyncratically and produce consequences which are apparently more independent of, and less tied to, those 'facts' (Reynolds and Sullivan, 1987; Mortimore, 1988).

This investigation was first inspired by an interest in the sociology of deviance and a whim to explore some of the social processes in primary schools that connect with it. The research in the end was driven by an interest in finding out how teachers interpreted the 'facts' of their classrooms and especially the 'social facts' of their personal and interpersonal worlds. It recognizes an important strand of sociological thinking in the notion of 'career'[1] — a concept which is in some respects the sociological equivalent of the psychological notion of child 'development'. 'Career' focuses upon how individuals are seen to be, are seen to develop, or seen to change over time. Its interest is perhaps less in how individuals *are* but rather in how they *seem*. The consequences for pupils as they journey through the processes of schooling are perhaps found as much in what teachers and others see them to be like as in the objective world of what they 'really' are like. Their careers are created in consequence of 'the definition of the situation' adopted by teachers.

Until the conceptual and methodological advances of the SI and phenomenological tradition (Filmer *et al.*, 1972; Berger and Luckmann, 1971; Schutz, 1967), it was not easy to investigate these phenomena with any rigour. Investigations of classrooms were often restricted to testing out limited hypotheses in the field of self-fulfilling prophecy theories and teacher expectations. This book is less narrowly focused and looks at the routine events, activities and processes of primary classrooms in which teachers form and continue to construct interpretations of the children who pass through their hands. It focuses on the ordinary — not the eventful. Like Nash (1973), 'I was interested in observing normal children in normal lessons in a normal school'. I didn't quite know how prophetic this quotation was going to prove until later it became clear that the 'normal' was to be more than just a starting point but would remain a significant category of classroom social structure.

This book looks closely at how children are viewed by their teachers. It relies on the social psychological tradition of sociology found in SI and phenomenology. From this perspective, the individual is not viewed as an entity with concrete or fixed qualities to be ascertained and then measured, or as a collection of traits to be checklisted, but is recognized as a more complex construction emergent out of a social process (Strauss, 1959). It focuses upon the SI model of the social world founded upon the central concepts of Self and Other (Mead, 1934) in which, as social interaction proceeds, there is a process of interpretation and definition going on in which Self and Other are continually constructed and reconstructed. This constant redefinition will be discussed more fully later but for the moment it will be enough to say that this book looks closely at how teachers engage in the construction of Others (the pupils and their parents) whom they encounter in their professional lives. Like Sharp and Green (1975), it examines 'the construction of pupil identities' and relates this to 'the practice of the teacher within the context of social structure in the classroom'. In the process of constructing Other, the image of Other which is assembled might be referred to loosely as an 'identity'.

The notion of 'identity' within the social sciences has been somewhat inconsistent. The psychological tradition has often emphasized the Self construction or Ego definition as the central constituent in identity (Erikson, 1966). Within the sociological tradition too, it has been used as a Self-concept to refer to the identity presented by Self to the social world for interpretation by Others (Goffman, 1971). It has occasionally been used as an Other-concept to refer to a Self viewed as an Other by an onlooker from a standpoint outside that Self (Glaser and Strauss, 1968; Lofland, 1969). Blum and McHugh (1971) and also McCall and Simmons (1966) at times use it in making reference to the role-identity imputed to Other. Its use here will be in this sense as a concept to refer to an imputed identity of Other.

Research into the Construction of Other and the Interpretation of Role-Identity in Pupils within Educational Settings

Many writers and researchers in the social sciences have explored these interpersonal processes. It hardly needs saying that the scope or adequacy of previous research in this field did not seem convincing enough in illuminating the processes as they operate in primary classrooms. In consequence, this study was conceived to attempt a more focused analysis. Examples of research in this field will be looked at more fully but in summary the impetus for this book derived from a belief that in general there had been a failure to get close enough to an analysis of the natural, undisturbed world of classrooms, or to examine classroom life in its ongoing continuity over a long enough time-scale, or to focus on the particular interpersonal settings of primary schools, or to respect the traditions of grounded theorizing rather than importing off-the-shelf models from Grand Theory to 'explain' the phenomena of classroom life.

Some writers have neglected to explore the social processes which are directly involved in the construction of Other, Other-role or role-identities. Instead, they have preferred to look away from classrooms towards the structure of society. Klapp (1962) was one of the earliest writers in the sociological tradition to look at Other construction. He recognized the 'social type' as an ingredient in the construction process: 'Social typing provides us with a convenient précis of the one with whom we wish to deal.' Typing was seen to be an important feature of social interaction in complex societies. Social typing was an element of life in:

> a mobile society where status is insecure, identities are uncertain and people do not know one another well ... It does what a personnel file would do (Klapp, 1962).

Klapp is perhaps more concerned with explaining *why* social typing occurs in the process of Other construction by focusing on its wider 'function' in society.

Rist (1970) looked closely at classrooms providing evidence of the emergence of those groupings which create social stratification at the micro-level of schooling. The social typing which might underpin such processes is mostly hinted at, however, rather than explicitly explored. Rist recognized the value of staying long enough in classrooms to expose their fundamental processes of social differentiation:

> There is a social process in the classroom whereby out of a large group of children and an adult, unknown to one another at the beginning of the school year, there emerge patterns of behaviour, expectations of performance and a mutually accepted stratification system delineating those doing well from those doing poorly.

Sharp and Green (1975) stayed longer in the classroom and have provided one of the most powerful sociological accounts of the construction of pupil 'identities' and of life in primary schools. They too, however, preferred to 'explain' the construction of identities in terms of a macro-perspective. It seemed the grounded theorizing or the grounding in data was for them to be no more than illustrative to make sense of an off-the-shelf macro-theory of stratification apparently adopted through hypothetico-deductive theorizing. The bolted-on theory of stratification seems to offer little advance on Rist and does not sit easily on, and at times bears little relation to, the data from which it is derived.

Some writers looked more closely at classrooms but seemed reluctant to approach them with unrestricted vision, preferring instead to structure their own, and the teachers' interpretations, through elicitation techniques of bi-polar constructs and repertory grid analysis (Nash, 1973; Ball, 1978). This was first used prominently by Nash and provided an important landmark for classroom analysis. He begins by using Kelly's (1955) Personal Construct Theory but gradually the analysis takes on a more sociological focus. Nash relied on the triadic elicitation technique derived from Kelly as a useful device for acquiring data about pupils. Yet the device is undoubtedly open to the criticism of simplifying reality within the artificial constraints of bi-polar boundaries. The teachers' typifications of pupils are artificially constrained by a contrived and logically ordered bi-polar relationship. So pupils are either 'quiet' or 'noisy' (or at some position between). Such a device seems to suffer the limitations of all pre-coded or structured devices for eliciting information in restricting the natural spontaneity of typifications. The result could be a distortion of the relationship between the elicited constructs and the 'natural' categories that might be employed by participants in authentic interactional settings.

For Ball, who came later, there seemed in some respects to be little advance on the work of Nash. His use of bi-polar constructs as he recognizes himself was no more than illustrative and, accompanied by the 'Guess-who?' test, seems to constrain the authentic data derived from the 'natural' processes of 'identity' and Other construction by teachers in schools or classrooms.

For several writers, the investigation of classroom identities has revealed a social construction of reality which acknowledges major or significant sociological boundaries in the interpersonal domain. Often a single boundary marking off a dichotomous, interpersonal world has been uncovered. Keddie (1971) examines the 'academic' categorization of pupils as the basic framework within which teachers construct their generalized types. It seems pupils are constructed within a dichotomized framework with a significant interpersonal boundary operating between the 'A stream' type of pupils 'who seem to be relatively unproblematic for teachers' and the 'C stream pupils' who 'disrupt teachers' expectations and violate their norms of appropriate social, moral and intellectual behaviour'. Later in this book there is a similar dichotomized framework recognized in teachers' categorizations of pupils. This is explored later in the distinctions between 'normal' and 'abnormal' pupils. As in the present study, the broad categories adopted by Keddie's teachers extend beyond the 'academic' into the more general notions of pupil role. It seems that 'A stream' pupils are seen by teachers to be 'more like themselves at least in ways that count in school' and 'C stream pupils disrupt teachers' expectations and violate their norms of appropriate social, moral and intellectual behaviour'. In this respect, the teachers appear to be constructing pupils in terms of their continuities and discontinuities with the world of the teacher. It seems Keddie's teachers are, like those in the present study, constructing a total pupil rather than relating to Other merely in his 'academic' role.

For Leiter (1974) the interest is in the differentiation of pupils into 'mature' or 'immature' types as teachers sort out a new group of children in a kindergarten. The distinctiveness of Leiter's approach is his use of ethnomethodological analysis as a means of uncovering the interpretative processes underpinning testing and selection situations. Leiter shows how: 'Social types are used in placement of pupils but also in justifications for placement decisions' (p. 153). Leither's research was narrowly focused on one single type of context (the pupil selection or testing situation) and so perhaps cannot be regarded as having general implications across the range of contexts in which typification or person formulation occurs in schools. Leiter recognizes that the construction of pupils is indeed a micro-sociological process:

> Social types are not just theoretical abstractions; they are grounded in the practical circumstances and interests of the user.... The teacher has linked the social types and the grounds for their use to the pragmatic task of maintaining the ability groups. This means that the social types and their definitions are not criteria which transcend the social setting in which they are used. Instead, the teachers' accounts demonstrate that the social types are embedded within the setting (p. 58).

For Woods (1979), typification emerges as a research issue in the course of exploring 'the concept of division' within a study of a secondary school. He draws upon the work of Sudnow (1971) to indicate, like Keddie (1971), how typification appears to be a process which operates upon stereotypes. He recognizes the similarities between the 'routines' established by teachers for the 'daily management of hundreds of children' and those operated in hospitals for the management of patients. The use of stereotypes is seen to assist the solution of such interpersonal management problems which apparently require that interaction proceed in relation to 'constant characters as social types'. Woods sees such typification as generating processes of stereotyping: 'As long as they are normal, conforming or non-disruptive their typification is a straightforward and institutionalized matter.' Woods treats such processes of typification as little more than the mere 'mechanics' of 'identifying cues' and relating them to stereotypes'. This book considers similar issues in later exploring how the teachers' use of highly generalized notions of the 'normal' and 'abnormal' type of pupil appear to be operated within their parameters of formulation. However, even the 'mechanisms' of this process in relation to 'normal' pupils cannot be merely treated as 'straightforward' without empirical investigation. This book has attempted such an investigation and also considers the processes by which 'special cases' (Sudnow, 1971, Woods, 1979) are constructed. There is an attempt later to explore some of the processes by which pupils may be seen to move between the categories 'normal' and 'special cases' over the course of their school careers -- which again perhaps cannot be assumed to be a 'mere' matter of mechanics.

For Tomlinson (1981), the significant boundary operates in the distinction between 'normal' mainstream children and those to be excluded as 'subnormal'. Tomlinson begins her analysis from the standpoint of those children who are outsiders to the 'mainstream' system. She documents the processes by which some children are categorized as 'subnormal' and so whose school careers become directed into educational settings beyond those of 'mainstream' classrooms. In the present study, the point of entry is the social setting of the 'mainstream' classroom attempting to understand the frameworks of categorization and formulation operated within them. Tomlinson outlines the parameters of formulation surrounding those processes of the social construction of 'subnormal' pupil identities culminating in their *exclusion* from mainstream classrooms. This book, by contrast, focuses upon those parameters of formulation which apparently support the construction of 'normal' pupil identities in maintaining the ongoing *inclusion* of pupils within mainstream classrooms.

For Hargreaves (1975), it was deviance and the construction of deviant and non-deviant identities which provided the reason for a substantial process account of Other construction. In identifying a number of phases in Other construction, Hargreaves and his team provide a genuine process theory of considerable sophistication.

Perhaps the longest running theme in accounts of Other construction in classrooms can be seen in the work of Becker. His 'ideal pupil' still seems to provide an off-the-shelf and ready-made analytical category for many writers (Ball, 1981; Sharp and Green, 1975; Pollard, 1985). Yet although a useful concept, it seems frequently to be used to permit researchers to organize thier *own* perceptions as participant observers rather than those of the authentic participants — the teachers. It seems rarely to have been fully tested as an account of the major yardstick of classroom construction. Indeed, it is perhaps not the 'ideal' but the 'normal' pupil who may well be the most significant yardstick of classrooms, as this book will propose later. There are suggestions of the importance of normal pupils found in the writings of Keddie (1971), Sharp and Green (1975) Hargreaves (1975) and Woods (1979). Though their work is consistent with a view that normal pupils may be an important classroom category, it is rarely fully explored or tested.

For many writers, the ideal pupil is seen as the major social process of the classroom. A prelude to sponsorship of those pupils categorized as of greater moral worth. The idea has assumed a prominent place in the sociology of education and seemingly been adopted as part of the 'taken-for-granted' by a sociology which sees inequalities and social stratification as a major feature both of society and the processes of schooling.

All research is conducted in a context. In pursuit of a nomothetically oriented ethnography this raises doubts about the potential generalizability of findings to other contexts beyond the research setting. Many investigations have provided accounts of individual schools. How typical are their findings as accounts representative of other schools or even of those in the same sector of education? Some studies are of primary schools (Sharp and Green, 1975; King, 1979; Hartley, 1985; Pollard, 1985); some are of secondary schools (Keddie, 1971; Hargreaves, 1975; Woods, 1979; Hammersley, 1980; Ball, 1981; Burgess, 1983; Evans, 1985). Can these findings offer indications of the social processes in primary schools? Even within the general context of their own sector, some are even more highly specific in their focus. For example, in looking at decision-making in relation to pupil grouping (Leiter, 1974; Woods, 1979; Ball, 1981), pedagogical practice (Keddie, 1971; Lundgren, 1977; Evans, 1985), exclusion (Tomlinson, 1981), the construction of gender (Clarricoates, 1980; Hartley, 1980; Davies, 1984) and ethnic identities (Verma and Bagley, 1982; Wright, 1987) or in exploring the more unique social world of the staffroom (Hammersley, 1980).

The present study was initiated because it seemed that the theme of Other construction had not been pursued rigorously or consistently as an issue to be investigated in primary schools, except as a secondary concern of research investigating other things. Where researchers had shown an interest in typifications in primary schools (Sharp and Green, 1975; King, 1978; Pollard, 1985), this was more usually in terms of their content rather than their process features and with an underlying macro-perspective which restricted the social psychological focus necessary to expose the dynamics of the emergence and use of typifications in classroom life. The formulation of children by teachers required a fuller investigation, especially in terms of the authentic natural typification situations of life in schools and classrooms free from the narrower focus upon academic differentiation, deviance identification, gender and ethnic identity construction and from bi-polar construct testing.

An Emerging Research Strategy

There were choices to be made about the research strategies and processes in this investigation. What should be the focus of research into the processes of Other construction, formulation and typification? For Klapp, Sharp and Green, and implicit in Rist, the ultimate focus is its place within wider social relations and systems. Although Sharp and Green and Rist looked closely at classrooms, the process of theorizing ultimately relies less on a grounded theorizing derived from an analysis of data itself. General theory comes to the rescue before theories of classroom dynamics are fully developed. A decision was made in this study to insist upon grounded theorizing and to resist the imposition of ready-made theory. Although links are later made with established theories of deviance and social interpretations of the classroom, it can be seen that these arise more naturally from the data. The focus, then, is deliberately kept at the micro-level[2] to give an account of the social world of primary schooling. Like Keddie, Nash, Ball and Pollard it was decided to restrict the analysis to the micro-level of school and classroom — a more realistic focus perhaps for a case study encompassing two institutions. Its claims to generalizability are more modestly limited to its account of interpersonal formulation within primary schools. It avoids the contentiousness of Sharp and Green, and Rist in moving from an ideographic case study of a single school to make nomothetic claims for the nature of society. The most that can be secured in the exploration of a specific micro-world is a specimen case with a potential for illustrating and facilitating the generation of hypotheses about broader social processes. The analysis of 'small segments ... throws light on the general' (Frankenberg, 1963) but of course cannot be regarded as a *test* of a more general theory of society.

This study was set up deliberately to take account of the ongoing features of classroom and school life and not to define from the research parameters those features of time, continuity and career appearing naturally in the authentic social construction of pupil identities. Because continuity of relations between one teacher and a cohort of pupils in primary schools can be for at least a year, often for two years and may occasionally even be for three years, there was a natural justification, or perhaps even an obligation, for respecting the nature of this interpersonal world itself and planning for ongoing continuous analysis of a group of pupils as they passed through the early part of the school system and as teachers 'accomplished' and maintained a construction of these pupils over several years. Other authors have also seen the justification and even the need for longitudinal investigation.[3] In writing of the absence of ongoing studies in respect of self-fulfilling prophecy analysis, Hurn (1978) has said

> clearly we need ... evidence that is derived from longitudinal studies over a four or five year period.... We need research that ... gives a better idea of how teacher expectations are formed over time.

Although this book does not set out to test self-fulfilling prophecy theory, its investigation of the teacher construction and interpretation of classroom careers over a four-year period might allow its findings to contribute to the controversies surrounding the theories of self-fulfilling prophecy and teacher expectations. Rist (1970) has also advocated longitudinal investigation: 'A major weakness of educational studies is that they don't provide for longitudinal analysis.' It is not uncommon to find observers trying to make sense of classroom data by making a single visit to an educational setting. However, as Rist recognizes, the 'interaction process within classrooms can't be discovered within a single two or three hour observation.' Such a research tradition is still not unknown even in recent years (Galton, Simon and Croll, 1980).

In investigating the construction and ongoing interpretation of pupil identities, it was decided to avoid the restrictions, limitations and artificiality of triadic elicitation techniques (Nash, 1973; Ball, 1978) or 'Guess-who?' tests (Ball, 1978). While others had given considerable weight to written reports (Woods, 1979; Tomlinson, 1981) which at least can be seen as more naturally occurring data, they were rejected for this study as being constructed in highly condensed language intended for specific audiences and somewhat removed from the 'natural' formulation of classroom processes.

It was decided that it was important to get as close to the real or live interaction itself. For Leiter (1974), this was possible by monitoring teacher-pupil interaction and recording talk at certain occasions critical for typification. In the present study this method was not feasible since it was not possible to know in advance what the critical moments of a pupil's career were going to be. For Leiter they lasted no more than half an hour or so while a child was tested to determine pupil grouping. In a career monitoring investigation spanning four years it was clearly impossible to follow Leiter's example!

Like many previous writers (Keddie, 1971; Hargreaves, 1975; Sharp and Green, 1975; King, 1979; Woods, 1979; Hartley, 1980; Hammersley, 1984; Pollard, 1985) it was decided to concentrate on typification talk. This was to allow the data to be as naturalistic and authentic as possible — as naturalistic at least as would be allowed in the constraints of an unnatural research interview. The naturalistic strategy was pursued by allowing teachers to talk fully about their classroom events rather than constrain them into bi-polar constructs or other pre-constructed systems for categorization. The talk was to be authentic by focusing on classroom processes and events and not upon decontextualized or otherwise highly generalized accounts of life with a reference point away from the chalkface, thus to avoid 'third party talk' as recognized by Hargreaves (1977). In addition to directing talk wherever possible towards the 'live' events of classroom life, the use of audio-visual recording provided another contextualizing strategy for locating typification talk in relation to reconstructed situations close to the original experience of the reality of classroom events.

In interpreting the events of the classroom, it was seen to be important to get teachers' accounts and not to rely on those made by the researcher. The teacher's perspective was deliberately pursued and attempts to avoid some of the unacknowledged 'omniscience'[4] of Rist (1970), Ball (1981) and Pollard (1985) in claiming to know what was going on, in Hargreaves (1975) in claiming to know whether what was going on was deviant or not, in Leiter (1974) in claiming to know what processes were to be found in the ongoing structures behind the verbal utterances of teachers (without interviewing them to clarify or probe) and by Sharp and Green (1975) in claiming to recognize a nomothetic macro-level of reality beyond that which is visible in the ideographic research setting.

Previous studies in looking at typification had rarely recognized the *emergent* nature of identity construction. The study by Hargreaves (1975) is perhaps the only investigation to do so. It was rare to find a continuous study of a single cohort lasting longer than a year. The dynamics of school careers have to be acknowledged. In this case, in looking at a single cohort over four years, there is evidence of how identity cannot even be treated simplistically in terms of clear-cut sociological categories. There are examples which follow of pupils moving, at different points in their career, from 'normal' to 'deviant' and from 'deviant' to 'normal' in their imputed identities. The constancy of categories then cannot be assumed by simply ignoring their emergent properties but should be tested by the very research process itself and not overlooked by defining out of the research parameters any notion of the problematics of constancy of category over time.

For many previous studies, typifications were explored obliquely from other standpoints when the focus of enquiry was to be found elsewhere. For Sharp and Green (1975), the main focus was social control. The understanding of typification then seemed to become subordinate to this task. For Hargreaves (1975) the focus was deviance. For Nash (1973), Woods (1979), Hammersley (1980) and Ball (1981) the major interest was the process of academic categorization. For this study there was a deliberate decision to suspend preconceptions about significant categories whether academic, deviant, gender or ethnic or whether derived from bi-polar construct, Guess-Who phenomena, etc. Even to suspend judgments about whether it really was *pupil* identity itself which was the basis of Other construction. It had been recognized by others (Keddie, 1971; Sharp and Green, 1975; Woods, 1979; Berlak and Berlak, 1981) that formulations of Other can often be broader and more all-encompassing than the mere 'academic' construction of Other in relation to pupil role. This study, then, chose to avoid predefined categories either for observation, interview, or analysis. Teachers were not restricted in what aspect of Other they could choose to talk about during research interviews. Indeed, this was kept as 'open' as possible placing no restriction on what aspect of Other or even *which* Other they would talk about in reporting the events of classroom life during research interviews. The focus was simply an Other. Any delimiting of Other in terms of identifying a category, role or within whatever parameters was accomplished naturalistically by the teachers themselves.

This study is a genuine *process* analysis, respecting the continuity of classroom events, and of children's careers within the classroom and the school. The very fast-moving nature of the ongoing processes were captured from a number of sources: by teachers in their recall as participant observers, by the researcher in observing and then 'reflecting back' or 'confronting' teachers with some of the observed sequences of classroom life; or by audio-visual recording of the fast-moving events which could then be slowed down, stopped and replayed for teachers to observe. The central focus was always the authentic participants' experiences of these events when being asked to talk through an audio-visual recording; to give an account in relation to a researcher's prompting, confronting or reflecting back on classroom events; or merely in giving their own unprompted reconstruction of classroom identities and events.

In the analysis of teachers' interpretations, it is important to go beyond surface meanings. There seems to be a tendency to treat references to such categories as the 'normal' or the 'ideal' pupil in teacher talk as self-evidently valid categories representing the first order (Schutz, 1962) constructs of teachers. Then to allow such meanings to pass into a second order usage by researchers with little further testing or clarification of constructs (Sharp and Green, 1975; Woods, 1979; Ball, 1981; Pollard, 1985) in an attempt to connect with traditional off-the-shelf theory relating to the 'ideal pupil'. This study has attempted to provide for deep structure analysis (Blum and McHugh, 1971). Like Hammersley (1980) and Sharp and Green (1975) it has been seen as necessary to recognize an underlying reality which is not always acknowledged by teachers.

The *raison d'être* of this study is to generate an account of processes of typification and formulation in primary schools from a perspective of grounded theory (Glaser and Strauss, 1968). It was pursued as a deliberate strategy in all stages of the investigation to maintain a phenomenological stance to the construction of reality to refuse to limit categories of formulation in advance, or to rely on members for supplying categories, and to be reluctant to adopt readymade 'theories' from sociology. What follows is an account of the emergence of a 'theory' from the data collected in relation to two primary schools. The hypotheses and theoretical constructions about the processes of Other identification emerge from the ongoing data collection generated from continuous observation in these two schools. They cannot claim to be representative of processes in schools in general nor of primary schools in particular. However, within the context of an ethnography of schooling it may contribute to a nomothetic re-appraisal of the nature of the processes underlying the social construction of reality in educational settings.

Notes

1   The concept 'career' was first introduced by Hughes (1937) referring to 'the moving perspective in which persons orient themselves with reference to the social order'. As such it is primarily a reference to Self-perception but has also been used as an Other concept (Cicourel and Kitsuse, 1963).

2   Compare Woods (1979) and Whitty (1977). Woods has seen the focus upon micro-processes as a mistake since the construction of the social world of the classroom in teachers' consciousness cannot be regarded as independent of the wider social structure. In choosing to adopt a 'naturalistic' approach in this study, wider social structures are perhaps ignored. Yet unless these 'structures' have empirical properties to be manifested within teachers' talk, it is difficult to see how they can be empirically observed or their inferred influences upon classroom typification verified.

3   Ball (1980) has argued for more longitudinal analysis. Tomlinson (1982) also recognized the value of a longitudinal time-scale although stopped short of doing this. Perhaps when the concern is to monitor pupils' crossing of a critical educational and social boundary with personal and political consequences for the pupil leading to exclusion from mainstream schools, there is less incentive to continue monitoring beyond that boundary once it has been reached. In contrast, the focus here is upon processes of inclusion and the identification of critical boundaries *within* mainstream classrooms.

4   By 'omniscience', I mean the tendency for social scientists to substitute their own meanings and interpretations of social reality for those of the participant social actors. (Douglas, 1971, p. 5).

Chapter 3

Central Concepts in
Person Formulation

Interpersonal relations in the process of schooling have increasingly become an interest of the sociology of education. Through the growth of interactionist perspectives, a greater range of concepts and methodologies have become available for exploring the interpersonal in educative processes. The perspective offered by symbolic interactionism (SI) has generated some of the most realistic frameworks for understanding life in schools and classrooms (Good and Brophy, 1978; Delamont, 1976; Stubbs and Delamont, 1976; Woods, 1983; 1986).

The symbolic interactionist model locates Self-Other interaction as the core process within any social setting. In the field of education the analysis of Self as an element of Self-Other interaction has received much attention by writers in the course of both theory construction and research (Nias, 1984; Verma and Bagley, 1982). It does seem, however, that the second ingredient in the interaction process, the formulation of the 'Other', has received less attention. There are fewer accounts available of social processes in altercasting, role-imputation, or the perception and construction of Others. These accounts are to be found in early attempts at model construction (McCall and Simmons, 1966; Goffman, 1961) largely inspired by the theoretical framework of Mead (1932) and perhaps owing something to the established discipline of social psychology and its research tradition within the field of interpersonal perception. Beyond these studies there has been little empirical analysis of dynamic processes in Other construction. One area of the social sciences which might be considered an exception perhaps, is found in those approaches to the study of deviance having connections with the symbolic interactionist tradition which have come to be known loosely as 'labelling theory' (Schur, 1971; Rubington and Weinberg, 1987). Even here the sociological focus has apparently been more concerned with documenting the social consequences of, and societal reactions to, the construction of Others as deviant types than with exploring any antecedent or constituent processes of interpersonal construction and formulation that may perhaps precede or generate these consequences. Not only is the analysis of Other in Self-Other interaction less frequently attempted in research, but the activity of theory construction has itself perhaps been slow to advance and seems hampered by a dearth of concepts for describing, exploring, explaining or understanding the process.

The SI tradition of Mead and his followers has itself moved on only a little since the theoretical accounts of Self-Other construction by its early exponents

(Blumer, 1962; Meltzer, Petras and Reynolds, 1975; McCall and Simmons, 1966). It has been left to writers from different social scientific traditions to attempt conceptual advances. Jones and Davis (1965) from a psychological tradition and using attribution theory have made an important step forward in the analysis of the dynamics of Other construction by focusing on 'acts' and 'dispositions' — an important distinction between the enduring personal and the more fleeting episodic parameters of formulation. Schutz (1963), within a sociological tradition, following earlier writings of Weber, suggests that Others are perceived as 'ideal types'. Schutz offers a possible conceptual advance on Mead for analyzing the dynamics of interpersonal relations in suggesting that Other is interpreted through a process of type-construction involving social typing or typification. Teachers and pupils, it seems, attempt to make sense of each other in the process of altercasting by formulating the Other as a social type (Schutz, 1967). Various writers have considered the nature of these types as they operate in educational settings. For Becker (1952), these were seen as predominantly social class types. For other writers (Nash, 1973; Ball, 1978) personality traits were seen as the more prominent types used in teacher-pupil dealings. Another interest has been an exploration of the emergence and use of types by teachers in relation to the interpretation of deviance (Hargreaves, 1975) and in relation to the construction of academic careers (Woods, 1979; Ball, 1981) in secondary school settings, and in primary schools (Sharp and Green, 1975; King, 1979; Pollard, 1985). It has become an established idea within the interactionist tradition that the 'social type' is the raw material of person formulation and typification. It is seen to provide 'a convenient précis of the one with whom we wish to deal' (Klapp, 1962).

The sociology of education has begun to explore the use of social 'types' together with the related concepts of 'typification' (Hargreaves, 1977) and 'construct' (Nash, 1973) in classroom interaction. Sharp and Green, following Schutz, have recognized distinctions between different categories of typification in the consociate and the contemporary. Before attempting an exploration of person formulation, then, some clarification of concepts is necessary.

A central concept frequently used in examining person formulation is that of 'typification'. The concept has been refined in the work of Schutz to a point which allows sharper distinctions to be made within the process of formulating 'Others'.

Schutz (1973) has made a useful distinction between constructing the Other as a 'contemporary' and as a 'consociate':

> In the dimension of time there are with reference to me in my actual biographical moment 'contemporaries', with whom a mutual interplay of action and reaction can be established. . . . Among my contemporaries are some with whom I share as long as the relation lasts, not only a community of time but also of space. We shall for the sake of terminological convenience call such contemporaries 'consociates' and the relationship prevailing among them a 'face-to-face' relationship (p. 315).

Schutz here makes an apparently useful distinction between contemporary and consociate constructions of Other but without indicating in any detail the empirical properties that might distinguish them as different kinds of formulation. Although he makes a clear reference to the dimension of 'space' as a basis for distinguishing consociate from contemporary relations, such invoking of the physical world through the dimension of space seems at first an almost positivist idea, far from the phenomenological concerns of his interpretative scheme. Schutz makes the assumption that when actors share space, a qualitatively different relationship is possible. But to treat *space* as the critical criterion rather than the *quality* of the relationship itself seems to be an unwarranted assumption about the influence of the physical world upon the quality of social interaction. Exactly what constitutes 'space' is not clear and this is perhaps a particularly critical issue for the investigation of educational settings. In the context of the present exploration of teachers and pupils in primary schools, it is not clear whether a teacher could be regarded as sharing the same space as a pupil if he or she is in the same classroom, or shares the same open-plan work area (and so has the pupil within his or her field of vision), or shares the same building (and so is in the spatially defined boundaries of the 'school' campus). The notion of trans-episodic Other-role, considered later, suggests a retention of what may be a consociate typification by the teacher even when the pupil is spatially away from the scene.[1] It seems the teacher is able to make use of a consociate typification so as to predict pupil action even when he or she is not there as a consociate within the immediate setting of the pupil.

The spatial aspect of typification certainly seems a relevant aspect of the typification process on which to focus, especially in schools, and particularly in the different 'open plan' and 'closed' socio-spatial features of the two schools of this research. But so far Schutz is not particularly helpful. The absence of operational criteria for empirically differentiating the two categories of typification leads to uncertainties in their use for constructing research categories. Are contemporary typifications and consociate typifications to be regarded as qualitatively distinct, conceptually distinct, mutually exclusive categories or merely the opposite ends of a continuum? Schutz's account of consociate relations indicates that in consociate relations, each partner relies on the immediately observable features of Other, such as body, gesture, gait, facial expression, as significant manifestations of 'the Other's thoughts'. Consociates experience a 'We-relationship' in which for each partner 'the Other is grasped as a unique individuality'. Schutz, however, is not very clear in indicating what might empirically count as grasping the Other as a 'unique individuality'.

The distinction becomes clearer, however, as the character of contemporary relations is outlined:

> In all the other forms of social relationship (and even in the relation among consociates as far as the unrevealed aspects of the Other's self are concerned) the fellow man's [sic] self can merely be grasped by a 'contribution of imagination of hypothetical meaning presentation' ... that is, by forming a construct of a typical way of behaviour, a typical pattern of underlying motives, of typical attitudes of personality type, of which the Other and his [sic] conduct under scrutiny, both outside of my observational reach, are just instances or exemplars (Schutz, 1963, p. 316).

So the Other is interpreted either as a mere contemporary who is not known in his or her individuality but only as a representative of a 'type' of Other, or as a consociate in whom certain 'unrevealed aspects' of Other's Self are outside observational reach and so are constructed as mere typical categories rather than in their 'unique individuality'. Yet there is still no indication of how these categories may be applied empirically.

The categories become clearer as Schutz refers to the qualitative differences in contemporary-consociate typification:

> ... an increase in anonymity involves a decrease of fullness of content. The more anonymous the typifying construct is the more detached it is from the uniqueness of the individual fellow man [sic] involved and the fewer aspects of his [sic] personality and behaviour pattern enter the typification as being relevant for the purpose-at-hand for the sake of which the type has been constructed. If we distinguish between (subjective) personal types and (objective) course-of-action types, we may say that increasing anonymisation of the construct leads to the superseding of the former by the latter (Schutz, 1963, p. 317).

So as anonymization increases, the fewer aspects of the Other's unique personality and behaviour patterns enter the typification. It can be assumed from this statement that in contemporary relations the Other is known only or predominantly through the construction of increasingly anonymous course-of-action types. This process provides an apparent qualitative differentiation that could be empirically applied to code typifications in teacher formulation of pupils. Yet if this qualitative aspect of interpersonal relations is *central* to understanding interaction it is unclear why Schutz takes us on a 'spatial', and apparently non-phenomenological, tour before arriving at the nub of the process of typification.

Even then there are no clear operational criteria for making empirical use of the concepts. Schutz (1963, p. 324) talks of an implicit continuum of interpersonal typification from the 'low degree of anonymity' and the 'high degree of fullness in the We-relationship among consociates' to their opposites in the Thou-relationship. The continuum is plotted in Figure 3.1. An application of Figure 3.1 then might permit a coding of typifications according to their position along this continuum if it were possible to specify what indicators could be used to recognize 'high' and 'low' measures of each. It suggests a substantial arbitrariness might result in relying upon a researcher's interpretation of 'low degree of anonymity' and 'high degree of fullness'. The interpretative process becomes even more problematic as 'anonymity' and 'fullness' cannot be regarded as themselves self-evident constructs. The difficulty of defining 'anonymity' and 'fullness' adds to the problem of empirically interpreting what is to count as an instance of a high or low degree of each.[2]

Schutz then incorporates notions of 'time' and 'space' in differentiating contemporary-consociate relations. His consideration of 'space' may provide at least a theoretical lever for understanding an important dimension of the formulation process in educational settings. 'Time' too may be critical in teacher-pupil dealings. The notion of 'career' incorporates a recognition of an Other formulated with reference to a time-scale. A construction which is seen to have emergent properties as the Other is gradually revealed in the first encounters with the teacher and then reconstructed from time to time over the course of a career in school. Schutz's concept of 'contemporary' might suggest that all pupils first

Figure 3.1: Continuum of interpersonal relations

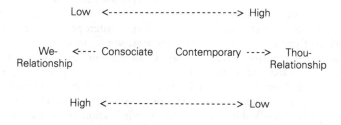

Degree of Anonymity

Low   <------------------------>   High

We-   <---- Consociate   Contemporary ---->   Thou-
Relationship   Relationship

High   <------------------------>   Low

Degree of Fullness

enter the teacher's experience as a contemporary since they are sharing objective time. In the passage of time it is likely that there will be an increasing consociality in the typification of each pupil as teachers continue to get to know them. In schools, the group character of interaction is noticeably different from the dyadic interaction perhaps implied by Schutz. Sharing both 'time' and 'space' with a large number of pupils may in some cases not easily permit contemporary constructions of even a high degree of anonymity. It might be necessary too, to recognize in schools a pre-typification phase of early formulation before teachers can separate individuals from the group.[3] In the present study it became clear that after the first few days there were some pupils who were no more than a name to the teacher. No typifications could be offered in the formulation of the pupil. Teacher was unable even to identify them. Yet such pupils are perhaps technically recognized as contemporaries according to Schutz. Perhaps at this point they are merely potential contemporaries. In schools teachers certainly have problems even of identification at first, when faced with twenty to thirty new pupils, let alone of moving towards individualized formulation of each child. Yet, at the point of pre-formulation, when apparently not known to the teacher, perhaps if pressed they would be able to offer a set of generalized contemporary typifications relating anonymously to new entrant children, of which the uni-dentifiable pupils will be regarded as typical unless they stand out to the teacher in some individualized way.

An additional issue in considering the typification process is the 'situation' as a dimension of an interpersonal relationship. It is apparent that the subjective situation is at the root of Schutz's notion of physical space. It might follow from this that teachers are likely to change perspectives in formulating pupils as they encounter them in different situations at different 'times' of the day or in relation to different 'spatial' contexts. In the same day then, perhaps pupils are experienced at one moment in time as a consociate (in spatial intimacy) and at other times are known in more anonymized constructions through contemporary typifications when they no longer share the same community of 'space' with the teacher within a classroom or teaching area. Teachers might be expected to change or modify their typification perspectives as they move from face-to-face encounters with pupils to more 'distant' relationships, perhaps continuously switching typification perspectives from one moment to the next as they each move around a classroom or teaching space. It becomes an interesting research problem to investigate how teachers accomplish the transformation between consociate and contemporary construction moment by moment. How do consociate typifications arising out of face-to-face relations become transformed into contemporary typifications and vice versa as the nature of an encounter begins to change? How do teachers maintain their own contemporary construction of pupils, derived from earlier face-to-face dealings, while observing the same pupil some distance away across a teaching space engaged in consocial relations with another teacher? Does Schutz's analysis imply that the pupil will remain a contemporary until he or she next becomes a face-to-face interactant with the teacher, until the pupil next occupies the same subjective 'space' as the teacher?

Schutz's differentiation of the concept of typification along a contemporary-consociate continuum has implications for research methodology and especially the nature of the interaction represented in a research interview. In this respect Hargreaves (1977) has identified the limitations of the interview situation as a tool for gaining access to the process of typifying in authentic consociate relations:

> Natural third party talk (such as staff gossip about pupils) and a respondents' third party talk (whether in the form of a test or an interview) both tap those aspects of the typification process by which a person conceives the other as a contemporary (p. 17).

Although a number of techniques are advocated to reduce the 'third party' feature of interview talk (such as contextualizing the talk in relation to both spatial and temporal locators) it appears that the research interview will always remain essentially a 'third party' situation in which the pupil is typified to another as a contemporary. This situation then, perhaps can never be overcome but only modified by such recommended strategies as contextualizing the talk. When a teacher is talking about a pupil to a third party, even during the playback of audio/visual data in which the teacher participated, it is possible that the pupil may be being experienced as a contemporary, rather than a consociate as in genuine classroom encounters. Although the teacher may be perceiving the pupil on video tape both visually and aurally, the situation is perhaps no longer equivalent to an authentic face-to-face relation, and certainly precipitates a situational change for the teacher adopting a role now of observer rather than of participant. So the pupil in this context may no longer be experienced in a face-to-face relation nor is he or she necessarily perceived from the same standpoint. The teacher's 'purpose-at-hand' (Schutz, 1963) is possibly now different. The purpose-at-hand is *now* perhaps to communicate, to justify, to survive an interview, or give an account to a seemingly inquisitive or critical outsider who continues to ask questions. [4]

Notes

1 The simultaneous holding of both consociate and contemporary typifications, and how these might be managed by teachers is discussed later. It will also be shown later how teachers may invoke contemporary constructions of Other even when en-

gaged in consociate relations with pupils. Drawing upon the pyschology of perception and the notions of 'figure' and 'ground' it seems possible that teachers may be able to move between consociate and contemporary constructions quite flexibly, treating each as either figure or ground.

2   There is an attempt later to explore some of the 'episodic' and 'trans-episodic' implications of the problems of defining these terms.

3   Schutz's scheme is perhaps well-suited to the one-to-one, dyadic or triadic relations of the small group encounters of everyday life. In schools, of course, the Other is at times not encountered as an individual pupil one-by-one but as a member of a group of many Others. For some pupils who do not appear in the psychological space of the teacher's construction at first, there perhaps is hardly a contemporary relationship at all but merely a pre-contemporary acknowledgment of their name on a register.

4   The situation governing the formulation of pupils is then communicated to the interviewer through a contemporary typification.

Chapter 4

Research Design

The aim of this investigation is to 'understand' the nature and course of those social processes which underpin teachers' formulation of the children they encounter as interactional 'Others' in the course of first getting to know them and in their continuing dealings with them as pupils in school and classrooms.

Objectives of the Research

There are two central concerns:

1 To understand the *nature* of teacher construction of pupils, including:
   — the framework of typification operated by teachers in interpreting pupils in schools;
   — the construction of interpersonal boundaries implicit in their formulation of pupils;
   — the facets of pupils as 'Others' typified by teachers.
2 To construct a theory of the *processes* underpinning teacher formulation of pupils including:
   — the processes by which teachers proceed to type pupils;
   — the typical sequences in which typifications of pupil are constructed over time;
   — the typical career patterns of pupil typifications;
   — the processes of emergence in typification;
   — any variations in typing to be found in different contexts of formulation (in various settings within schools, between different teachers, and between different schools).

Research Strategies

Every ... social science sets as its primary goal the greatest possible clarification of what is thought about the social world by those living in it (Schutz, 1967, p. 222).

Compared with some of the previous research in this area, this book gives a greater emphasis to understanding the processes of construction and formulation from the 'subjective' standpoint of the participants and has attempted to mini-mize the personal imputations of the researcher as an observer of classroom events. It is essential to move closer to the social world of the actors themselves. Consequently qualitative methodology has been adopted as the general research strategy (McCall and Simmons, 1969; Denzin, 1970; Lofland, 1971, 1976; Schatz-man and Strauss, 1973).

Within qualitative methodology and the sort of micro-research which limits itself to the analysis of small samples, or even single cases, the selection of the sample for study is critical. An 'atypical' sample case will threaten any generaliza-bility in research findings. As generalizability from individual cases is always a problematical enterprise it is especially important in ethnography to minimize the occurrence of atypicality.

In the present research the phenomenon under investigation is the process of person formulation. Throughout this research it was important to allow any 'natural' variations in the typification process to emerge and not to preclude the appearance of alternative forms by the selection of limited cases. For each identi-fiable feature of any social process it is important to allow opportunities to observe variations in its occurrence, including not only instances of its occurrence but also instances of its non-occurrence or absence (Lofland, 1971). The pursuit of methodological rigour should take account of well-established procedures for constructing with measured care the observational setting to be investigated. For example, following the tradition of experimental design, it is important to take account of variations in the 'dependent variable'. The variation in the nature and forms of typification, whether in terms of the distinctions between contemporary and consociate or between individualized and anonymized constructions, is perhaps unlikely to be as strong as 'occurrence/non-occurrence' but will probably be something like 'more present/less present' or 'stronger/weaker'. For this reason it was advisable to examine a variety of teachers and in at least more than one school setting, in contrast to some previous research cases where single schools seem to have been examined (Rist, 1970; Nash, 1973; Hargreaves, 1975; Woods, 1979; Hammersley, 1980; Ball, 1981; Sharp and Green, 1975). It was decided, however, that more than two schools would be unmanageable and would seriously limit opportunities for investigation in any depth.

The schools were not selected randomly but for the opportunity they pre-sented in yielding potential theoretical gain according to the notion of 'theoretical sampling' (Glaser and Strauss, 1968). In the use of theoretical sampling one exercises judgment about the phenomena under investigation and the likely 'independent variables' that may be related to the 'dependent variable'. It was hypothesized that the processes of teacher formulation of pupils (the 'dependent variable' under investigation) may perhaps be related to two 'independent variables':

1 Extra-school variables such as social differences in school populations or 'catchment areas';
2 Intra-school organizational variables such as pupil grouping practices.

It might then have been profitable to select two schools varying in the organizational 'variable' of pupil grouping. A reasonable working hypothesis to

27

adopt might be that school organization will be related to inter-school differences in pupil typification. Alternatively, the sociology of education has continually recognized that 'social class' is a major 'variable' influencing the process of schooling. Consequently, it can be hypothesized that 'social class' differences of 'catchment area' will be related to inter-school differences in the formulation of pupils. One method of providing for 'class' differences in typification would be to select a single school of mixed catchment area in which, within the same school, there would be an opportunity to discover the influence of 'social class' upon processes of formulation in the careers of children of different 'home background' in the same school. Any variations in categories or processes of typification might then prove to be related to 'perceived' or 'actual' social class differences in pupils, as was well-illustrated by Nash (1973). This would be assuming too much, however. Without first being in a position to identify all other 'variables' in the setting, it would not be possible to state with any confidence the influence of social class upon typification independent of other variables. More important, this study was not concerned with examining social class properties of typification but in analyzing the *processes* of formulation. It was regarded as more important to allow for variations in the processes of formulation themselves rather than test a general and somewhat narrow hypothesis frequently recurring within the educational literature. It was decided that to select a 'working class' and a 'middle class' school would allow for any variations across different 'social class' settings to appear and, additionally, would allow for variations across two different schools as organizational settings. Whether 'social class' produced variations was a matter which would be allowed to emerge in the course of research. The schools were selected so as to correspond with the respective categories 'working class' and 'middle class' populations without being extreme cases of their respective types. Consequently, the 'working class' school selected is in a well-established local authority housing estate some distance away from the more 'extreme' inner city catchment areas of the town. The 'middle class' school is again not an 'extreme' type but takes in a cross-section of children from lower and upper non-manual occupational groups in its recruitment. Both catchment areas have a population quite varied in the criterion of social class and so allow for some intra-class variations within schools to emerge, especially through the perception of possible socio-economic status differences in families who pass through the area during the period of the research and so influence the socio-cultural composition of the sample under investigation.

The two schools selected, in addition to being located in different 'social class' catchment areas, were different in other respects. These differences meant that in the traditional sense of representative sampling this would not provide for a simple comparison of schools varying only in the control 'variable' of 'social class'. Any variations in the dependent variable may then be attributable to these other 'variables' and not to 'social class'. However, it should be clear from the discussion so far that the purpose of this study was not to provide generalizable findings derived from highly controlled settings but simply to uncover a process and to allow for possible variations in that process to appear within the research samples and case studies by increasing the variety of settings to be investigated. Consequently, from the viewpoint of 'theoretical sampling' (Glaser and Strauss, 1968), the two selected schools had a number of advantages in that they allowed for variations in:

— social class,
— pupil grouping practices,
— organizational and pedagogical ideology.

Additionally, within the opportunities offered by the longitudinal time-scale the point of transfer from infant to junior schools, at the end of three years, provided for the investigation of a variety of 'process' variables in the movement of pupils from one form of grouping and ideology to a school of differing grouping and ideology. In each case the associated junior and infant schools had different arrangements for spatial organization and pupil grouping. In one school the pupils (at the point of transition from infant to junior) move from a 'structured' to an 'open' setting and in the other school from an 'open' to a more 'structured' social world.

In effect, although 'social class' difference in catchment area was selected as a major variable of theoretical sampling, the variation in pupil grouping provided an additional justification for the selection of the two schools. It was hypothesized that pupil formulation may be related to inter-school differences in ideologies and practices of school organization. So, in selecting a school in which 'normal' horizontal grouping had been suspended (by adopting vertical grouping) it was hypothesized that teachers may adopt different frames of reference in formulating children in a teaching group which is organized on criteria quite distinct from notions of 'normal development' in their chronological age group. It was additionally hypothesized that formulation may perhaps become increasingly problematical to teachers. In consequence, this provided an opportunity for additional theoretical gain in allowing for the investigation of processes of 'Other' construction as they operate within such a unique or 'strange' world itself, and also at its junction with ideologically and organizationally differing educational and social worlds as the pupils pass from one school setting to another. Also, since typification is not unrelated to practices of pupil differentiation, any variations in the ideologies of pupil differentiation would themselves provide additional theoretical sampling opportunities.

In qualitative analysis it is not a goal of research to acquire measured and controlled variations in 'dependent' and 'independent' variables or to acquire the systematic quantitative data sometimes seen as necessary for the search for 'causes'. The danger of doing so is clear:

> If the observer gets himself [sic] into a strongly quantitative frame of mind he [sic] is likely to have his [sic] attention drawn away from the major features of the ongoing setting itself (Lofland, 1971).

This study is focused upon the dynamics of the 'ongoing setting'.

As a consequence, the search for 'causes' has not been a primary goal of the present investigation, although this does not preclude the exploratory and tentative examining of apparent relationships as a subsidiary task. The major research goal has been the understanding of the *ongoing* processes of person formulation and typification. For this reason the longitudinal dimension of research was regarded as essential so as to allow opportunities for appropriate monitoring of the *emergence* and *maintenance* of typification careers over time. It was decided that a period of four years would be long enough for this purpose.

Summary of Methods

1 Qualitative methodology (McCall and Simmons, 1969; Denzin, 1970; Lofland, 1971; Schatzman and Strauss, 1973).
2 Theoretical sampling (Glaser and Strauss, 1968): Two infant schools selected taking account of inter-school variations.
  Major sampling 'variable': 'Social class' of pupil population.
  Subsidiary sampling 'variable': Pupil grouping (practices and ideology).
3 Sample of pupils: All pupils starting school at the beginning of the school year in year one of the research in the autumn term were treated as the research cohort (fifty-two children).
  Sample of teachers: All teachers encountering the target group of pupils throughout the four years of the study.
4 Longitudinal investigation: Four years continuous monitoring from entry to primary school.
  The longitudinal framework was to allow a continuous monitoring of the same research cohort. It provided opportunities for examining processes of formulation and typification occurring as ongoing social phenomena and so follows naturistically aspects of emergence and continuity in the construction of pupil identities over a lengthy and sustained period of their early schooling. Additionally, it also naturally incorporates their transfer between infant and junior school (hypothesized as a possible critical point in the organizational processing of typification careers) making it possible, within a theoretical sampling framework, for a process which may prove to be of some importance to fall within the scope of the study.
5 Data Collection: Participant Observation (McCall and Simmons, 1969). Depth Interviewing (Cicourel, 1964; Denzin, 1970) to collect teacher talk about pupils in the research cohort. The research proceeded by depth interviews varying from forty minutes to about two hours in length. Interviews were to provide general formulatory talk about the cohort pupils or specific and more focused talk following either a period of classroom observation by the teacher and researcher or on some occasions the video recording of a 'slice' of classroom life.

Summary of Research Procedure

The research began by monitoring the entire pupil intake in two infant schools at the start of the new school year. These two samples were the research cohort. They were followed through the first four years of primary schooling so as to identify, describe and analyze the construction of their perceived identities:

— throughout the entire phase of infant schooling;
— over the period of infant–junior transfer; and
— through the first complete year of junior schooling.

The present research was conducted by employing the methods and techniques often loosely referred to as 'participant observation'. Indeed, the whole research was conceived within the notion of 'taking the role of the other' (Mead, 1934) as a means of attempting to understand the processes of classroom life as they were experienced by teachers. The methods and techniques of the tradition of 'participant observation' have been well-documented elsewhere (McCall and Simmons, 1969; Lofland, 1971, 1976; Schatzman and Strauss, 1973; Burgess, 1982; Woods, 1986) and need not be repeated here. The account by Schatzman and Strauss is perhaps one of the most considered treatments of the approach. It is particularly illuminating in its indications of both the negotiative and the ongoing character of the role of participant observer and its continuing tensions and problems. The present research was set up by going through processes of negotiation in which the researcher explores with his contact in the field 'a mutually voluntary and negotiated entrée'. In the initial negotiations, the teachers were made aware of the longitudinal nature of the research and its concern to monitor pupils' classroom experiences, through the teacher as the 'participant observer', and their passing on of these observations to the researcher during depth interviews. (In effect then, the research was cast squarely in the 'naturalistic' mode.) Teachers were not required to artificially constrain their observations into typifications, constructs or typologies devised by the researcher. Nor were the teachers to engage in any construction of pupils for purposes imposed by the researcher but were to engage in natural 'observation', acting as informants of classroom experiences. Over the four-year period of this research, 'entrée' was inevitably an even more extended process than is usual in classroom research. Schatzman has referred to it as 'a continuous process of establishing and developing relationships'. As the children moved on from one teacher to another over the period of this research, the process of negotiating 'entrée' continued sometimes from term to term and usually from year to year.

The method of 'participant observation' practised in this research corresponds with what Schatzman has called 'limited interaction' in which the researcher's 'interventions in the flow of interaction are confined mainly to seeking clarification and the meaning of ongoing events'. This was often done at the time, when spontaneous but brief exchanges with teachers became possible as classroom events proceeded, but was pursued more rigorously in depth interviews at the end of teaching sessions. The purpose of the interviews was to get from teachers, as the authentic 'participant observer' a clarification of meanings. The researcher's role of 'participant observer' was merely as an onlooker, able to bring to the interviewing situation a sense of the preceding classroom events which could then be employed in an attempt at taking the role of teachers so as to pursue the clarification with greater sensitivity to the possible underlying meanings and processes.

As the key participant in the formulation of children and the main supplier and user of typifications, the class teacher who was assigned to each target group of pupils received most attention in interviews. Other teachers having some contact with the target groups were also interviewed from time to time to provide a more complete coverage of in-school typification careers, to allow for inter-teacher variations in typification, and to provide comparative data as pupils were formulated from different standpoints within the same school.

In each year of the research the teachers given the most attention were the teachers assigned by each school as the *class teacher* to the cohort group. Before the next academic year began, when it was known which teacher would next be assigned to the target group, preliminary interviews were conducted where this was possible to identify some of the interpretive procedures or formulatory processes practised by each teacher, in advance of their first encounters with the target group. These preliminaries made it possible to be ready to 'test hypotheses' relating to these processes from the moment of their first encounters with the target group, and permitted an exploration of any pre-encounter formulation of the pupils. This preliminary interview with the next teacher often proved difficult due to the practice in both schools of only assigning the next teacher in the last week of the preceding term, thus giving little opportunity for extensive probing. Because of the usually hectic atmosphere of end-of-term activities in schools it would have been unreasonable (and also quite impossible) to ask for more than one interview in the final week of term. The continuance of this sort of research depends so much on retaining the goodwill of the participants that in spite of the potential for theoretical gain it was judged to be inappropriate to pursue the end-of-term teacher interviews any further. Such is the reality of field research that on occasions the research process inevitably becomes methodologically constrained or compromised.

Strategies in Data Collection

The main focus of the investigation has been to identify some of the central ongoing processes found within the formulation of pupils in schools and classrooms. This has required attention being given to *two* elements of the dynamics of typification:

1   Processes of emergence over time (Longitudinal study);
2   Processes of maintenance, continuity and change within the dynamics of interpersonal relations in classroom settings (Interactional monitoring).

While the longitudinal aspect has not presented any problems (other than not always knowing in advance which teacher would next take the target pupils, thus limiting opportunities for intensive early or pre-typification investigation of future teachers) the interactional or contextual analysis of typification processes has sometimes presented problems. In order to give prominence to the *interactional dynamics* of typification careers within classroom settings several strategies have been employed.

For example, the data has been contextualized whenever possible by encouraging teachers to locate their talk in particular settings, contexts or episodes of classroom interaction rather than encouraging the elicitation of more generalized non-contextual formulation talk. Although teachers have in fact often shown a tendency to move away from the specific to generalize about pupils in the course of their formulation, nevertheless a continuing interviewing strategy was adopted to re-direct their typification talk to specific contexts of social action (so as to move some way towards gaining data that may permit some understanding of the dynamics of processes of typification naturally occurring in schools and classrooms).

Naturalistic samples of classroom life were collected by video recordings, and teachers were asked to provide a commentary on these. Teachers were

directed to talk about the pupils who appeared before them in the video recordings so as to generate Other construction while viewing the playback of video
tapes of 'live' interaction. The playbacks simulated the 'natural' observation of
pupils contextualized in authentic classroom settings and permitted some recording of the reconstruction of the teachers' 'natural' formulation of pupils in
quasi-authentic interactional classroom episodes. (Teacher formulations are inevitably less accessible to researchers directly during the authentic interactional
encounters themselves when teachers are immersed in the fast-moving events of
everyday dealings of classroom life. However, participant observation combined
with depth interviewing makes possible a reconstruction shortly after the events
by probing some elements of recently experienced classroom life).

Participant observation by the researcher of sequences of classroom life
provided a focus for the questioning of teachers about recent events or sequences
of episodes and so encouraged teachers to typify sequences of classroom life that
had only recently occurred. This technique encouraged a less generalized framework of formulation and reduced the risks of 'losing' the typifications in long-
term recall.

The focusing of typification talk upon precise moments was encouraged
rather than upon more general phases of classroom life. Through the use of a
random time sampling technique teachers were encouraged to engage in Other
construction of a, usually randomly selected, pupil at a randomly selected moment
of classroom life. The formulation thus becomes grounded or anchored in specific moments of classroom life and counterbalances the tendency otherwise to
give more generalized and trans-situational or trans-contextual typification that
can easily become a feature of interview talk. It must be recognized that this
technique is a partial move away from the naturalistic intention of the research.
It directed teachers' attention to specific pupils (which otherwise may not have
occurred) and to specific moments (which otherwise may have been ignored
in the fast-flowing stream of classroom life). However, the introduction of
this non-naturalistic method was only an *addition* to the existing data collection. It did not become the *only* data collected in the later phase of the research
and did not prevent teachers continuing to give both the generalized and the
incident-specific typification data as previously.[1] It thus is unlikely to have done
any irrecoverable damage to the 'natural' research setting.

Year One of the Research

In the first year of the research, weekly visits were made to each school for
observations of the sample pupils and to collect teacher talk in relation to the
target pupils. All teachers having contact with the pupils were interviewed so as
to collect a full range of data on in-school careers of *all* the pupils in the sample.

In School A *one* class teacher was predominantly in contact with the pupils
so weekly interviews (of about forty-five minutes in length) were conducted with
the class teacher. Additionally, there were occasional interviews with the headteacher and others, who had occasional contact with, and some knowledge of,
the cohort pupils.

In School B the research sample was spread across *three* teachers operating
across an 'open plan' setting in which the research cohort was distributed across

three separate vertical groups. At certain times of the week the sample group was brought together for teaching by a part-time teacher. All four teachers were interviewed each week (for approximately thirty to forty minutes). Occasional interviews with the headteacher were conducted to acquire additional data on the interpretation of the children's school careers.

Year Two

Participant observation and depth interviewing was continued together with occasional video work. The observational and interviewing visits to the schools were continued on a weekly basis for the first two months but were then reduced to fortnightly visits at the request of the teachers. They were finding that they had nothing new to say about the pupils. We had been talking in weekly interviews for the whole of the preceding year and the teachers were beginning to feel increasingly uneasy at having (in their opinion) nothing 'new' to say about the children. In research terms it was felt that there was likely to be no significant loss by reducing the frequency of visits and, indeed, it was thought wise to reduce the visiting so as to avoid losing the goodwill of the teachers, on whose support the research so crucially depended. In order to revive what seemed to be (by now) flagging interest on the part of the teachers and maintain the interviews as authentic talk situations, thus ensuring that they remained situations for talking about the pupils when there was something to say and formulating pupils when there was an authentic reason for doing so, it seemed appropriate to switch to fortnightly visiting. This frequency was continued throughout the year and the next two years of the study.

Analysis

Interview transcripts were analyzed for indications of the processes, constructs and typifications employed in the formulation of pupils. Although occasional written data (as in school records) were available, this was largely discounted as being highly condensed language and so not easily allowing opportunities for a clarification of meanings. In any case, it was regarded as having been constructed for a specific audience, and so its intended meaning was regarded as, in some respects, problematical for this research. However, it was sometimes used as a basis for interview talk, especially at those times of the school year when the writing and preparation of these records were naturistically a current concern of the teachers.

The formulation data given in interview, and available in transcripts, was analyzed for evidence of interpretive processes and for providing key linkages in theory construction. This analysis indicated the nature and course of the ongoing process of 'Other' formulation in the children's school careers.

Analysis of formulation processes was made from interviews with teachers reporting their observations of classroom encounters with the children. An additional source of data was provided in teachers' own commentary on the playback of video tapes of classroom life so as to get closer to, and illuminate, some of the processes in action. Teachers, in effect, provided an 'action replay' of the preceding classroom events as they attempted to talk through a video recording. Video recordings were an essential addition to compensate for the tendency otherwise to generate decontextualized and somewhat generalized data in post-interactional interviews. It was regarded as important to maintain the contextual focus of data so as to increase its authenticity as an account of a genuinely interactional formulation process. It provided an opportunity to develop a *dynamic* model of typification and person formulation embedded in ongoing episodes of classroom life.

The Emergence of an Interpretative Framework

The focus of formulation has remained open throughout this study. The area or range of typifications has not been reduced as it might have been by limiting teacher talk to any particular facet of classroom identities. Each succeeding year of the school career had to be regarded as a potentially unique experience for the pupil and it was necessary not to foreclose on any features of career at any point in the research. It was not possible to know in advance what aspects or elements of pupils' career patterns would later emerge or prove to be critical. So there was no opportunity, say in the second year, to discard certain aspects of role-identity without prejudicing the analysis of such careers in the third. Consequently, the range of teachers' typification talk was not knowingly limited by the researcher.

In a study of this kind the emergence of an interpretative framework is a process generated during the research and not something which is worked out in advance and then put to the test in an empirical setting. In the early part of the research a systematic interpretation of interviews and the generation of categories was deliberately delayed so as to avoid imposing any artificial limits on the 'natural' typification and person formulation of the teachers. Therefore no aspect of formulation was deliberately unloaded from the research and no pupil was dropped from the research sample. At the same time no systematic testing of the developing models was attempted. Instead, data collection continued (in much the same way as Hammersley, 1980, has referred to as 'trawling') not wishing to leave out anything that might turn out to be invaluable at a later stage of analysis.

Note

1   This interview technique became a methodological antidote to tendencies of generalized (i.e. trans-situational) typification and tendencies to otherwise focus upon deviant or extreme pupils rather than the 'normal' unobtrusive ones.

Chapter 5

The Parameters of Person Formulation in Classroom Life

Emerging Categories

This book follows the procedures of analysis advocated by writers and re-searchers in the interpretative tradition of sociology (Cicourel, 1964; Lofland, 1971; Glaser and Strauss, 1968) It is particularly sensitive to the ideas of Schutz (1963) recognizing that the practice of analysis is itself a problematical one. It is a point at which one is aware of the danger of easily doing damage to the data. The phenomenological tradition being followed here insists that the analysis be not only derived from, or arise out of, the data but be 'adequate' as an account of it. Critics of this empirical tradition have quite rightly exposed an apparent hypo-crisy in researchers claiming to collect samples of the world as it is seen by the participants and then, during analysis, imposing an outsider's meaning upon it (McNamara, 1980). It is hoped in the present case that at least a sensitivity to the nature of the data has resulted in a not too invalid account of the interpretative world of the teachers.

According to the tradition of this methodology (Lofland, 1971) the categor-ies and hypotheses spring from the data and are not imposed on it. This puts the researcher into a self-critical frame of mind in which one is always reluctant to interpret the data, condense and oversimplify it, and is particularly cautious when attempting to categorize it. It was not until well into the second half of the first year of data collection that any systematic attempt was made to engage in strategies for sorting data into categories. Several reasons influenced this decision.

For instance, the continued interview data collection generated more tapes than could be transcribed and so there was always a backlog of transcripts to work on. (A problem noted by other researchers in the ethnographic tradition, Hammersley, 1980). The need to continue fieldwork and transcription was itself a major inhibitor of sitting back and reflecting about the process, especially as the real action of classroom life was still happening in the two schools. There seemed to be little point in attempting to reduce to simple patterns what was recognized as a complex process which was still, in effect, actively going on for this cohort of pupils.

The perspective of phenomenology perhaps oversensitized me to the dangers of imposing structures and meanings upon the data. Therefore to delay inter-pretation as long as possible seemed a justifiable strategy — so as to avoid an early 'closure' on the analytical framework. The data was left intact as a first order account of the careers of the fifty-two pupils. After all, the data would still be there to be analyzed when appropriate. (However, it does mean that in pursuing this strategy some opportunities are lost for conducting follow-up interviews to further clarify meanings from previous interviews).

Since the goal of the research was to take account of two dynamic aspects of formulation:

1 the ongoing/developing careers of pupils,
2 the authentic interactional grounded features of typification embedded in action rather than in third party situations generated from mere interview talk,

it was assumed that there was little point in developing general categories merely to produce a generalized theory when a *contextualized* theory was looked for.

Imposing categories carries with it the assumption of common properties in patterns of conduct, or presumed equivalences between apparently similar events and processes that must always remain empirically problematical. It was also adopted as a basic premise that every context in schooling and in school careers may be a unique social setting and in consequence there was little point in doing follow-up interviews referring to past interviews (as suggested as a possible strategy above) in order to take them to a 'deeper' level since, acknowledging a sensitivity to situations, it may impose either the researcher's or the teacher's *previous* purposes from a previous situation into a *present* and possibly different one. Each situation was approached with some attention to the possibility of uniqueness and so interviewers' questions were limited to current situations and teachers' talk was directed towards the construction of present or very recent classroom encounters. Contextual relevance in the elaboration of formulatory accounts was given priority over a hasty hypothesizing or verification of a theory.

Consequently, in the first six months the interviews were predominantly limited to exploring meanings elicited in the course of the current interview itself (and therefore required little continuity of content from previous interviews). However, the practice of note-taking during interviews did allow some opportunity to explore unclear meanings that had arisen in previous interviews in advance of a full transcript being available (although, of course, as these referred to previous contexts of meaning, then the present accounts, given one or two weeks later, may have had only partial relevance to teachers' meanings in previous settings). Attempts were made to elicit talk about *all* children during interviews (rather than selecting samples for research purposes) so as to avoid imposing any artificial boundaries constructed by the researcher. It was seen as important to respect the naturalistic world of the teacher and leave undamaged the teachers' formulations in respect of whatever individuals and facets of identities appeared salient to them in the interviews. In effect, any talk about pupils was regarded as relevant during research interviews. Consequently the deliberate delaying of selectivity was actively pursued as a research strategy.

Once categories begin to be imposed in the course of analysis then they may have two distorting effects. First, by increasing the selectivity of perception of the researcher in affecting interpretation of all subsequent data. The process of verification then might proceed by building up supportive data and so a process is introduced which creates a vested interest in confirming the analytical categories and relationships which have been developed and acts against the process of rejection and refutation.[1]

Second, the collection of all subsequent data may itself be influenced so that the researcher's questions then become designed to test the categories and their presumed connections, so distorting the 'naturalistic' talk towards the direction of researcher salience and away from the authentic concerns of the teacher. This might then threaten the interactional authenticity of the formulation since it would preclude or restrict talk about teacher-experienced *situations* and about teacher concerns. The investigation of participants' perspectives and of genuine classroom encounters has been given high priority in this research in order to investigate *authentic* and *interactional* processes of formulation in schools and classrooms.

Categories of Formulation

As the process of assembling and sorting of data proceeded and the preliminary strategy of generating 'classes' and attempting 'analytic description' (Schatzman and Strauss, 1973) of the data was undertaken, it became clear that teacher talk fell into four major categories. Although there were many possible categories encompassing the range of talk generated by the research interviews it seemed to occupy four main focuses[2] in relation to the formulation of pupils. This point is where researcher interference may have a significant impact. The categories are 'invented' and so inevitably relate to the researcher's own understandings, from whatever conceptual or ideological source, yet at the same time must 'adequately' represent the phenomenal world of the teachers. This process is referred to by Schatzman and Strauss (1973) as 'discovering classes' and attempting to find 'key linkages', the beginning of the process of 'analytic description' which generated the major categories operated by teachers in their formulation of pupils, and perhaps is where the role-taking and role-making processes possible in the method of participant observation begin to influence the course of the research. The researcher's increasing immersion in the research setting creates a developing appreciation of meanings apparently operated by members. At this point a sense of teachers' 'background expectancies' (Garfinkel, 1969) in formulation was emerging both in the interview talk about pupils and in the spontaneous exchanges occurring beyond it.

The four areas of talk do not provide discrete categories but merely represent a *focus* of orientation in teachers' construction of pupils: first, in focusing upon the *personal* or *dispositional* with some degree of anonymity and suggestive of more fundamental identity construction; second, in focusing upon more *individualistic* constructs of courses of action and seemingly more situated categorization, often invoking an interpretation of a pupil in highly specific situations or categorizing the pupil in relation to an act, or typical acts, within a limited area of school life and not in itself immediately suggestive of more fundamental identity construction. Each of these two focuses is in turn related to the teachers' interpretation of processes of conformity and deviation which seem to dominate their classroom dealings.

Explorations in the Major Categories of Person Formulation

Analysis of teacher talk suggested four focuses of classroom formulation and revealed above all that 'normality' was a major organizing category in teachers' interpretation of children. This provided a major sorting device for 'discovering classes' and 'exploring key linkages' since teacher talk revealed a frequent and prominent use of constructs of 'normality' as a members' device for pupil construction. At this point, of course, in focusing on the notion of normality no claim is being made about its ultimate significance, salience, persistence, or pervasiveness as a construct. It is merely a starting point which can be empirically justified in the teachers' use of the 'normal' and the related concept of 'average' as a prominent category in Other construction. It is also an implicit concept underlying the four focuses of formulation evident in teachers' talk about pupils.

Constructs of Normality

School A

Lynne: 'a pretty average kid',
        'middle of the road-y',
        'just average. . . . [What does average mean?] Sort of a
        norm. . . . Just OK. Copes with most things.'

James: 'never does anything completely out-of-the-ordinary',
        'thoroughly average',
        'normal',
        'Mr. Average',
        'generally just OK',
        'just an ordinary little boy.'

Valerie: 'normal',
        'average',
        'nothing outstanding characterwise.'

Andy: 'a pleasant kid.'

School B

Alan: 'should be helped to feel that he's normal and that he belongs to the group and that children *do* things together.'

Sally: 'just average at anything . . . not brilliantly clever . . . not terribly poor.'

So far of course the category of 'normality' has been genuinely generated by the research and not imported from hypothetico-deductive theory. The present research had been generated from a familiarity with the field of deviance, as an area of sociological research and a particular interest in the interpretative processes relating to it. The early interest in deviance was abandoned well before setting up the research framework since a preliminary exploration of infant school life had suggested the notion of deviance as employed in traditional sociological theory did not sit easily upon the social world of primary school classrooms. As in Jackson's (1968) seminal work on the construction of classroom worlds, it was considered more appropriate here to attempt a quite open analysis of classroom life avoiding any focusing on preconceived sociological categories. The legacy of deviance research led the present researcher to recognize the problematicity of not only deviance as a sociological construct, but to a realization that *all* construct categories imported from general sociological theory had to be regarded as problematical in the micro-context of a single social setting. Therefore, instead of focusing narrowly on the doubtful construct of deviance, the research proposed to look at the *entire* issue of inter-personal Other construction or person formulation in primary schools. In any case, it had seemed that in addition to the construct problems of focusing upon the phenomena in primary schools, even the occurrence of deviance may perhaps be (at least in the traditional sociological sense) a less frequent phenomenon in infant classrooms. The operation of formal rules and concerns about their infringement seemed to be a notion often quite foreign to the seeming informality and apparent flexibility of classroom life and structure. What use, then, in framing a research activity around a phenomenon or a construct that might have to be strained to fit the social reality of early schooling and may not necessarily correspond with the 'first-order' interpretations of classroom life of the participants? It was regarded as more appropriate to recognize the legitimacy of phenomenology and attempt to do justice to the authenticity of classroom life by examining *what* interpretations of pupils are made by teachers. The phenomenon of deviance would be something that would emerge if indeed it was prominent in teachers' construction of children. Previous literature (Sharp and Green, 1975; Rist, 1970; Nash, 1973), documenting research in primary schools, had given it little coverage. It seemed coincidental, then, to find upon first serious analysis of transcripts what in traditional sociological theory is a construct closely related to the notion of deviance and social deviation — the construct of 'normality'. (However, whether such teacher constructs 'average', 'normal', 'typical' at a first order level are part of a cluster of meanings that may be directly equated with sociological constructs of 'deviance' or 'normality' has yet to be examined). The conceptual connection between deviation and normality within traditional sociology cannot in itself provide grounds for regarding the occurrence here of a cluster of constructs around the notion of 'normality' as indicative of a central and enduring concern with deviance in the teachers' construction of pupils. The use of a collection of constructs apparently related to the notion of 'normality' would also be quite consistent with what could be a more limited and situated strategy, particularly in the early encounters with pupils, for teachers to engage in a rough sorting of pupils into crude categories as a convenient way of dealing with an otherwise undifferentiated intake of new pupils (Hargreaves, 1975). This sorting and labelling might suggest the identification of some central or middle position as a crude but convenient yardstick for easy reference by teachers in the early categorization of children. As a category this 'yardstick' might then be only a preliminary sorting activity and not a continuing reference point for interpreting aspects of normality and deviation in the ongoing processes of classroom life.

Constructs of Abnormality/Deviation

School A

Adrian:	'misfit.'
Gavin:	'mum's not one of the lot round here', 'difficult to analyze.'
Michael:	'bit of an odd-man out.'
Peter:	'most other children can appreciate that but Peter doesn't understand.'
Roseanne:	'stands out as a ... I can't put my finger on what it is.'
Robert:	'a bit of an odd one on his own as well.'

School B

Susanne:	'certainly not the sort of normal parent that we have.'
Jilly:	'hadn't got the basic security that the others seemed to have.'
Alan:	'the only one who uses baby talk', 'the only one who goes home for dinners.'

Two children in the cohort have apparent 'clinical' (Cicourel and Kitsuse, 1963) or 'psychiatric' careers. This is apparent in the quasi-psychiatric language employed by the teachers and the implicit pathological model operated in their formulation of pupils:

School A	*School B*
Adrian	Jilly
'never seems quite right',	'Practically incapable of doing anything herself without getting in a panic',
'Psychologists have seen him', 'funny',	'Absolutely ... almost hysterical',
'always lazy, sleepy.'	'A very nervous child.'

In both cases 'psychiatric' constructs are present in the teachers' first order Other construction.

Interestingly for Adrian the typification is always in terms of an acquired contemporary typification. He is never experienced consocially by the teachers in psychiatric terms. His case is regarded by the teachers as situationally specific or contextually contingent: 'Outside of school his personality seems to change completely ...' This typification is apparently received from the child's parents and adopted as a formulation by the teacher.

With Jilly the teachers experience her directly in consocial relations through such 'psychiatric' constructs as 'panic' and 'hysterical'. In this case her career seems to hover between a 'clinical' and a 'deviant' category boundary.

In these first two focuses of formulation teachers' differentiation of pupils seems to rest upon a notion of 'norm' or 'average'. The data considered so far suggests teachers are using a norm-based framework for constructing identities. The apparent formulation of pupils in relation to various aspects of 'normality' suggests that for certain facets of a pupil such a norm-based procedure might be in use by the teachers.

Significantly, perhaps, the pupils who are seen to represent the 'normal' or 'average' are not talked about as much as others during the interviews. When talk is offered about such pupils, teachers seem unable to articulate at any length, even when prompted or probed. This, of course, could perhaps be a mere feature of 'third party talk' that might occur in any research interview situation, or it could indicate a difficulty of articulating Other to a third party or even a difficulty in Other construction itself for such pupils. One can only hypothesize and turn attention to such issues in later analysis. Is the lack of talk about these 'average' pupils because their 'normality', their 'average-ness', is so unremarkable or taken-for-granted it requires no further exposition? In the analysis of data from the early interviews it was noticeable that those pupils who were seen as 'average' had the shortest case records. In this research there was a deliberate strategy of not directing the interview talk so it might be assumed that the teachers' tendency to talk less about these pupils is significant and relates in some way to the teachers' own systems of relevance, either in their role as teachers or as interviewees.

Those pupils typified as deviating from the classroom world appear to present the teachers with a greater problem for understanding and so occupy much of the interview time in struggling to make meanings and engage in person formulation to communicate to a researcher as an enquirer, perhaps even indicating a struggle reminiscent of the events in teacher-pupil dealings of classroom life. This may throw some light on the difficulties frequently encountered during this research in attempting to get teachers to talk through video playbacks of classroom life. As most of the video data, like so much of classroom life, is mundane and routine, it is perhaps thought to require little exposition since it is unremarkable. In this case the very 'normality' and 'average-ness' of the typical pupil may be what makes him or her also difficult to talk about — his or her very unremarkable qualities. It might perhaps be postulated that the normal or average pupil is the very basis or fabric of the teachers' taken-for-granted world (a view also taken by Sharp and Green, 1975, Ch. 6). The teachers, thinking-as-usual about how to deal with infant pupils, embraces 'recipe knowledge' of how typical pupils are likely to behave, think and act. They are understandable as typical pupils through the generalized formulatory categories that render them explicable and the typical motivations that may be attributed to them. The 'normal', 'average' or 'typical' pupil thus apparently presents the teacher with no challenge to her or his thinking-as-usual and so requires only routine person formulation in order to relate to the pupil. The child's very typicality renders her or him manageable through her or his assumed typical motives. The deviant pupil, however, is one who presents the teacher with a classroom situation that is not easily managed within the teacher's thinking-as-usual[3] and so requires more complex person formulation in order to relate to. The process of typifying the student involves the search for an appropriate formulation of Other through a more *individualized* construction than the apparently more *anonymized* notions of 'average' pupil. A 'first order' indication of this can be seen in the case of Gavin who, as a deviant pupil, after abruptly presenting the teacher with a challenge to her thinking-as-usual is suddenly rendered understandable by getting to know he is 'an outdoor child', a more individualized formulation which leads to a consequent motivational understanding for the teacher. In the construction of this pupil the teacher has been able to move some way towards constructing a more individualized typification which now provides the key for understanding his typical actions.

Constructs of Action or Behaviour: Conformity

Classroom life is active and yet lived within constraining rules. Teachers' formulations of pupil action seemed to amount to a generalized summary of pupils' actions in typical situations. Such summary descriptions usually contained explicit or implicit motive imputations.[4] They appeared to be a motivational description of a pupil's actions or typical actions. Once again, implicit in the teachers' early formulations was a similar use of categories of normality and deviation and so the imputation of motives in respect of pupils conforming or deviating in relation to the rules of classroom life. It is difficult to be certain that a simple rule-based model of conformity and deviance is applied by teachers, especially in relation to infant children in the early part of their career. It may be that rules are not seen as applying to new entrants to the school. Or the breaking of rules may not be seen as 'deviance' in that for such children rule-breaking may be viewed as 'normal' (Pollard, 1980). Most pupils are referred to in terms of apparently normal constructs of action. The following are examples:

School A

James: 'No problem at all. James is a conscientious little worker.'
        'You set James his jobs to do and James gets on with them usually.'

School B

Sally: 'She fits in so well into ... it's like into the classroom'.
        'As if she's trying very hard just to be normal. And just sitting there as being ... a conforming member of the group'.
        'gets changed at the normal rate'.
Susanne: 'average sort of in that way, in fitting in'.

Constructs of Action or Behaviour: Deviation

Identifying those constructions which suggest deviation is not easy for researchers. Even those working on the same research project (Hargreaves *et al.*, 1975) may find it difficult to acknowledge explicit criteria by which they recognize constructs of deviation. Following a labelling position (Schur, 1971; Plummer, 1979), the analysis might begin by adopting an operational definition of deviance to be founded upon a teacher 'blowing the whistle' or engaging in some 'societal reaction'. Yet the labelling position on what is to count as deviance is rarely clarified. It is difficult to identify what would count as a teacher reaction. Is the use of a typification itself to count as a form of reaction? Is it necessary to distinguish between shrill blasts on the whistle and gentle whispers? How can a deviant construct be recognized? The analysis of such constructs is fraught with difficulties and must remain tentative. In this book the interest is only in presenting a general picture of teacher frameworks of formulation. There is no intention to investigate deviance as such. It is enough merely to recognize that certain typifications fall within the range of categorization frequently recognized as the concern of the sociology of deviance. This book relies on contextual data to identify the nature of typifications used by teachers. Any attempt to treat such typifications as necessarily corresponding with the second order constructs (Schutz, 1962) of deviance used by sociologists would always be problematical.

Two pupils in the cohort from School A are apparently seen as significantly deviant: Gavin and Peter. (Peter is lost from the sample after only a few weeks when his parents move away from the area.) They are presented here to illustrate the range and diversity found in the interpretation of pupils' actions:

Gavin: 'Our friend has bloomed',
       'being anti-school',
       'trying to make as much trouble as he can',
       'very violent, extremely so',
       'been trouble every playtime we've had',
       'generally making a nuisance of himself',
       'just doesn't conform',
       'always the last one in',
       'has a very loud voice',
       'he's the one who's kicked somebody or he's the one who's bumped. Or I believe he's scratched as well',
       'last week had difficulty controlling[5] him. I can now',
       'been trouble every playtime we've had',
       'generally making a nuisance of himself',
       'he's all right when he's in stories',
       'once you've got him on his own he's alright',
       'It's the violence that's most worrying',
       'It's disturbing',
       'We're still battering our heads against a brick wall'.

Peter: 'tends to wave cutlery about, in the air',
       'stood out there as not watching',
       'must look down and he must look here ... that type of child',
       'naughty',

> 'a bit cheeky',
> 'very rough',
> 'a breaker',
> 'he'll destroy something rather than build it',
> 'a fighter',
> 'rough and ready',
> 'a bit vicious',
> 'can be aggressive'.

Both Gavin and Peter quickly establish a reputation which results in the imputation of a deviant identity in each case. Other pupils are also seen as potentially deviant and yet rarely appear to become typed by the teacher. Their *actions* are apparently seen as deviant but the formulation of them as deviant *persons* does not appear to occur:

> Adrian: 'uses every swearword under the sun' [outside school],
> 'swears, kicks ... aggressive' [outside school],
> 'appears to be quite a normal child'.

The teacher's comments about Adrian are an interesting case in that in school he is seen as quite 'normal' and yet the typifications received by teachers (through the parent) result in his being redefined in terms of his out-of-school deviant and clinical career.[6]

> Roseanne: 'a bit shy sometimes',
> 'can be a bit naughty'.

Although deviant typifications are used tentatively she is never seen as centrally deviant. Later comes to be seen as:

> 'hasn't been particularly naughty ... is just a boisterous child',
> 'just a noisy boisterous little girl really'.

> Ellen: 'the one who still sucks her dummy'.

The Range of Constructs of Deviance in Early Transcripts

In addition to the cases from School A already referred to, the following constructs of implied deviation and imputation of deviant motives provide an indication across the whole cohort of the range of teacher concerns in the interpretation of pupil actions in the first few weeks. A richness of individualized formulation that seems missing in the talk about normal pupils.

School A	*School B*
'can be a little devil'	'very loud'
'gets quite bumptious'	'extremely noisy'

'going through a silly phase'
'can be very shy'
'a bit of a tale-teller'
'fussy'
'noisy'
'flighty'
'more giggly'
'obstreperous'
'out of spite'
'pushy'
'a bit of a bind'
'flibberty gibbet'
'a bit arrogant'
'bit of a bully'
'a chatterbox'

'a bit of a nuisance'
'difficult to discipline'
'can't sit still'
'always where they shouldn't be'
'they'll never be told'
'shouting to children on other tables'
'still very boisterous'
'not yet learned to wait her turn'
'always scratching other children'
'quite mischievous'
'so rough with the boys as well'
'always kicking and punching'
'has to thump and hit'
'an irritating child'
'constantly tells lies'
'stubborn'
'sheer awkwardness'
'tears and sulks'
'cheeky grin'
'chatterbox'

Boundaries in Classroom Life

These constructs and typifications suggest the implicit boundaries operating in teachers' formulation of the classroom actions of children in this cohort, as though teachers' concerns are focused upon the categorization of pupil actions as conforming or deviating in relation to the rules of classroom life. However, some constructions seem to be of typical *actions* and not perhaps of *persons* as centrally normal or deviant identities. The distinction between the construction of actions and identities is an important one to recognize, particularly in exploring processes of labelling. While some constructions are quite general, conveying a categorization of the whole person, some are highly specific and seem to carry no implications for identity. It seems evident from the context that certain constructs are to be treated as potentially deviant categorizations but it is always necessary to acknowledge that such typifications might be seen to apply to 'normal' children in some situations and that for these children the act of deviation or of rule-breaking might not reflect serious deviance if seen in the context of their inexperience of schooling.[7]

The first phase of data analysis required the generation of categories. Using the strategy of what Schatzman and Strauss (1973) have called 'discovering classes' and 'analytic description' it became clear that teachers' formulation of pupils was centred upon a notion of the 'normal'. A teacher's talk about pupils hinged upon constructs of normality and deviation. It was clear that a dominant classroom process was the interpretation of children in relation to recognized processes of normality-deviation. In making constructions of both normality and deviation, teachers recognized distinctions in the categorization of persons (a generalized and holistic summary of the pupil) and the categorization of actions or typical actions (a formulation of the pupil as actor either for the duration of a particular episode only, or as an actor in typical situations of a specified kind).

Notes

1 Negative case analysis was practised during the category formation so as to reduce this skewing of data. In following through the two deviant and four normal cases later there is an additional opportunity to check the appropriateness of the frameworks from episode to episode in sampling four years of the school careers of these critical cases.

2 These categories are merely focuses rather than discrete categories. They contain three polarities in formulation: conformity-deviation; anonymization-individualization; act-disposition.

3 (Schutz, 1971). A teacher's 'thinking-as-usual' presumably will be highly specific in nature, perhaps even operating as thinking-as-usual-for-first-year-infant pupils.

4 Usually these 'motive imputations' were what Schutz has called 'in-order-to motives'.

5 This use of 'control' as a first order construct lends some support to the interpretation of these typifications as instances of deviance. The conceptual relationship at a second order level between deviance and social control suggests that social processes of deviation are an implicit element in teachers' construction of pupils.

6 Parent is here a typification carrier who imports the idea of deviant identity from the social world outside the school.

7 A more enduring formulation would then in effect be operating as a higher order and ongoing process beyond the more limited action of rule-based formulation (which would be episodic or momentary).

Chapter 6

Normal Pupils: A Key Linkage in the Social World of Primary Classrooms

Developing Interpretive Frameworks

In the social world of the two primary schools it became apparent that the teachers were relying on the 'normal' or 'average' pupils, and the 'deviant' or 'extreme' pupils, as the significant reference points in the construction of 'group life'.[1] It would have been inappropriate early in the research to regard such boundary markers as anything more than an indication of the strategies employed in the first exploratory formulation by teachers when encountering a quite large group of unknown pupils (Hargreaves, 1975). Gradually, it became clear that such processes were continuing to operate much later. In constructing a tentative framework of formulation arising from the emerging data, the tendency for teachers to rely on normal and average pupils needed to be recognized.

Previous researchers have attempted to identify the basis of teacher typification of pupils (Becker, 1952; Nash, 1973; Hargreaves, 1975; Sharp and Green, 1975) by constructing a model to account for the process. Although each model postulated differences in the facets, traits, characteristics and dimensions of pupils incorporated in the process of Other construction, all adopted a similar perspective in that they were *single* models of typification. In looking more closely at the two case study schools, it seems that previous researchers may have been too ready to generalize the process of formulation in assuming that *one* model may apply in all situations.

This study at first revealed the apparent use of *several* models by teachers in formulating children in primary schools. A 'normal' model is adopted as the foundation of the formulation process in conjunction with two 'abnormal' models. The three models are outlined below. All three, however, are centred upon what is seen to be the core social process of classroom life: conformity–deviation. In the course of Self–Other interaction, teacher engages in a process of constructing pupil as Other in relation to processes of normality and deviation. The basic process of classroom formulation proceeds by invoking norms against which some comparison or matching of Other is made. A notion of the 'normal' pupil appears to be used as a bench mark and continuing unit of comparison in primary school classrooms.

Basic Model: Normal Model (Normal Distribution)

The basic model of Other construction is founded upon a process of 'normal matching' in which children are formulated by comparison with a teacher's notion of the 'normal' pupil. This is quite different from Becker's claim that teachers engage in 'ideal matching' in which the matching of each child is against a notion of the 'ideal pupil'. Formulation in the two case study schools suggests a process of matching against the normal. Perhaps a more attainable yardstick than an 'ideal' which might otherwise appear as the ultimate limit within a hypothetical distribution of pupils.

The basic model suggests that teachers in primary schools construct pupil groupings in a distribution not unlike that of a frequency distribution, statistical distribution or Gaussian curve. In effect it is a trichotomous model. A pupil is not matched against the 'ideal', as in Becker, but against an 'average' or 'norm'. The significant reference points in the trichotomous distribution appear to be 'average', 'above average', and 'below average'. The trichotomous distribution appears to be used in the early phases of typing for *all* pupils, and for the majority of pupils throughout their 'normal' typification career so long as they are perceived to remain as individuals who fall within the parameters of the 'normal' distribution of pupils[2].

It seems that teachers begin formulation with a basic norm matching model and then, if the pupil falls outside the perceived 'normal' parameters, there is apparently a shift to a dichotomous model. Those outside the 'normal' category are consequently beyond the parameters marking the limits of 'normality' and so are viewed as being in an 'abnormal' or 'deviant' category requiring additional models to be invoked.

For certain 'abnormal' typifications in the formulation of pupils falling entirely outside the 'normal' parameters, the model switches to one of two 'abnormal' models within a dichotomized framework.

'Abnormal' Model 1: Pathological (Discrete Dichotomy)

For pathological typifications pupils are typified as either normal or abnormal in a dichotomous framework. In the construction of all identities beyond the normal, including 'deviant' and 'clinical', the formulation is in relation to a framework of distinct or discrete categories. Children can be seen to be either normal or beyond the normal parameters. Other is either on one side of the boundary or the other, either normal or in one of the abnormal categories such as 'deviant' or 'clinical' (see Figure 6.1).

'Abnormal' Model 2: Divergent (Continuous/Variable Dichotomy)

Another 'abnormal' model is a more open framework (see Figure 6.2). It does not recognize such discrete boundary categories. This model is similar to the

Figure 6.1: 'Abnormal' model 1: Pathological (discrete dichotomy)

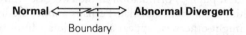

Figure 6.2: Abnormal model 2: Divergent (continuous/variable dichotomy)

pathological one above in that pupils are formulated along a dichotomized scale but the dichotomy is a continuum rather than representing the two distinct all-or-nothing categories of Model 1. The two sides of the dichotomy are less clearly differentiable than in the pathological model. For example:

> Alan: Most children sit on a table in a group. But he'll go away over there from everybody to do his work.

Here the pupil is formulated in relation to the majority of children. The boundary between his apparent divergence from the 'normal' range of pupil action is not sharply defined as a discrete demarcation as it seems that the 'norm' itself is only tentatively expressible since only 'most' children follow it. There appears to be an absence of clarity in stateable norms but nevertheless this pupil's conduct is seen to be diverging from the 'norm' identifiable in what 'most' children do. Here the pupil Alan is typified in relation to the majority of children. He is presented as a member of a minority outside the 'normal' range.

Norm-Matching as a Basic classroom Process

It is important to question whether the teachers' continuing use of 'average' and 'normal' during research interviews really is an indication of their use of a 'norm' as a standard of judgment or as a significant referent in the formulation of children in primary schools. It is possible in some cases that formulating children in relation to such terms as 'average' could be a mere 'cop out' (a term used by one of the teachers during an interview on this question) — a linguistic device perhaps to avoid committing themselves in the formulation of a pupil when they are genuinely unsure about the identity of a child, or even to cover up their lack of knowledge about a particular pupil. In previous research (Hargreaves, 1975) the use of 'normal' and 'average' has been identified as an early feature of typification used: 'in a particular sense to indicate that the pupil concerned did not as yet "stand out" in any striking way either positively or negatively'.

This usage may correspond with that of the teachers in the present sample. Indeed, in the early phase of a teacher-pupil relation perhaps this definition is what is meant by the terms. But when the ascription of 'average' or 'normal' persists beyond this early typification it may mean that teachers are in no position (in an interview situation at least) to say anything about a pupil other than in the generalized category of an anonymized type. Such a pupil is seen either as one whose unique characteristics are still unknown or if known is regarded as having no remarkable characteristics but rather as falling within the broad parameters of a general 'normal' type. Such pupils are typified with a high degree of anonymity. However, while the teachers may find it difficult to talk about such a pupil they may well know how to deal with him as one who shows all the usual qualities of a typical or 'average' pupil and so is manageable, in teacher-pupil relations, according to their recipe knowledge for handling such highly anonymous 'average' types of pupils (in the manner regarded by Schutz as 'course-of-action' types perhaps).

This situation suggests a possible methodological problem of relating *real* situations of interactional typification with the less authentic third party interview typification situation. Is the use of such constructs as 'average' and 'normal' perhaps a mere feature of interview talk?

Supplementary Matching Processes

The 'norm-matching' model is the core process of formulation in primary school classrooms. The construction of children proceeds in relation to the 'norm' and within the parameters of the 'normal' as they are constructed by the teacher. Beyond norm-matching in the construction of Other there is a process permitting more precision in the generation of more individualized typifications. Further formulation refinement is made possible by supplementary matching processes. In this way matching proceeds by incorporating certain additional processes in the formulation of both normal and deviant pupils.

Specific Other Matching

One feature of teacher talk which has frequently been identified in this research is the tendency to match children with specific Others as referents. For example: 'She's quite ... she isn't as exuberant as they are'. This tendency perhaps indicates that norm-matching or any single model will inevitably be too simplistic to reflect accurately the *dynamic* nature of teacher typification, or even perhaps to permit the finer differentiation of pupils *within* either the normal or the abnormal categories. Other-matching is apparently a teacher's method for formulating Other more precisely once the major differentiation in deciding between normal or abnormal identity has been accomplished. Teachers frequently employ specific Other-matching. The matching of pupils with specific others can be seen in the following examples:

> I'd said to Ellen ... that she was zooming along. You know. Just to ...
> Perhaps the ones at this end I would say a little bit more to just get them going a bit more.

Here in the interpersonal dynamics of the classroom, the teacher decides her action in the light of her categorization of a particular set of Others: 'the ones at this end' compared with Ellen.

Again Other-matching precision in formulation for generating highly specific and appropriate strategies to allow the teacher to decide how to organize an individual pupil in the classroom:

> People like Ellen will just scribble gaily off and get over there. So I quite often say something else to do … Cause … the ones on that table will spend a bit more time and add a bit more. But Ellen's obviously just copying. So she zooms off a copy and she's finished long before anybody else. So I tend to give her something else to do … to keep her going.

From this example it seems that in order to understand the dynamics of typing it needs to be recognized (as perhaps teachers also find) that the 'norm-matching' model is too general. To deal with specific situations and specific pupils perhaps the matching model has to be refined. In the interview situation, when a pupil will be experienced with a high degree of anonymity as a mere contemporary (who may be matched with general norms) a generalized model is perhaps enough. The pupil will be reduced to anonymous generalized typifications. In the authentic interaction of classroom life, however, norm-matching is possibly too general a process. Perhaps specific Other-matching, according to the particular purpose-at-hand of the teacher, will then be more appropriate. The teacher here switches from a perspective of the class norm to a more specific concern for 'the ones on that table' or, as in the previous example, 'the ones at this end'.

Of course, specific Other-matching appears frequently in non-contextual talk too and so is obviously relevant to the purpose-at-hand of the teachers during interview sessions: 'She's a similar child in a way, I think, to Kathy'.

> … and in a way there's perhaps a similarity between Jilly and Alan in wondering how far you can go with them and what sort of things.… How in fact … it's going to be possible to establish this relationship with them that will make for exchange of talk and ideas and so on … Although it's possible to say Jilly is listening because she will look at you and … she realizes that something's being said to her. Alan doesn't. He will turn his face away …

Here two 'abnormal' pupils were matched. This suggests that abnormal Other-matching can also be used to formulate abnormal pupils.

Previous research (Hargreaves, 1975) has also indicated that teachers compare pupils with specific others:

> The first two or three pupils to emerge as individuals serve as a kind of yardstick against which an emergent individual can be matched: a pupil is described as being 'similar to' or 'the opposite of' or 'not at all like' those pupils who have already acquired a degree of individuality (p. 147).

In the two case study schools such matching is also seen but it continues beyond the early phase of typification and so appears not to be just a temporary method of matching. Teachers use certain pupils as comparisons or referents long after the initial phase of typification. It may, of course, depend entirely on the context of formulation as in some cases comparison appears to be used to refer to pupils mentioned earlier in the interview. In this respect the research interview is much like everyday conversation and so may also perhaps be just like staffroom talk which itself is a significant arena of typification (Hammersley, 1984).

Family or Sibling Matching

A particular form of Other-matching is that of the family and sibling group. This method has also been identified by Hargreaves (1975, p. 160) as the 'sibling phenomenon':

> If a pupil has an older sibling, then the older brother (or sister) acts as a yardstick or model against which the new pupil can be matched.

The family and sibling group is also available for providing insight into the typical motives that might be imputed to pupils. Ellen, for example, is interpreted first through the 'abnormal pathological' model, and then is further motivationally scrutinized (perhaps for finer formulation) by locating her within the context of her family and sibling group:

> Seems to me to be growing much more self-reliant. And I would say is learning a great deal about how to live without an overpowering sister ... She has always licked her sister's shoes and done everything her sister has demanded of her.... Ellen's sister is a very forceful person. She's very forceful indeed. Very domineering. Very dominating.

In this case the sibling matching also provides some motivational typification of the inferred sibling relationship. Teachers appear to proceed on the assumption that sibling pupils will be similar. It seems that teachers operate family typing as a form of anonymous contemporary typification, with all members of a family group being typified within the framework of the anonymous type, perhaps as a family 'course-of-action' type.

Typification Exchange

Another form of matching in the present research is found within the process of interpersonal exchange. It takes the form of interpersonal typification matching, which involves the comparison of categories and constructions offered by other typification 'carriers'. In this example, the negotiation of an identity from different sources proceeds with the pupil's mother as a typification 'carrier' providing the teacher with additional, though competing, knowledge with which to continue her construction of the pupil:

> What mother says about her doesn't correlate at all with what I think about the child's performance.

The next example suggests it can be another teacher rather than a parent as 'typification carrier'. After anticipating a possible deviant identity in a pupil some indications are recognised: 'That's the first sign' ... This comment was said by a teacher who has apparently begun to *scan* this pupil's behaviour through a tentative 'pathological' model after having been told of his previous 'abnormal' career. When teachers discover a pupil has earlier had an abnormal pathological career it presents them with alternative models for use in scanning. Consequently, they are able to scan either with a norm-matching or an abnormal pathological model, but presumably the latter takes precedence. In the present case, until this point in the pupil's career, his formulation had proceeded through a 'normal' phase. The teacher had taken note of him and was apparently operating a norm-matching model. In scanning his behaviour within the ongoing events of class-room life it seems that as everything appeared to be 'normal' in his case then there was nothing striking to be noticed. However, the researcher himself was perhaps in this case a typification 'prompt' rather than 'carrier' since in the course of questioning the teacher probingly about this pupil she may have been triggered into a reformulation. It is possible that the implicit message of the interview may have been received by the teacher in this case as 'Does the normal model really fit his case?' Or: 'Have you tried abnormal pathological model with him?'

It has to be recognized that some occurrences of norm-matching may perhaps be a product of the interviewing technique used in this research. Instead of directing the interviews according to researcher concerns, teachers have been encouraged to talk about the pupils according to their *own* frame of reference. Sometimes the questions explicitly (and perhaps understood implicitly throughout) were in a form such as:

Anything worth commenting on?
Tell me how each of them has been.
Keep me up to date with pupil X or Y (when chosen randomly from the sample for interview purposes).
Can you give examples?
Any incidents you can recall?

Such interviews would perhaps encourage a form of norm-matching in their formulatory talk since only those occasions or those pupils who deviated from a notional norm would perhaps be seen to be worth commenting on as being out of the ordinary. Nevertheless, the quite overt and continued naturalistic use of norm-matching by the teachers unprompted suggests it does form part of their method of person formulation, quite independently of its prompting by some of the strategies of the research interviews themselves. For example:

I know her but there's nothing quite outstanding about her. She's quite normal. In a way. Not like Alan ... his moods ...

This pupil is typified by reference to an abnormal pupil. By contrast, she is seen to be normal and is clearly not like Alan against whom she is spontaneously compared and who is recognized to be abnormal. All that the teacher could say here is that she is normal. It does not get elaborated further. She says what the pupil is like by saying she is *not* like an abnormal type of pupil. Then the teacher invokes an implicit 'normal' model:

> But Sally's always quite bright and ready to work and doesn't really object. She'll do it if she's told to.

And so by apparent implication she fits the normal type.

A Framework of Formulation:
Ongoing Processes of Typification in Primary Classrooms

Having indicated a number of models for understanding typification, it is necessary next to consider how the models, as somewhat static constructions, may relate to the ongoing or *dynamic* processes of Other construction. How do teachers employ the models in the ebb and flow of classroom life? Do teachers proceed as though persons and events can be regarded as 'normal' until something signals that the frame of reference should after all be 'abnormal'? Are teachers processing the interpersonal information through a filter of the 'normal' as they look around the classroom, so that when something 'abnormal' occurs it becomes instantly noticeable? If teachers do indeed view the classroom through a haze of normalcy, it would account for the sparsity of Other formulation often found in teachers' talk during action replays of classroom life in video playback sessions. If, during video playback, teachers were operating a 'normal filter' and situations on the screen registered 'normal' then no explicit formulation would be occurring and no typifications would be offered, as the teachers' 'scanning mechanism' would presumably register 'everything normal'.

Normal Scanning

The suggestion of a normal scanning 'mechanism' can be seen in the following teacher-teacher talk during one of the interview sessions. Teacher 2 (T2) interrupts the talk by asking Teacher 1 (T1) about an 'abnormal' pupil transferred from Teacher 2's group and who Teacher 1 has had in her class for a couple of weeks. (In fact, the pupil is Adrian who was earlier referred to as an 'abnormal pathological' type and who temporarily moves out of the main sample):

> T1: I haven't really given it a great deal of time, [T2], because I've been getting to know my new ones. And to me they're first priority. I know he's there but I haven't taken any time to study him at all.
>
> T2: It was the same last time ... he didn't stick out at all.

As teachers appear to operate a 'norm' or 'normal' scanning mechanism it might then be asked how they arrive at their awareness of the 'normal'? It has already been noted how Schutz and Luckmann suggest constructions arise from their prior experience and their stock of knowledge. This would perhaps be acquired in professional training in professional experience and in their contact with the staffroom culture of 'what everyone knows'. In this way it is possible that 'social structure', both within school and beyond (in notions of wider 'society'), is incorporated with teachers' typification processes perhaps in a manner suggested by Sharp and Green. It would be possible then to 'explore' this relationship as prevailing definitions of the 'normal' impinge upon teacher consciousness. It is perhaps unlikely that teachers would acquire anything more than a highly generalized notion of 'normality' from their 'professional socialization'. The problems for teachers in applying generalized frameworks to particular settings has been referred to by Mardle and Walker (1980) and Edwards (1980). They refer to the problematic relationship in making comparisons from a generalized to a particular frame of reference. The problem is apparently in deciding upon the appropriateness of comparisons between generalized notions of 'situations of that kind' and their connections or continuities with 'the features of any present encounter'.

Situated Norms

Teachers seem to recognize that norms are themselves contextual and specific to particular settings: 'Certainly it isn't normal for children in this school ...'

In another example a new teacher to School A sees her 'abnormal' pupil differently from the standpoint of norms relating to her previous school:

Interviewer: (Leading question)[3] But I wondered if actually had he been at your old school would he have seemed as naughty?

Teacher: No. No. He would've been a minor problem because our children were aggressive in a lot of ways to one another.

The teacher indicates a relative view of deviance. It seems that this pupil's behaviour would not have been seen to be so deviant in her previous school (a process of inter-school norm-matching).

The same teacher six months later is still operating her inter-school norm comparisons in talking about the same 'abnormal' pupil:

He's very changeable ... Well. I think he's unusual for a school like this in any case ... These children don't know how to deal with Gavin at all....

The teacher is claiming the process is a complex interpersonal one. The pupil is not merely 'abnormal' in context but in his interpersonal dealings in the classroom the 'societal reactions' of other pupils makes him 'appear' abnormal.

The role of staffroom talk in shaping teachers' awareness of a norm is revealed in the following:

I've just found out that the lot I had last time were far below par for this school you know. Not half as good as they're 'used to'! Quite! But I didn't realize 'cause I'd always taught in rough schools. They were all pretty good, you know. You forget what the norm is after a while!

You're either with schools with loads of children who're below or above
or ... you know. There's no such thing is there?

The teacher's use of the term 'normal' and the introduction of the idea into the
talk is entirely spontaneous and so perhaps of some significance. (The use of
naturalistic methodology and the attempt at phenomenological sensitivity required the deliberate avoidance of any researcher imposed meanings being imported into the situation.)

The teacher typifies the whole class in relation to her recognition of an
inter-subjective notional norm for the school. She also overtly acknowledges at a
first order level an interest in 'norms'; it is part of her spontaneous use of
constructs, though of course its equivalence to the use of 'norm' in the present
research or with established sociological usages cannot simply be taken for
granted. It also indicates the difficulties for new (and younger) teachers in
learning to identify norms and take them over into their 'stock of knowledge'
(Schutz, 1963) in spite of their likely exposure to implicit norms as generalized
notions during their 'professional socialization'. It is likely that school experience
and exposure to staffroom culture during training, together with the prominent
literature (Douglas, 1964; Plowden Report, 1967; Goodacre, 1968; Craft, 1980;
MacBeath, Mearns and Smith, 1986) will foster this process.[4]

Teachers also recognize that school norms themselves change:

T1: But on the whole the children that we do have at this school are
    well-balanced and polite. They have good manners and say please
    and thank you ...
T2: Yes ... Yes ... But they're not prepared to listen. They're far
    more like Gavin, aren't they, than they used to be.

Here the process is reversed as deviant pupil matching. The deviant pupil is used
as the referent against which the school is matched!

In addition to norms for schools it seems teachers recognize norms in
relation to family life and, in particular, for parental roles. There are norms
relating to typical parents:

She isn't ... she's unusual ... She's certainly not ... the sort of usual
parent that we have.

Family norms relate to siblings too. We have already referred to sibling matching. An example of sibling matching after a preview meeting (to allow teachers
and pupils to meet each other before the start of the school year) indicates the
strength of sibling matching even in the pupil's absence and after only a brief
contact with her(!):

These are the Robinson children and ... I will be getting Deborah back.
And Susanne was in the nursery. Now Susanne is old enough to come
over. So I will be having Susanne.... Well I didn't meet her yesterday
but I have seen her before but not had a great deal of contact with her.
Only her sister. So I've an idea about her.

The process of sibling matching starts ('I've an idea about her') with the teacher apparently proceeding on the assumption that an older sibling who is already known to the teacher can be adopted as a base for the formulation of younger, and as yet unknown, siblings (as a working hypothesis) in spite of the fact that the teacher 'didn't meet her yesterday' and so far has 'not had a great deal of contact' with the new pupil. It may be that such sibling matching is only provisional as the starting point for person formulation. However, the ease with which such early 'speculative' typification might move into type 'stabilization' (Hargreaves, 1975) indicates the potentially powerful influence sibling-matching may have upon the emergence of pupil careers.

Norm-Matching

Examples of the norm-matching process can be seen in the following illustrations of teachers typifying pupils:

> But compared to the other children the other people in the group ... in Susanne's group I think she is ... Yes ... Average sort of in that way, in fitting in.

Here, even in School B where the child-centred ideology might perhaps be expected to discourage norm-matching, the teacher appears to search around for an appropriate construction but then settles on 'average sort of' as a rough approximation to what she means.

> When you're talking to her she's on a level with you. You know. She's super. Where the others tend to treat work as work she doesn't. You know. She comes and has a chat with you.

Here the teacher talks about Susanne by matching her with 'the others' in her class.

Another norm-matching situation relating to a previously 'abnormal (pathological')' pupil suggests once again the operation of a norm scanning 'mechanism' registering (apparently) 'everything normal':

> You see I can't remember, quite honestly, whether I praised him or not in that ... in PE ... in the Movement. I most probably have, 'cause I try and mention all their names. I try to ... so that they don't feel inadequate ... But I don't know. I can't say he has ... he hasn't stood out as being either terribly poor or terribly good in that activity.

The teacher's norm scanning mechanism appears to operate by being set to ensure that children are at ease in the activity and that 'they don't feel inadequate'. In the context of this activity then the pupil appears average. Additionally, this example illustrates a naturalistic bi-polar continuum ranging from 'terribly poor' to 'terribly good'. This spontaneous use of bi-polar continuum and based around a norm-matching framework indicates the apparent model switching process. In this activity, at least, and for the teacher's current purpose-at-hand it seems her scanning 'mechanism' was set to ensure all pupils fell within this 'normal' range. The spontaneous use of bi-polar relationship in this instance has a 'naturalistic' authenticity rarely found in research which employs repertory grid analysis and triadic elicitation techniques of construct data collection. It may however, be that after all the teacher is only outlining more explicitly the outer boundaries of each end of the 'normal' distribution rather than stating what otherwise could be seen as a bi-polar construct in the sense used by Kelly (1955). In research focused on the elicitation of constructs then, the nature of the boundaries and relationships between them ought to be an area that is investigated[5] rather than taken for granted by, and incorporated within, its methodology as though it were an unproblematical phenomenon. It is necessary to ask in research contexts:

> *When* do teachers operate bi-polar models?
> In what *circumstances*?
> And for what *purposes*?

In School A the use of norm-matching is also evident:

> It isn't that he's not very good at it himself. But in comparison to the other children ...

It seems that in order for the teacher to formulate the pupil (for the research interview at least) the typification had to be understood within a norm-matching context. Norm-matching appears to be the teacher's method for rendering typification meaningful to others in third party situations too.[6]

Models in Use: Sequences of Formulation

While it seems teachers are operating a 'norm-matching' model as a general strategy, it is clear that after applying a norm-matching model, if the pupil proves to be a poor match in relation to pupils within the parameters of normality then teachers appear to switch to the use of 'abnormal' models. It has been suggested in this research that teachers operate two types of 'abnormal' model.

Abnormal Model 1: Pathological Model: (Discrete Dichotomy)

The following are examples of teachers apparently operating this model:

> 'he's still not like the others.'

> 'She hadn't got the basic security that the others seemed to have in school environment.'

> 'I don't think that I've come across anybody that's as disturbed as Jilly in this way ... that she has all these external symptoms that've brought those problems to our attention. Because we must've had ... there've probably been other children that've had problems like this but you don't detect them quite so early.'

'She's funny. She's not like the rest of them ... She fends for herself but in a manner that's alien to everybody else.'

'He's one of the very children who should be helped to feel that he's normal and that he belongs to the group.'

'She's just come ... very unusual little girl ... I don't know what's funny about her really.... A very individual type of person ... Just totally different ...'

In this example the teacher may even be moving through a 'divergent' model into a 'pathological' model. It perhaps illustrates a move through all three models at one go! The process is represented in Figure 6.3.

Figure 6.3: Norm-matching model

NORM MATCHING ----> ABNORMAL DIVERGENT ----> ABNORMAL PATHOLOGICAL

in one move!

The teacher appears to be operating a procedure that might be expressed as follows:

'Test for normality' (i.e. norm–matching)

Result: pupil immediately falls at abnormal end of scale.

'Therefore try abnormal divergent model' (i.e. 'very unusual').

'Then test for pathological abnormality with abnormal pathological model' (i.e. 'totally different').

Another example:

Obviously most children wouldn't want to wander. So he's not upset in the normal upset sort of way. I think he's just come from a different world into something he just can't understand personally.

In this example the teacher tries a normal matching test leading (rather than switching) into 'abnormal divergent' test. Then switching into 'abnormal pathological' model.

Normalization in Processes of Reformulation of Abnormal or Deviant Pupils

Teacher talk suggests the model sequence may operate in reverse as a process of normalization when reformulating or retyping previously categorized 'abnormal' pupils. The following examples illustrate:

It could've gone either way that. There could've been some horrific problems there in the child's make-up. But it just seems as though there isn't.

The teacher has here moved from an 'abnormal pathological' to a 'norm-matching' model. She is aware that the two models are perhaps qualitatively different or something of a perceptual watershed as shown by her statement, 'it could've gone either way'. But after 'abnormal pathological' scanning he has now moved out of the pathological category. 'Pathological' scanning was operated for a while: 'there could've been some horrific problem in the child's make-up' (i.e. look out for this quite likely manifestation!)

Another example is of a pupil who started his second year in school with a new teacher who apparently either forgot about or never knew about his previous 'abnormal pathological' career. Instead she appears to operate 'norm' scanning:

'a bit untidy',
'funny little boy' [still a potential abnormal divergent or abnormal pathological?]
'I would say he's average'.

The new teacher then has no doubts about the operation of norm-matching in his case and his career has been normalized. The pathological scanning was introduced later, after my probing helped her to recall his previous 'abnormal pathological' career.

Abnormal Model 2: Divergent Model (Variable or Continuous Dichotomy)

Through the process of norm-matching, pupils appear to be identified as deviating beyond the parameters of 'normality'. They are at the 'abnormal' end of the 'normal' distribution but they are not seen as a totally discrete category as is the case with the 'pathological' model. Here there is something like a 'normal curve' or distribution which encompasses most children. Certain pupils are outside the 'normal' range and so fall into an 'abnormal' category along a continuous or variable dichotomy. The following examples illustrate the models in use:

Most children sit on a table in a group. But he'll go away over there from anybody to do his work.

By operating a 'norm-matching' model leading into an 'abnormal divergent' model, this pupil becomes identified as potentially abnormal.

'Socially they're ... all quite sociable except for Alan Knight'. Here is a different use of abnormal divergent. Rather than a dichotomy in which most children are regarded as being in the normal range while certain pupils are outside, the use of abnormal divergent here is of continuously variable *construct* dichotomy (Sociable-Unsociable) and with this pupil lying just outside the 'normal' range. (In this case, in fact, most children are perceived as falling within the 'normal' range on the construct 'sociability' and so it serves as additional matching). Note how the two above examples are different uses of continuously variable dichotomy. In the first, the *children* are the variability. In the second, the *construct* is a variability.

'He was more advanced in that way than most of the other children ...' This statement is an example of the 'abnormal divergent' model operating at the other end of the continuously variable dichotomy and suggests the model may even perhaps be a trichotomy (in the manner of authentic 'normal' distributions in which increasingly divergent or extreme cases are to be found towards the 'tails' at both positive and negative ends), allowing the formulation of pupils at the positive divergent end of the distribution. The example also illustrates a *positive* typification in respect of one dimension of Other for a pupil whose identity was usually formulated from an 'abnormal pathological' framework.

> 'I know a lot of children do this. But she does it to my mind in the extreme.'

> 'She won't look away like a lot of children do.'

> 'Gavin ... whereas most children say "Yes please" and try anything, Gavin's not one of those at all.'

In this case it is difficult to know whether the teacher is using a straightforward norm-matching model or switching to abnormal divergent. It seems that to use abnormal divergent, teachers may perhaps pass through norm-matching. Norm-matching is perhaps the first move in the use of the 'divergent' model. Abnormal divergent is then perhaps an extension of norm-matching. The pupil is definitely abnormal. He is typified in relation to his not being one of the normal ones.

> And she isn't as quick as the other children but getting it into perspective, she would be a lot brighter than a lot of other reception children in other areas.

Once again the teacher does not say how the pupil *is* but how she matches with others generally and with 'reception children' generally. The teacher says nothing relating to the inherent qualities of the pupil as such but every statement is a comparative one involving a matching process. It also begins with an abnormal divergent model and then switches to a norm-matching model for children 'in other [school catchment] areas'. So for in-school matching it is abnormal divergent, for extra-school matching it is norm-matching.

> ... Most children are fascinating, or interesting or something. You can say something about them. Ellen's just a bit wishy-washy, babified. But she's not babyish, she's just *there* ...

The teacher goes through a norm-matching model into an abnormal divergent model. Ellen, compared to most children, is very different i.e. 'just *there*'. Perhaps the pupil is seen to be unremarkable, but the teacher is as yet unable to say what the pupil will be like as she doesn't match the norm. This is the case on the second day of the pupil's school career!

Self-Matching (Perceived Self as Biographical Other)

Along with norm-matching, it seems teachers engage in the matching of a present construction of pupil with former constructions of pupil (i.e. biographical

Other). It seems that teachers carry with them highly anonymized typifications of the pupils as contemporaries derived from former encounters and which they seem to use by a process of matching when formulating the pupils in current consocial relations. This process might suggest some process of transposition of typifications from an anonymized form to an individualized, from biographical Other to present Other, and also from contemporary to consociate typification (as teacher moves towards face-to-face relations with pupil). This problem has been previously referred to and will be further examined later.

Self-matching may prove to be a key to the dynamics of the formulation process and is likely to be at the root of the emergence of typification careers. It seems likely that the pupil is carried forward through time (by the teacher as typifier) in the form of an anonymized contemporary typification and then formulated comparatively against an individualized consociate typification in the context of face-to-face encounters. Although research in the past has given prominence to the construction of a largely decontextualized theory of typification, the dynamics of typification in the course of the ongoing processes of interpersonal typification has hardly yet been explored by researchers. This will become a focus in a later section. The following examples are drawn from interview data and so are often decontextualized or interaction-free forms of typification. The Self-matching process of the typification of pupils in research interviews may prove to be different from those processes in authentic face-to-face relations, of course. Whenever possible, however, the focus of interview talk was deliberately made as context-related as possible and so may go some way to providing an indication of the dynamics of formulation in authentic face-to-face interaction. In the first example teacher interprets pupil in present by comparing his previous behaviour:

> ... which never happened before ... But I think that he is becoming more confident in my presence and with me ... It's just ... it's something I've noticed ... 'Oh, here's Alan again'. ... And it seems as though ... that I'm tripping over him more than I ever did ...

In this example there is recall of how the teacher apparently scans the scene at the time ('Oh, here's Alan again'). It suggest both Self-matching and scanning more generally may be an important aspect of the dynamics of face-to-face typification.

> ... has settled nicely this term. She's much more cooperative and ... how shall I say ... She'll play with the children more than she did when she first started. She was very ... on her own when she first started ...

The teacher begins by matching with pupil's previous Self: 'She's much more cooperative.' Then in order to explicate more fully she pauses: 'How shall I say?' Then she continues with overt Self-matching of Other in the past. But it is not clear whether this is a process employed for the benefit of the interviewer or an authentic simulation of how the teacher invokes typifications of the pupil during live interaction:

> She'll play with the children more than she did when she first started. She was very ... on her own when she first started ...

Interviewer:	What made you feel that she'd tried very hard?
Teacher:	Because of the presentation. Sometimes ... well quite a lot of the time she's doing something off a card in front of her. She'll do it quickly and not really try. But you could tell looking at this today that she had ...

The teacher evaluates the pupil's current work through a Self-matching biographical formulation of pupil as she normally is 'quite a lot of the time ... But you could tell looking at this today that she had [tried]'

> ... used to in the dining hall. He used to sit at the end of the table and just eat his dinner completely to himself. And that was a task to get through that dinner ... And now it's 'Yes please. I like that one. Don't like that one'. Before you even ask him! Whereas before it was ... a nod. Rather than anything. And he told me the other day that Matthew wanted some potatoes.

The teacher's account of current incidents relies centrally upon a process of Self-matching. The meanings to be employed in making sense of the pupil's current actions rely upon a comparative process matching Self in current episodes against a construction of former Self.

Dynamics of Pupil Careers

It seems likely that individual pupil typification careers can only proceed through a process of perceived Self- (or biographical Other) matching. The notion of 'career' makes reference to the emergence over time of an individual identity and therefore must have a reference point in the past to allow the relating[8] of the pupil as perceived Self (or biographical Other) in the present to a perceived Self at some previous reference point. This process, in effect, becomes a longitudinal form of relativity allowing biographical Other matching. There are also additional processes of horizontal relativity permitting comparison with Others in peer and norm-matching of various categories of typical pupils as course-of-action types in relation to the appropriate age and stage of schooling.

Irrespective of which Others are selected as additional referents in typing (e.g. cohort peers, age norms, catchment area norms) it seems likely that the only way in which an individual pupil can be constructed and carried forward by the teacher as a continuingly known contemporary is by distilling from the teacher's experience of a pupil a constructed essential Self (biographical Other). Such processes are perhaps implicit in the following:

> 'At the beginning she was very shy. But she's come on tremendously'.

> 'more confident',
> 'doing very well with reading now',
> 'more fluency.'

This pupil is continuously Self-matched by reference to temporal indicators such as 'more'.

He's becoming more ... a normal boy. Because his behaviour is so
different to when I last saw him in the group situation ... But he's
deviating ... His behaviour has deviated from his former norm.

In this example the teacher's constructs seem to actually include an overt reference to Self-matching ('his former norm'). It is noticeable how many of these are
contextual Self-matching situations. Teachers in specific face-to-face contexts are
interpreting pupils specifically in relation to contemporary typifications imported
into the situation.

Nevertheless, teachers seem to find some children difficult to formulate and
so their typification careers present some difficulty for distilling sedimentary
(Hammersley, 1980) typifications to carry forward: 'I often wonder which is the
real her!'

It seems likely that Self- (or biographical Other) matching lies at the root of
such interpersonal processes as labelling and self-fulfilling prophecy, which is
apparently recognized by teachers themselves:

If you get a name when you first come into school it's passed around
and it's very difficult to get rid of. I mean it ... I find it very difficult to
be objective myself and not to relate his present behaviour to his past
history.

Interpersonal Negotiation in Typification

It can be seen that teachers typify pupils within a complex interpersonal network.
They encounter formulations relating to their pupils from a variety of sources,
including other colleagues and even from the pupil's parents. It seems likely, then,
that teachers are occasionally in positions requiring them to resolve apparently
conflicting or differing typifications received from others and so they reconstruct
or negotiate a usable type. The process of matching may provide a clue to
teachers' methods of resolving such competing typifications.

The previous example indicated how negatively sedimented divergent
typifications are passed around. The teacher says 'I find it very difficult to be
objective myself and not to relate his present behaviour to his past history'. In
this case the teacher has only been a member of the teaching staff for a month
and so can only have encountered the pupil's 'past history' through received
typifications.

The same teacher goes on to illustrate apparent interpersonal Self-matching:

When he's had a naughty period like he has just this past week then, yes,
he is talked about because then it affects children in other classes ...
When you know the other staff are saying to me 'He's a naughty boy'
and I have to pull myself up a lot and say ... well find out for yourself
whether he is first. And you know, use your own judgment ... But I
feel sorry for him because I feel as though ... in the school where I've
just been this would never have occurred with him.

This example illustrates the complexities of typification matching. The teacher engages in:

1   Self-matching of the pupil,
2   interpersonal Self-matching of the pupil,
3   inter-school norm matching of the pupil.

It seems here the teacher has her own intuitive or common-sense version of what some researchers have recognized — that the social construction of deviance is a phenomenon relative to the prevailing norms of the school and the particular strategies adopted by teachers in 'reaction' to pupil actions (Reynolds and Sullivan, 1979).

In addition to typification matching with colleagues, the teacher may perhaps encounter a variety of other typification 'carriers'. Parents are a frequent source of information in infant schools because of the tendency for frequent informal talk between parents and teachers at the end of each day.[9] Other pupils may occasionally act as typification carriers too. For example, they may provide information on how a certain pupil was when the teacher was not present, e.g. at lunchtime, in the playground, or in another teacher's lesson. 'Professional' typifiers, such as educational psychologists, may also contribute to the teacher's knowledge of a pupil. There are references later to pupils in the research sample who were referred to educational psychologists and so provide illustrative data on this aspect of negotiation in the process of Other construction.

Emerging Models

So far the analysis of data resulted in the construction of three models to represent interpersonal typification processes. The models previously outlined as a norm-matching process emerged as an underlying feature apparent in formulation processes of teacher typification in both schools. It seemed that teachers operated a 'norm-matching' or 'norm-scanning' process in their dealings with pupils and so formulated pupils in relation to a notion of the 'normal' or 'average' pupil. Pupils who could not be fitted within the 'normal' range and so fell outside the boundaries of normality were interpreted through one of two 'abnormal' models. Whereas the norm-scanning process seemed to suggest the teachers' recognition of a continuum of pupils (within a trichotomous range) from one divergent extreme (perhaps not unlike the 'ideal' pupil identified in Becker) to the other extreme of a pupil at the deviant end of the continuum, the abnormal models assumed instead a clear dichotomous categorization in which quite sharp boundaries were drawn between the abnormal and the normal pupil. In the abnormal pathological model, pupils were sharply marked off qualitatively (in a discrete dichotomy) from the normal population. In the abnormal divergent model, the deviating pupil is apparently marked off only quantitatively (within a continuous dichotomy) in comparison with the normal pupils who lie within the normal range beyond a less sharply defined boundary.

In the basic norm-scanning process, 'normal' pupils are typified by comparing them to the 'normal'. The 'normal' pupil becomes the yardstick against which other pupils are matched. In the 'abnormal' models, the 'normal' pupil is used as a yardstick against which the abnormal pupil is contrasted, either in terms of quantitatively formulated variations from the norm (divergent model) or of a qualitatively discrete distinctness from it (pathological model).

The transfer of the pupils to a new school with a new set of teachers in the fourth year of the research presented an additional opportunity for testing the emerging models and offered further scope for developing, revising or even replacing them. In addition, of course, the continuously emerging nature of the pupils' formulated identities or 'typification careers', as they were carried forward through time and into 'new' organizational contexts, could be further explored.

Notes

1 Erikson (1966) has suggested that deviant forms of behaviour may be seen as 'marking the outer edges of group life'. His view of deviance, as in that taken here, moves away from notions of rule-transgression to recognize the creation of deviance as an issue rather of personal categorization and interpersonal relativity.

2 Becker's 'ideal pupil' would correspond with the 'above average' reference point of this model. However, the 'ideal pupil' for many of the teachers represented in this research corresponds more with the 'average' who is seen as a 'model pupil'.

3 The 'leading question' is introduced into the interview so as to elicit and verify meanings which had been stated earlier, before the 'formal' interview started. So much valuable data was often presented at such times.

4 Exposure to the 'sociological myth' suggested by Hargreaves (1972) and tested by Nash (1973) might also affect this process.

5 The use of bi-polar and repertory grid techniques in personal construct theory can seem a sociologically naïve approach if this method is not acknowledged.

6 It may, of course, be the case that the entire norm matching model is merely a third party occurrence only! However, even then it would still have relevance for understanding those 'natural' third party situations that are found in schools and particularly in staffroom talk (Hammersley, 1984).

7 In the career case studies of individual pupils presented later, it can be seen that in the ongoing dynamics of school and classroom life the interpretation of an individual pupil's identity involves a continuing comparison and inter-relation of present constructions with previous formulations.

8 The achievement of a reference point is apparently accomplished by processes of emergence and in particular the discovery of a 'theme' which links the present and previous constructions (McHugh, 1968).

9 Examples are to be seen in the later case studies.

Chapter 7

The Social Construction of Pupils in Relation to a Critical Boundary: Normality-Deviance

This book grew out of an academic interest in the social processes involved in deviance and a professional concern to try to employ these insights (Merton, 1957; Becker, 1963) in the analysis of schooling, particularly in understanding the early years. Accounts of deviance in educational settings seemed to be predominantly of secondary schools (Cicourel and Kitsuse, 1963; Werthman, 1963; Hargreaves, 1967, 1975; Lacey, 1970; Woods, 1979; Reynolds and Sullivan, 1979; Bird, 1980). Where primary schools had been looked at, the focus in some cases seemed to be heavily influenced by a macro-perspective (Sharp and Green, 1975) even when interpreting the interpersonal processes of classroom life. Whatever the merits of the various systems or structural frameworks for analyzing deviance, at least at a micro-level, the analysis of deviance can perhaps more profitably be examined within the conceptual framework of interactionist sociology. The research of Hargreaves (1967) and Lacey (1970) had already begun a move in this direction but, although focusing upon the subcultural origins of deviance, had not moved very far into an exploration of the interactional processes in which deviance was created or sustained. These processes tended to be assumed as either a given or as an apparently self-evident element in the creation of deviant subcultures. Some attempts have examined more fundamental interpersonal processes, however. The work of Cicourel and Kitsuse (1963), Hargreaves (1975), and Sharp and Green (1975) was a further move towards providing an account of interpersonal processes in the creation of deviance. The latter two works, by adopting a phenomenological methodology, coupled with either a symbolic interactionist or a Marxist perspective respectively, have contributed significantly to the micro-analysis of processes underlying deviance in schools. The emerging phenomenological framework in the sociology of education had, by the early 1970s, continued to question the nature and use of members' constructs within educational settings. The work of Keddie (1971), Young (1971), and Esland (1971) had raised as problematic the range of academic constructs employed in accounts of education. One of the most valuable attempts to explore the social construction of meanings by participants in schools was that of Cicourel and Kitsuse (1963) who examined the social creation of 'academic', 'deviant', and 'clinical' identities in an American highschool. Like Cicourel and Kitsuse, this book has not begun from an analysis of 'problems' as defined by academic sociology, for example, by researching into deviance or academic differentiation. Although a sociological interest in deviance fostered a research focus on pupil categorization, this merely recognized processes problematic to teachers themselves as they struggled to make sense of those pupils who deviated from the taken-for-granted social world of orderly classroom life. It is in the clarification of participants' attempts to construct interpretations and meanings within these processes of interpersonal typification and person formulation that the central concern of this book has emerged.

Established theories in the sociology of deviance cannot easily be imported into educational settings without either straining the theories or distorting the 'realities' of life in schools. In looking at primary schools, which are perhaps in social and interpersonal terms somewhat distant from the source fields which generated many theories of deviance, it is even more important to abandon the hypothetico-deductive approach to the formulation of research problems and its reliance upon a closed set of issues to investigate. 'Adequate' social science requires an open approach to research.

The naturalistic study of a particular setting and the generation of conceptual and analytical frameworks which are grounded in that social world act against the straining of imported frameworks from abstract hypothetico-deductive theory. In this book it would have been against the spirit and intention of the approach to social inquiry to allow the sociology of deviance to predominate. Established frameworks within the sociology of deviance merely sensitized the researcher to those aspects of the social construction of reality to be treated as problematical. It is in this way that notions of typification and person formulation can be seen to have connections and continuities with some sociological accounts of deviance.

In any single social setting such as a primary school, it cannot be assumed in advance that a phenomenon will be present. It is always a matter for empirical investigation. In attempting to examine the particular social setting of an infant school, which was a 'strange' world to the present researcher, the nature of meanings could not be taken for granted in advance so as to make the sociological construct of deviance itself the focus of inquiry. It would be presumptuous to assume:

a) that as a phenomenon deviance *does* appear as an element of the members' construction of reality;

b) that deviance could be studied from an imported conceptual framework as though it were a phenomenon having direct continuities with other previously researched settings.

Consequently pupil typification and person formulation, as more general and pervasive social processes, were made the focus of this study. This focus did not preclude the possibility of making connections with sociological accounts of deviance if such social phenomena were found in the research setting and they could be interpreted as an expression of, or an element in, the social processes of deviation.

Although deviance may be analyzed from other more traditional perspectives, such as those operating within the structural functionalist tradition (Merton, 1957; Gibbs, 1966), such approaches tend to frame their focus in terms of questions about the structural origins, functions and relations between deviance and other structural phenomena. It is clearly outside the scope of a micro-analysis, of the kind provided in this book, to do any more than *explore* the possible origins, consequences and implications that may arise beyond the particular social setting under investigation. It would be possible, perhaps, to attempt to explore implications for wider social relationships as others have (Sharp and Green, for example) in embracing the macro-world but this book has chosen to limit its field of analysis to the micro-world of social processes in person formulation.

In the micro-sociological perspective of this investigation, it is more appropriate to consider teachers' formulation of pupils from those frameworks available within some of the interactionist accounts of deviance. The approach has been pioneered by Becker (1963) who has recognized that deviance, rather than referring to an absolute category of social reality, is a rather more negotiable phenomenon relative to time, place, situation and to the definitions of participant actors:

> Deviance is not a simple quality present in some kinds of behaviour and absent in others — it is the product of a process which involves responses of other people to the behaviour (Becker, 1963).

The labelling perspective which is evident in the work of Becker sees as worthy of special attention such questions as:

> Under what circumstances are actors labelled deviant?
> Why are some people successfully labelled deviant and not others?

This perspective offers a useful conceptual framework for exploring the processes by which teachers categorize 'deviant' pupils.

The emphasis in the labelling perspective is on deviance as a product of the 'responses of other people'. Whether an act is deviant or not is both operationally and theoretically a matter of whether other people react to it. Writers and researchers working within the labelling tradition, although operating from this premise, have rarely clarified what empirically might be meant by a 'societal reaction' (Schur, 1971). In respect of teachers' classroom typifications, it is not clear whether a teacher's cognitive action in engaging in the formulation of a pupil would itself count as a 'reaction', or whether it would only be a 'reaction' if the formulation became an element in a teacher's *overt* action and so was transformed into an 'observable' act. Would it perhaps count as a 'reaction' if the formulation only became overt in the form of a typification expressed by a teacher in the course of a research interview? Or only if it naturally became overt by being communicated to others as, for example, in the course of staffroom talk (Hammersley, 1984), or in the more general contexts of teacher-teacher exchange (Ball, 1981). Perhaps it is not important ultimately to resolve this conceptual unclarity as the focus of this inquiry is not upon deviance. It merely employs an interpersonal perspective which is shared with certain established frameworks for the analysis of deviance. The question of whether what is really being investigated here is deviance in a strict interpretation of the sociological construct is not an issue. It will remain problematic throughout. In the precise sense in which

Figure 7.1: A traditional definition of deviance

Rule-Breaking - - - - - - - - > Deviance

Becker defines it, covert processes of typification alone, without the overt action of 'blowing the whistle', would apparently not constitute deviance. Pre-'whistle-blowing' formulation or talk that never leads to whistle-blowing would perhaps not count as deviance.

Previous research in educational settings has also focused on the social construction of deviance. The research of Hargreaves *et al.* (1975) was focused on teachers' interpretations of deviance and, as one of its particular concerns, analyzed processes of typification. Its approach was in the established tradition of sociological analysis in which deviance was seen to be constituted in the action of breaking social rules. This approach was different in two respects from the present investigation.

1 It does not appear to show the same concern for theory construction as a process to be generated by the 'first-order' analysis of ethnographic accounts of episodes of interaction but begins instead from an established standpoint in sociological theory.
2 It studies deviance *per se* rather than the processes of person formulation or identity imputation.

Hargreaves *et al.* operationalize deviance as an act of rule-breaking. They examine processes by which teachers apply school and classroom rules and from which they engage in the construction of pupil identities. The starting point is to be found within sociological notions of rules or norms as regulators of behaviour. The present inquiry seeks to avoid any prior assumption of the place of rules or sociological norms in classroom life but has merely chosen to examine teachers' attempts to interpret and make sense of pupils in their accounts of Other formulation. 'Rules' or 'norms', if relevant, can be expected to appear within teacher talk and so perhaps should not be regarded as having an *a priori* relevance. Many writers in traditional labelling theory (Schur, 1971) seem to regard deviance as shown in Figure 7.1. Therefore any act of deviance imputation is assumed to be contingent upon a perceived instance of rule-breaking. This presupposes that all deviance imputations relate to acts of rule infringement. There is also a tendency to assume that in the interpretation of such acts the social construction of reality, on the part of the labeller, will have a focus upon the transgression of rules in a current incident. By choosing to focus upon rules, researchers have indirectly overlooked those processes of person formulation that may be antecedent to, or not directly traceable in, the episodic boundaries of rule-breaking incidents. Whether in the course of person formulation the constructor of Other *does* relate to a rule-breaking situation must be regarded as an empirical issue. Are there no occasions when even the interpretation of acts committed by those with deviant identities may relate to phenomena other than rules? Is the process of interpretation of persons and their acts within rule-governed situations in everyday life itself something that can be taken for granted as though it were a logical sequence of events which justified beginning the process of social inquiry at the occurrence of rule transgression? It must be empirically a matter for investigation to discover the extent to which deviance is, or is perceived to be, contingent upon perceived rule infringement. Deviance cannot, by definition, be reduced to a sociological phenomenon which is contingent upon rule infringement unless the notion of 'rule' is to become so loose and vaguely defined[1] as a concept that it relates to, or can be assumed to be implicit in, all aspects of everyday person perception, interpretation and construction.

Nevertheless, this inquiry into the educational careers of children in early schooling has eventually led to the use of perspectives from the sociology of deviance. This assimilation has proved to be appropriate on two counts. First, although empirically it must always be an open question whether deviance, or anything like its manifestations as a sociological phenomenon, would be found in the infant classrooms of the case study schools, in fact within a few weeks it became clear that at least *one* pupil in each school so deviated from teachers' conceptions of 'normality' that processes of perceived deviation became central to both teacher concerns and to the research interviews. Second, the models of pupil formulation and typification generated from the study of the two schools suggested that the teachers' formulation of all pupils was related to their perceived correspondence with the 'norm' and their deviations from it, either to a point *beyond* certain 'normal' boundaries (as in the dichotomous models) or *within* 'normal' boundaries (as in the 'normal range'[2] of pupils represented by the normal distribution). It seems that whether or not deviance involves the perception of individuals in relation to notions of rule-oriented conduct, apparently all teacher-pupil interaction is formulated in the categorization of persons and actions as operating in, and bounded by, recognized interpersonal and societal boundaries which act as reference points. Whether or not these reference points are indeed rooted in rules must be treated as a matter of empirical investigation.

Labelling theorists, in their work within educational settings, have been inclined to focus upon the *instance* of rule-breaking itself rather than exploring the associated *ongoing processes* of person formulation. This investigation focuses upon the process of person formulation as this emerges and proceeds over time. The emphasis then is less upon the analysis of classroom episodes (whether involving rule-breaking or not) and more upon the inter-relationship between isolated classroom episodes and ongoing processes of person formulation.

There are continuities here with the sociological (Sharp and Green, 1975) and social psychological (McCall and Simmons, 1966; Lofland, 1971) notion of 'identity'. Schools, both wittingly and unwittingly, engage in the process of constructing or at least imputing pupil identities. Sharp and Green (1975) have attempted to explore

> the relationship between the construction of pupil identities and the practice of the teacher within the context of social structure in the classroom, school and wider society.

It is here, of course, that a researcher must be conscious of the possible continuities with existing concerns in the sociology of education, such as the inequalities of pupil attainment, and of social differentiation and selection within schools and in 'society' (Floud, Halsey and Martin, 1956; Halsey, Floud and Anderson, 1961; Hargreaves, 1967; Little and Westergaard, 1962; Lacey, 1970; Barker-Lunn, 1970;

Halsey, Heath and Ridge, 1980). But while Sharp and Green provide a useful link between the micro-world and traditional macro-sociological theory, this inquiry has attempted to move more closely into these micro-processes and leave the exploration of extra-school relations as an activity for others.

This phenomenological orientation has recognized the construction of social reality within schools as a major issue and the central focus of researcher interest. The deliberate longitudinal perspective has given a major methodological thrust to the examination of processes of 'identity' imputation over time, as reality is defined, modified, redefined, changed and reconstructed during an extensive period in a pupil's career. The ongoing dynamics of reconstruction are more accessible to long-term observation and analysis in the course of the continuing research process.

Sharp and Green have recognized 'social structure' as a 'human, indeed, an intellectual construction' which may be seen as a 'result of the network of consciousness' as people 'acquire in their socialization a "sense of social structure"'. The possibility of the reconstruction of social reality or a redefinition of the situation, however, needs always to be considered:[3]

> Identity is never fixed, once and for all ... Teachers are in the process of constructing pupils' identities through the differential management of pupils' careers (Sharp and Green, 1975).

The emergence of pupil careers in the social construction of normality and deviation in the cohort of pupils is the concern of the remaining section of this book.

The concept 'career' was introduced by Hughes (1937) referring to 'the moving perspective in which persons orient themselves with reference to the social order ...' As such, it is primarily a reference to Self-perception rather than to Other formulation. However, the symbolic interactionist framework (Blumer, 1965) recognizes the Self as an interactional process. The relation of Self to the social order is itself often expressed in Other terms (in the 'generalized Other') acknowledging that even Self is a process rooted in Other perception (Blumer, 1962; Mead, 1934). Within schools teachers are clearly powerful contributors to a 'definition of the situation' and their formulation of pupils provides a basis for pupils' own construction of Selves (Nash, 1973; Brophy and Good, 1974). This book, however, rather than examining pupils' Self-construction, has purposely drawn its boundaries artificially at the limits of teachers' Other interpretation of the pupils in an attempt to salvage some clarity from an otherwise vast, complex and methodologically problematical territory.

A framework for considering the negotiation of pupil identities and the consequences for in-school careers has previously been offered by Cicourel and Kitsuse (1963). Their analysis examines teacher typifications in 'academic', 'deviant', and 'clinical' careers as they relate to pupils in a highschool. The 'tracks' or 'careers' to which they relate are followed for each area of these acknowledged typification careers. In following up deviant careers, Cicourel and Kitsuse are not following labelling definitions of deviance as a rule-breaking phenomenon but are engaging in an analysis of person formulation. It is the formulation of persons that receives primacy of attention and not the question of deviance or its definition. Cicourel and Kitsuse's concentration upon the negotiation of a pupil's identity between teachers, and between teachers and parents, appears to be a more profitable way of illuminating the social construction of pupil careers than would be the case in a more rule-oriented sociological analysis of deviance. They rightly relocate the analysis of deviance within the field of person *formulation* rather than *rule-transgression*. There is a strong case for relating and retaining both these approaches, but it should perhaps be acknowledged that the focus of enquiry for fully understanding Self-Other interaction in educational settings has to be centred predominantly upon the formulation of persons rather than the inter-pretation of classroom rules.

The pupil case studies in Part II show the interpersonal processes which contribute to the emergence and maintenance of deviant careers over a period of four years within each of the two schools. In each school the apparent deviation of one pupil seemed to dominate both early teacher interactions and interview talk. Whether such apparent deviation really does constitute a case of deviance in the strict labelling sense is not an issue in this study (though in fact the struggle experienced by each set of teachers to resolve the perceived threat to classroom life posed by their particular deviant pupil is perhaps enough 'evidence' of societal 'reaction' to justify such an interpretation). The issue for the present inquiry is the ongoing formulation of pupils as Others. The construction of deviant pupils seems to represent for teachers an extreme case of Other formulation since the boundaries of everyday teacher-pupil relations appear to be threatened by the deviant pupils presenting a challenge to the teachers' taken-for-granted world. The occurrence of deviant cases in social research provides a significant oppor-tunity for researchers also to uncover some aspects of the 'normal' processes in everyday dealings since these may remain covert unless they are otherwise exposed either by the researcher asking questions which probe beneath the overt features of classroom life or are exposed by a naturalistic challenging of these 'normal' processes by individual pupils. The deviant pupil seems to present such a naturally occurring challenge and is not unlike a case of natural 'Garfinkling'[4] which disrupts or disturbs the taken-for-granted world of classrooms. In the interviews with teachers there was an attempt to explore some of the features of this assumed territory. Yet the methodological limits of such interview explora-tions are inevitably complemented by the fortuitous occurrence of deviant cases. Teachers are then not merely encouraged to talk about the taken-for-granted as a basis of Other formulation but are compelled to employ it and even act upon it in the presence of an observer and as they try to relate to such key classroom figures as the deviant pupils who continually question it. It is perhaps a more genuinely interactional 'questioning' of the taken-for-granted — a naturalistically fortuitous gift to a researcher!

It was suggested that in the early weeks of the investigation each of the two deviant pupils was interpreted as apparently deviating from the social world of the classroom:

Week 1

Gavin	Alan
'misfit'	'very uncooperative'
'from a different world'	'the only one ...'

Exactly what, however, is deviant about these supposed deviant cases?

For the present inquiry, of course, the issue is not one of defining deviance but of exploring the *emergence* of deviant identity. How such pupils acquire an identity over time, whether deviant or not, which, within the social structure of a particular school, empirically indicates a taken-for-granted reality for the school personnel. Nevertheless, these examples are perhaps, in any case, not at odds with traditional sociological definitions of deviance since clearly the teachers' formulation is implicitly based upon a recognition of rule-transgression. Gavin, seen as a 'misfit' and 'from a different world' is one who appears to be overtly challenging the taken-for-granted 'culture' of the classroom. Many examples of his deviant actions in the classroom are seen as confirming this. Alan's challenge to the classroom world is more negative, however. Compared with Gavin's excess of participation, Alan's divergence is an under-participation which is disturbing to the teachers for the very reason that it is challenging to the highly participatory and more overtly 'child-centred' culture of School B. The 'logic' of child-centredness is adopted to provide a strategy for dealing with him. He is left alone quite often to participate in events as and when he decides he is ready to.[5]

The pupil case studies presented later reveal something of the ongoing processes of emergence in two deviant identities. In each case the deviant identity remains with the pupil throughout the entire period of investigation. It continues as a backcloth against which each pupil is constructed, although the extent of deviation is seen to vary so that at different times it is seen as either more or less appropriate as a basis for person formulation. From time to time each pupil goes through occasional phases of being formulated as potentially normal, when the deviant identity is seemingly suspended, qualified or neutralized. In the case of Gavin, the deviant identity is sustained throughout the period and professional help is sought. Such use of outside specialist help is often regarded as a significant turning point in the 'official' labelling of pupils (Tomlinson, 1981) often leading to amplification processes. Yet, the school in this case seems to delay the process of referral to outside agencies quite deliberately and it would be an unjust trivialization of the professional and personal concern shown to this pupil by the teachers to interpret their actions as mere 'amplification'. If anything, perhaps the 'official' labelling could be said to be the culmination of ongoing and complex processes of negotiation rather than a mere instance of simple amplification processes. Indeed, the school seems to be operating an incorporative strategy not unlike that indicated in Reynolds (1979). In the second school, Alan's deviant identity comes and goes throughout. Finally, he seems to have either moved onto a normalized career line *or* the school has successfully managed to avoid situations in which his deviant identity becomes apparent either by deliberate structuring of his interactional opportunities or by the use of the child-centred ideology whose boundaries of normality are perhaps redefined by his very presence. Again, 'incorporative' strategies predominate as though oriented to ensure a negotiated 'inclusion' rather than 'exclusion' from the 'normal' world of the classroom.

The problem in this study is how to conceptualize, analyze and theorize about these deviant cases. Recognizing that they fall within that domain of sociological territory which has already been extensively and powerfully contributed to by researchers into deviance, one is tempted to draw upon their well-developed framework. It would be inappropriate, however, to employ directly well-developed frameworks in advance of preliminary data analysis. It is important for the nature of the data to determine the framework of analysis and not the other way round. The frameworks have no inherent worth or validity but are merely a means for sorting and assembling data.

To be realistic in the ethnographic research tradition, it is impossible to be free from commitment to certain perspectives and frameworks. The researcher's awareness of significant literature in this substantive area will inevitably colour and selectively affect perception and interpretation during data analysis. This can, to some extent, be guarded against and its effects minimized by providing opportunities for refuting the theoretical account and more deliberately by the employment of negative case analysis while pursuing the search for validity.

Notes

1 This suggestion of a somewhat oversimplified use of the construct 'rule' within the sociology of deviance is not to deny that the notion of rule could be defined with sophistication to incorporate the routine elements of everyday life. Harre and Secord have made a convincing case for recognizing rules at the core of social interaction, while Cicourel has exposed the use of rule in processes of interpretation by which actors construct reality.
2 The view of social organization contained in the norm-matching model and its associated normal distribution seems to correspond with that of Erikson in his investigation of deviance in New England during the period of witchcraft hysteria. Erikson has suggested that in the life of a community there is a tendency for human actions to vary across a vast 'range'. This 'range' tends to be limited in practice, however, by the symbolic markers which set the outer boundaries of the 'normal' way of life. Most members of a society restrict their actions to those encompassed by the inner 'zone' of acceptable conduct.
3 The acknowledgment of this constant potential for reconstruction presents a strong case for engaging in longitudinal research. Recognizing the ongoing nature of the construction of reality, particularly in an emergent phenomenon such as identity, encourages research over a longer time-scale than is usually attempted.
4 'Garfinkling' is a term which seems now to be popularly used to refer to the strategy advocated by Garfinkel (1969) for 'doing' sociology. It requires the deliberate and sometimes abrasive disturbing of the taken-for-granted.
5 This treatment is similar to that referred to by Sharp and Green in relation to the pupil, Michael.

Chapter 8

Identities in Interaction: The Construction of Identities in Classroom Episodes

Basic Processes of Emergence and Relativity in Classrooms

Having outlined a theoretical framework for 'understanding' the basic elements in teachers' formulation of pupils, it is now possible to turn our attention to the second and more important interest in the emergent processes. This will be an attempt to understand the *interactional dynamics* in processes of Other construction as teachers live through their ongoing classroom encounters with pupils. So far an attempt has been made to generate a 'situated'[1] analysis of the formulation of children by grounding the data wherever possible within episodes of face-to-face interaction and in contextualized talk rather than relying upon the looser, more generalized and wide-ranging formulation that otherwise may occur naturally in research interviews. By the methodological strategy of contextualizing talk, the general theory of typification has been tied in with the micro-social world of classroom events with the intention of strengthening its validity as an authentic account of ongoing classroom processes. The primary interest has been in discovering the essential properties of Other formulation. Additionally, the contextualization of a theory has been pursued by continually pushing teacher talk towards episodes of classroom life.

To change the plane of analysis the intention now is to focus *exclusively* on the moment-by-moment construction of Others in the *ongoing* processes of classroom life. Particular attention is given to:

1   the longitudinal dynamics in processes of Other formulation as identities are seen to emerge and are maintained over the four years of schooling covered by this study,
2   the minute by minute ongoing processes in Other formulation as episode follows episode in the fast flowing stream of classroom life.

The procedure for analysis will be that of *grounded theorizing*; (Glaser and Strauss, 1968) as followed throughout this research. This adherence requires a resistance to the direct employment of established theories or accounts from other research settings and, instead, insists upon a systematic analysis of the data itself in order to generate concepts and theoretical structures grounded in the data of the present empirical settings under investigation.

So far it has been revealed that significant interpersonal 'boundaries' are operated by teachers between 'normal' and 'abnormal' pupils. In the next phase of analysis, the approach of grounded theorizing requires a systematic working through of the operation of these 'boundaries' in the week by week emergence of pupil careers over the entire four year span of the work. The practice of *theoretical sampling* had earlier led to the selection of a number of critical cases in relation to these 'boundaries' and so these cases will now be followed through in a sample of episodes from the first four years of their life in school. This practice is an attempt to examine dynamic processes of formulation, both in the longitudinal emergence of careers over a substantial period of early schooling and in their moment-by-moment accomplishments within episodes of classroom life. Certain pupils in each school had emerged as critical cases: one as a distinctly deviant or 'abnormal' case and several examples of pupils who seemed to epitomize or personify the 'normal' pupil. These 'normal' pupils, although shifting across the 'normal' space[2] towards the outer boundaries of the normal world from time to time, were instances of pupils who, for most of their careers, were regarded by the teachers as quite 'normal'. Their occasional movements of divergence towards the outer boundaries in fact provide an opportunity to examine the nature and extent of shifts in identity *within* the categories of normal careers. Any attempt at constructing a representative selection of normal or deviant cases from the pupils who make up the cohort would, of course, always be problematic and is particularly so in long-term studies since *constancy* of category cannot easily be presumed throughout several years of a longitudinal study. The purpose is not to examine a representative sample of *actual* cases, either normal or abnormal as examples of a prominent 'ideal type' construction in classroom life, but merely to explore the operation of certain critical types in relation to the interpersonal boundaries operated in the dynamics of social interaction. It should then be possible to offer an account of formulation which follows the 'natural' dynamic framework of emerging and ongoing careers in which pupils constructed by teachers.

Before exploring the case study data of the selected children, it is necessary to explore a framework for conceptualizing the dynamics of social interaction in classroom life. The analysis of the present cases has suggested certain concepts that are critical in the investigation of episodes in the school careers of children. These concepts are found in the notions of 'emergence' and of 'relativity' which are prominent in the writings of Mead and some of his followers.

Emergence

The dimension of *time* has rarely been given prominence in sociological research. Even longitudinal studies of early schooling have rarely provided accounts of the continuous ongoing emergence of data over time. They have, instead, often presented essentially static accounts of phenomena at selected points in a research time-scale (Davie, Butler and Goldstein, 1972; Douglas, 1964). Continuous monitoring has rarely been practised. Other researchers (Hargreaves, 1967; Lacey, 1970) have acknowledged some measure of emerging reality within a finer time-scale as found in such time units as the school 'year' as pupils in successive years were monitored in moving between streams or between subcultures. It seems that the 'year' has often been the smallest temporal unit to receive any significant scrutiny. Within-year movement is usually ignored, except in Hargreaves' later work (1975), providing a theory which recognizes phases in typification as a sub-unit of the time-scale within the first year of pupil careers in secondary schools.

The conceptualization of *temporal* dimensions of reality owes much to the work of Mead. His notion of 'emergence' recognized social reality as a phenomenon rooted in and spanning across time. This area has rarely been taken up by his followers within the SI tradition but was later given some attention by ethnomethodologists (McHugh, 1968).

Mead (1959) drew attention to the changing of meanings with time, as reality is capable of different construction from different standpoints in time. The extent of change or continuity in pupil identities as they are viewed by teachers from different temporal 'systems' is attempted in the case study explorations later.

Since action or interaction is a continuous or dynamic process it should be acknowledged in the selection of research strategies and recognized in the attempts to piece together a meta-theory of interpretative accounts. Mead has made the point that a social event is a *continuing* phenomenon: 'An event is ... always becoming and never complete. It is continuously achieved'. And, perhaps particularly important in the fast-moving world of classrooms in the early years of schooling, that, 'the process of emergence *is* the present, for it is the point at which all the impingements on behaviour contemporaneously intersect' (Mead, 1932, p. 69).

The point of entry for investigation in this book has been classroom 'events'. In looking at the nature of Other formulation processes, there have been many opportunities to explore the extent to which there is continuity or momentum in careers, or temporal boundaries[3] operating between 'earlier' and 'later' events.

One feature of social reality seen as important in this study and recognized in the writings of Mead, and later in McHugh (1968) is that of the framework for social construction:

> in a causal account of an *event*, any unanticipated change in the character of the event requires a change in the accounting system (McHugh, p. 27).

How teachers engage in motivational 'accounting' in relation to the unique properties of a current event or episode as against the more enduring properties of the concept of pupil identity is an issue explored in each of the case studies.

So far the attention to emergence has been quite general in relating to long-term time-scales of past, present and future. However, there is also a temporal or emergent aspect to the focus upon micro-situations in looking at events as they unfold. McHugh (1968) quotes Mannheim (1952) on the process of constructing present events:

> Karl Mannheim has suggested that 'patterned' definitions depend upon relating previous interpretations to present circumstances, a process in

which the actor searches for homologies that 'underlie' the behaviour of the moment. It is a 'search' for documentary meaning, for an identical, homologous pattern underlying a vast variety of totally different realizations of meaning (McHugh, p. 35).

It can be assumed that in each episode or event within classrooms, teachers will be continuing the search for meaning as they piece together an identity for each child from the fragments of information before them. The intra-episodic time-scale of emergence is itself worthy of investigation. An important aspect of the social construction of reality to explore is that of interpretation within the episode and beyond it in relation to the more long-term dimensions of time-scale.

As action proceeds it does so with an *episodic* dimension of emergence:

as patterns are discovered they are documented by the actor in his immediate ongoing situations ... [which] ... allows [the] actor to integrate temporally discrete events by giving them a *baseline of meaning* and thereby ascribe order to the general environment (McHugh, p. 35).

In this way typification may be recognized as an element in the intra-episodic search for patterns of meaning as teachers engage in the process of constructing pupil 'identities' as 'baselines of meaning' which are transposed from episode to episode. Although it has so far been possible to identify the general framework of 'normal' and 'abnormal' models, it is not yet clear how these models relate over time, how they operate at the micro- or episodic level of action, or even whether they are used as a continuing 'baseline of meaning'.

The work of McHugh has shown how intra-episodic elements of emergence can be identified in social encounters. This possibility offers a clue to potential processes by which teachers impute identities to children as the events and episodes of classroom life unfold. He has identified what he calls 'theme' as an element of intra-episodic emergence:

actors assume that a pattern of meaning will be discovered in the events they observe ... theme thus generates a definition of current activity not by describing the immediate moment itself but by describing the immediate moment's relation to other moments ... theme is past and future homology that informs the present (McHugh, 1968).

In the construction of pupil identities from moment to moment and from year to year, what then is the relationship between the 'immediate moment' and 'other moments' in the teachers' framework of formulation?

Similar conceptualizations have been made by Smith (1978), whose work also derives from ethnomethodology. Her account has suggested a means for exploring processes of emergence as they appear to operate in any social setting. Following Smith (1978, p. 46) it would seem that as a means of acting or operating as a participant in an emerging setting, an actor needs to know the situated meanings that may be attributed. In dealings with children, except in the very early days of a relationship, teachers will have knowledge of their pupils from previous encounters. It is probable that the teacher transports from previous constructions of Other (in terms of *time* and *space*) meanings which make a present event meaningful. The event would otherwise have no meaning other than that which would be evident to any newcomer or 'stranger' (Schutz, 1971) to the setting who experienced the episode as a novel set of events[4] without benefit of a key to unlock their meanings. Familiarity with Other means that episodes will rarely be interpreted anew but will be constructed from a 'baseline of meaning' rooted in previous encounters. Following Smith, it might be said that, in looking at the dynamics of formulation in typification careers, we are in effect looking at the documentary method for transporting constructions of *persons* and for transporting constructions of *situations* from previous episodes into the present[5].

McHugh has made the claim that continuity of otherwise discrete events is accomplished by the ongoing use of the documentary method:

> Events are connected by conceptualization not observation. . . . The 'tye'
> between . . . events is empirically chronological and conceptually social,
> a family of chronological cases connected by our emergent concep-
> tualization of them (McHugh, 1968, pp. 41–2).

The inter-connectedness or otherwise of 'chronological cases' is examined in this final section of case studies. How teachers 'connect' the episodic and the trans-episodic in their social construction of pupil identities from moment to moment will be of particular interest.

McHugh has provided an empirical account of *two* significant elements of interaction originating in the work of Mead: 'emergence' and 'relativity'. Both emergence and relativity rest upon the notion of 'boundary' — a fundamental element of social interaction and one which has been shown to be a major component in teachers' formulation of pupils. The boundary between 'normality' and 'abnormality' appears to figure largely in teachers' relations with, or at least their construction of, pupils. Its relationship to the construction of ongoing *action* now becomes an increasing interest in later chapters.

Relativity

Relativity is a spatial concept. 'It characterises an event in its relationship to other events across the boundaries of space' (Turner, 1962, p. 28). It focuses upon the 'situatedness' of meanings. Teachers can be expected to be operating notions of *boundary* in their formulation of pupils and in their differentiation of Others across the interpersonal 'space' of classroom and schools. This process, and the concept of boundary, can be seen in the later case studies.

Turner (1962) has suggested that the placement of boundaries is always a matter of perception. It places limits on how the Other is seen:

> the placement of any one of these boundaries, whether for a fleeting
> instant or for a longer period limits the identification of other roles
> (p. 22).

The case studies allow an opportunity to look at the placement of boundaries as teachers accomplish their construction of, and dealings with, pupils. Although in the present two schools the normal-abnormal is a significant boundary operated by teachers, we have yet to explore the placement of such boundaries 'whether for a fleeting instant or for a longer period' and in relation to the accomplishment of pupil careers in episodes of classroom life.

Turner sees the process of formulating Others in interactional settings as one of interpreting roles:

> It is this tendency to shape the phenomenal world into roles which is the key to role taking as a core process in interaction (p. 22).

In this investigation there is a concern to understand the ongoing processes of teachers' attempts 'to shape the phenomenal world into roles' as they proceed to interpret and relate to pupils in the fast-flowing stream of classroom life.

Boundary construction seems to be at the core of Turner's discussion of role in the accomplishment of interaction with Other:

> The role becomes the point of reference for placing interpretations on specific actions, for anticipating that one line of action will follow upon another and for making evaluations of individual actions (p. 24).

For Turner then, 'role' seems to operate in a manner similar to McHugh's 'baseline of meaning', providing a 'documentary method' as the 'point of reference in placing interpretations on specific actions'. Obviously the interpretations *do* have to be placed! This placement involves drawing quite sharp boundaries so as to extract meaning. The setting of such boundaries is a key process in social interaction and figures largely in this analysis of primary school classrooms.

Continuing the notion of boundary implicit in relativity, it is important to give prominence, as indeed Turner has, to the *active* process of boundary construction by participants: 'Role-taking and role-making always constitute the grouping of behaviour into units ...' (Turner, 1962, p. 24). Turner then recognizes 'role-taking' as the basic boundary formulating process. The active process of 'grouping of behaviour into units'.

Although this active process has been of central interest here there is perhaps another dynamic element which is more critical for understanding its ongoing or continuous nature. Turner sees the process of role-taking as a 'tentative process' in which roles are marked out and given substance on 'shifting axes' as events continue.

This view is critical for the analysis of continuing classroom careers. It recognizes the exploratory and active strands of the process of identity imputation. First, the 'tentative process' acknowledges the potentially evolutionary or emergent feature of 'boundary' organization or 'grouping of behaviour' over time. Second, it allows for the possibility of changing or shifting frameworks in the 'stream' of interaction. Although earlier it was possible to identify the basic models of Other which are apparently operated at a general level by teachers-formulation their appearance within the ongoing dynamics of pupil careers in classroom interaction has yet to be considered. Exactly *how* they might operate, or what their relationship is, in the moment-by-moment accomplishment of classroom life, is not yet known. Later there will be an attempt to deal directly with examining the possible 'shifting axes' of person formulation as interaction proceeds and to provide a framework that allows for such changing or 'shifting' processes.

proceeds and to provide a framework that allows for such changing or 'shifting' processes.

Longitudinal research has the considerable strength of permitting analysis of the temporality of social reality. Researchers have often presumed *constancy* of meanings over the entire time span of a research project or within, and between, different phases of data collection. In the case studies the focus will be upon the temporality of frameworks as a major element of Self–Other formulation. Turner has expressed something of the importance of shifting frameworks in discussing role-taking, which, although perhaps written from the viewpoint of Self as role-taker, provides a theme which is just as apt in understanding the present concern — imputing to Other an identifiable role within a framework of roles and boundaries. As interaction proceeds, the roles and their content, according to Turner, experience 'cumulative revision'. In the ongoing processes of social life, roles become relatively fixed for only so long as they offer a 'stable framework for interaction'. The focus in this investigation is upon the extent to which teacher formulations of pupils *do* experience revision; whether formulation *is* 'cumulative'; whether imputed identity does become 'fixed for a time'; for *how long*; and its *relationship* with 'frameworks for interaction'.

Turner's discussion of role-taking and role-making, although apparently centrally concerned with the problem of the sociological concept role, seems to sum up person formulation and typification quite convincingly. Attention is focused upon the dimension of *continuity* which is implicit in the process. The perceiver is seen to be continually engaged in a process of assembling an image of Other and constructing it from a constellation of components pieced together over a period of time.[6] The empirical context of such occurrences, of course, are examined later in the case studies of 'deviant' and 'normal' pupils.

In Turner's view, and in the later case studies, concern can be seen for 'deeper' rather than 'surface' constructions of Other. Instead of the mere formulation of what might immediately be apparent to an onlooker at the 'surface' there is a recognition of a significant element of construction which sees beyond the immediate and relates *present* to *previous* and 'surface' to 'deeper' construction. This process is particularly evident in the imputation of motives, purposes and goals to Other — which by their very nature can only be introduced by imputation. Such constructions of reality may relate perhaps to deeper or possibly even to trans-situational views of Other which are beyond the immediate surface appearances. The highly active sense of search*ing* beyond the mere surface manifestations of appearances is conveyed by Turner. He recognizes that in the interpretation of Other, it is not a specific action that is the focus of perception but the recognition behind it of an Other-role which is directed towards some 'ends' and 'expressive of the sentiment which dominates the role in question'.

This view is well-suited to the present investigation. It provides a framework for viewing teachers as actors engaged in the formulation of children in their classrooms through imputed Other-roles. It also allows for the possibility that teachers may be operating pre-defined notions of Other role from earlier encounters. The present behaviour of children may be interpreted from a previously operating frame of reference suggesting that once a role is imputed it may become a yardstick against which to compare current actions of Other. In current episodes then, the Other-role is imputed to the extent that the individual's actions are:

susceptible to interpretation as directed towards the ends associated with the other role expressive of the sentiment which dominates the role in question.[7]

The main argument is that the relativity of interpersonal relations centres upon the process of role-taking — of casting Other within a framework in which meaning is assembled by the recognition of a dominant and encompassing personal and interpersonal boundary. Turner has suggested a tendency for actors to presume that Other's various actions spring from the adoption of some role. In turn, this adoption generates a strong tendency to organize the interpretation of Other's role behaviour as though it were following a single role. There is an active searching for an interpersonal boundary that could encompass the Other's actions within a presumed single role. Such processes receive attention here, especially in exploring the extent to which such single roles are transported continuously through time in notions of 'identity' and of the 'deep structure' of interaction, implicit in the idea of 'core typification' or 'sedimentary type' (Hargreaves, 1977) and 'pivotal category' (Lofland, 1969).

The dynamics of such a process require an examination of the frames of reference employed by teachers in their formulation of present pupil action. For Turner, the key to the interpretation of action is to be found in a 'matching process' in which current behaviour is checked for its consistency with that associated with a recognized role. Turner conveys the notion of a *process* as an ongoing or dynamic perspective in which Other formulation is recognized as a *continuous* and *active* phenomenon. So far it has been suggested in this study that a matching process is prominent in teachers' construction of pupil identities. As the case studies are explored later, it will be important then to examine the extent to which teachers *do* operate matching processes, whether the comparative referents remain constant and to consider any shifting of perspectives which may take place over the longer term of a pupil's career.

The formulation of pupils as Others, of course, takes place within an organizational setting and so the wider organizational processes in the formation of possible 'deep structure' and its communication within a community of formulators is worthy of attention. It is possible that teachers receive from colleagues certain 'deep structures' or frames of reference which may operate independently of *present* or *immediate* pupil behaviour, and promote in the formulation a sense of continuity in pupil identity beyond what is otherwise available to the onlooker in the appearances of present episodes. The professional community of teachers may play a key part in identifying, fixing, promoting and maintaining the interpersonal boundaries perceived in other roles. Turner recognizes collective or cultural processes in the validation of interpretations of a role. A role imputation acquires greater legitimacy in finding that the behaviour also indicates a role to 'others whose judgments are felt to have some claim to correctness'. This is most simply demonstrated in discovering the existence of 'a name in common use for the role'. Here, then, is a clear account of the possible relationship between typification and role. Teachers are in effect likely to be constructing commonly recognized roles and calling to attention the typical motives and actions of a typical actor who plays the role in question. The staffroom processes of the formation and use of typification talk 'in common use' for typical pupil 'roles' has been explored elsewhere (Hammersley, 1980).

In the later case studies, however, attention will be focused upon the temporality, endurance and use of such communal constructions as teachers proceed with the formulation of emerging pupil identities. Turner has suggested that it is the possibility for a form of behaviour to be readily given a name which immediately transforms its interpretation by invoking an externality and constraint recognized in Durkheim's (1953) notion of 'collective representations'. The present interest is in exploring the extent, and possible internal mechanisms, by which pupil formulations appear, are used and invoked within an organizational culture. Staffroom culture may perhaps recognize and treat typified pupils as reified Others providing an 'exteriority' of reality within the taken-for-granted, permitting teachers to invoke staffroom knowledge as part of the possible 'deep structure' of pupil identity. Such staffroom knowledge might well operate as an ingredient in the mechanisms by which enduring pupil identities are maintained and accomplished.

Surface and Deep Structure in Other Formulation

The idea of 'deep structure' has been explored within a psycholinguistic framework by Chomsky (1957) and from a sociological perspective by Garfinkel (1967). Both ideas can perhaps be related to the present usage. The notion of transformation from deep to surface structure may provide a metaphor for understanding the process by which teachers make connections between their immediate and direct observations of pupils' *present* actions and the formulations of pupil identity at a 'deeper' level, pre-existing and continuing beyond the manifestations of Other in the current episode. The issue is to understand how teachers transform their view of the pupil within a current episode into a trans-episodic construction which may tap a social reality beyond the appearances of the mere surface features of a current episode.

In ethnomethodology, the idea of deep structure is employed in the concept of 'documentary method', a term introduced by Garfinkel to refer not merely to a sociological *process* but to the very *method* employed by members for the active interpretation and construction of social situations or events. Garfinkel has claimed that actors extract from, or inject meaning into, events by supplying a 'theme' to act as a baseline of meaning for the 'surface' behaviours. It is this base of meaning which actors use to transform the otherwise ambiguous surface features of situations into meaningful events. McHugh has identified its temporal significance:

> the documentary method is a formula used by actors to maintain temporal congruity in the environment and to keep meaning extensive in time (p. 35).

In this way meaning is recognized as having a temporal dimension. It is this very notion of meaning as it endures both within and across episodes which is critical for the present task. There will be an attempt later to examine the emergence and endurance of pupil identities both within and between episodes. A focus then upon the relationship between trans-episodic and intra-episodic formulation. In the present analysis the notion of a 'figure-ground' relationship will be referred to as a means of conceptualizing the idea of an enduring or trans-episodic formulation of Other. It will be suggested that the perception of a current episode as 'figure' may be transformed into a trans-episodic construction as 'ground' by the interpreter merely switching perspective from the immediate to the enduring properties of social reality.

The idea of the documentary method (of identifying the underlying meaning), suggested by Garfinkel as a means of making sense of situations or events, may have implications for understanding *person formulation*. It is quite possible that the formulation of persons is similarly a process of being concerned not just with the directly observable manifestations of Other, as he or she appears at present before the perceiver, but perhaps also with the more trans-episodic meanings attached to Others in *general* (as cultural notions or cultural stereotypes), or to a specific Other in the form of an identity which is seen to pre-exist, and endure beyond, the present manifestation of social reality as a form of continuing or trans-episodic Other. This notion seems to be implicit in the idea of enduring formulations to be found in the concepts of 'core' or 'sedimentary' typification (Hargreaves, 1977), 'pivotal category' (Lofland, 1969) and 'identity', suggesting a notion of deep structure and underlying meaning — that at the heart of everything the person does, the 'core typification', or 'pivotal category' will be *the* answer to the present search for meaning in Other's actions.

The work of Smith (1978), in studying the categorization of persons as mentally ill, has provided a framework capable of handling some of the less explored dynamics of person perception. Her analysis recognizes the problematic nature of social reality and its changing meanings when a new standpoint of perception is adopted, or when the framework of interpretation is shifted by restructuring the inherent ambiguities of data. Smith's analysis has some continuity with Garfinkel and the ethnomethodological tradition. She attempts a further conceptualization by incorporating the established notions of 'figure' and 'ground' from the field of the psychology of perception. Her incorporation provides a framework for exploring the *accomplishment* of constructed social reality in the face of potential ambiguities and the presence of dissonant elements from which actors piece together a definition of the situation. In situations of potential ambiguity, a constructed account is a process of constant searching which might then give prominence to one set of dissonant items, treated as figure, or to another set and so transform the overall construction: 'once you identify one facet as figure then the other is ground and vice versa' (Smith, 1978, p. 26).

This idea is seen by Smith to be particularly relevant for understanding the problematic nature of categorizing a person as 'mentally ill'. It involves the resolving of dissonant elements within a collection of inherently contradictory information where the assembled data may appear to have competing or contradictory features or even some fragments which are potentially dissonant. This resolution of dissonance would be most evident when attempting to categorize persons at critical boundaries within the social world — as between the 'normal' and the 'mentally ill'. Such a boundary is a significant social boundary since the stance taken in relation to it has powerful consequences for the imputed identity of the person under formulation. In schools and classrooms an imputation of pupil Other-role can be seen to have similar dramatic consequences for long-term identity, as, for example, in the identification of 'exceptional' or 'gifted' pupils or those with 'special needs' or categorized as 'sub-normal'. The potential for reification of identity in the social structuring of pupil careers has been well noted in educational research (Sharp and Green, 1975; Tomlinson, 1981). The present investigation has revealed an apparently similar boundary of critical significance in the social world of the classroom — that between the 'normal' and the 'abnormal' pupil. The same notions of 'figure' and 'ground' may then prove to have conceptual strength for handling the dynamic properties in present data, especially for examining long-term identity.

It can be seen that the figure/ground conceptual framework does provide a means for exploring some of the *dynamics* of person formulation — as a *process* of shifting between different elements of constructed images. Traditional work in the psychology of perception has provided a model of processing stimuli in which perceptually discrete elements within a perceptual frame contain certain prominent features (i.e. figure) which dominate the construction and result in the other elements (i.e. ground) receding in the constructed image. In those instances of specially constructed 'illusions' used in perceptual experiments, the ground element is usually so constructed as to be displaced by figure elements and so precluded from the construction when it is 'seen' to recede. And yet each element has the potential for appearing as either figure or as ground. It becomes theoretically possible for the perceiver to continually shift the 'figure' from one element to the other. In this way the construction becomes a *continual shifting* between two competing constructed images.

Continual shifting provides a useful and powerful metaphor for attempting an analysis of the construction of Others within a dynamic frame of reference. If it is assumed that social reality has no constancy of form but may be perceived and constructed from more than one standpoint, then clearly there are interpretative and selective processes that may operate when perceivers decide to adopt one perception or another. If we transpose the analysis from the psychological base of perception to the present sociological field of interpersonal relations and the domain of social psychology, it is likely that the process of constructing Others (as more than two dimensional 'objects') is a process involving even greater choice and more active construction than is the case with the two-dimensional stimuli of ambiguous 'figures' (which are specially constructed to be viewed from one standpoint or the other). The perceptual boundaries within the social psychological domain of everyday life then, may be assumed to be even more complex than such a simple dichotomy. The framework of constructing Others in the present study will begin its exploration from this basis as a means for viewing all the pupil careers as an ongoing or dynamic journey continually shifting through the figure-ground framework of teachers' accomplished constructions.

Episodic and Trans-Episodic Constructions of Reality

It is important to emphasize the sociological focus being employed here in referring to 'figure' and 'ground'. The conceptual framework originates in the psychology of perception and so perhaps more usually relates to the perception and interpretation of static, and more often inanimate, stimuli. In the present analysis, as in that of Smith, the use is *sociological* and will attempt to account for dynamic formulations within the ongoing construction of social reality. It is related to the notion of 'documentary method' (Garfinkel, 1967), of 'emergent theme' (McHugh, 1968), of 'core' and 'sedimentary typification' (Hargreaves, 1977), and of the identification of 'pivotal category' (Lofland, 1969) within the field of sociology.

Following what has already been discussed in respect of role-taking and the construction of Other as a process of placement of boundaries upon pupil roles, it now becomes possible to regard teachers' interpretations of pupil Other-roles as either *figure* formulations or *ground* formulations. The surface manifestations of *present* pupil role behaviour may be considered to be figure phenomena while the deep structure of *previous* or trans-episodic constructions contained within the notion of identity regarded as ground. Both elements may be present in the course of assembling a construction, with one or the other of either figure or ground possibly becoming dominant. This presence and possibility both provide a conceptual framework for handling the two potentially discrete elements of the teachers' perceptual frame and can incorporate two dimensions of temporal Other within it — the present episodic manifestations of Other role (figure) and the temporally distant or remote trans-episodic Other (ground). It is then possible to examine teachers' construction of pupils in figure-ground relations. The ground and figure may appear to the teacher as being in congruent relations when the present role or its manifestations are consistent with emergent or continuing identity but as being incongruent when the present manifestation of Other in a current episode is at odds with previous constructions of Other as enduring identity. The pupil's present actions or manifestations (i.e. figure) may be seen to be either congruent or incongruent with established constructions of Other (i.e. ground).

In this attempt to examine the dynamics of Other formulation over the temporal dimensions implied by the emergence of school careers, we are here incorporating the continuing or ongoing construction of reality within the notion of ground. Ground changes little with time (or at least is certainly less resistant to change). Figure is more shortlived and temporally fleeting. The longitudinal design of the present study allows for the monitoring of both short-lived and enduring forms of typification that may be conceptualized within the notions of an episodic figure and a trans-episodic ground. It is noticeable that much short-term research, with its emphasis on the observation of current behaviour[8] as 'figure' (Bennett, 1976; Galton, Simon and Croll, 1980) has offered less opportunity for temporal dimensions and enduring ground phenomena to emerge as an aspect of classroom reality — in fact it is often defined out of the research parameters! In such short-term research, the researcher is often guilty of approaching each observational unit of data afresh as though it were discrete and independent of previous observational settings. In educational research there is often an absence of any *long-term* longitudinal frame of reference equivalent to that which is naturally operated by teachers who are continually present within the same educational setting. Researchers are usually only occasional visitors to the situation and inevitably approach observation not from a frame of reference of continuity but of immediate, and so more usually figure, observation.

In the notion of ground is a reference to those enduring forms or constructions, of Other embraced by the concepts 'identity' and 'career'. 'Identity' is the perceived enduring, or relatively permanent, 'underlying theme' — a 'ground' for persons.

In this discussion the reference to role-taking, the formulation of Other-roles and the imputation of purposes to actors, permits connections to be made with the literature of person typification (Schutz, 1967) and that of role-taking (Turner, 1962):

> The unifying element [of a role] is to be found in some assignment of purpose or sentiment to the actor. Various actions by an individual are classified as intentional and unintentional on the basis of a role designation ... (p. 28).

Following this view it is possible to conceptualize ground or pivotal identity[9] as a long-term or enduring Other-role. It has already become noticeable how teachers seem to distinguish between 'normal' and 'abnormal' Other-roles in pupils. Such role distinctions are references to the actor's imputed typical motives or purposes. Consequently, the assignment of a pupil to a normal or an abnormal Other-role simultaneously fixes the typical motives or purposes he can be assumed to operate from. The 'abnormal' or 'normal' identity can be seen along with the typical operation of 'abnormal' and 'normal' motives. In the formulation of ground as well as in the recognition of identity, an additional element might perhaps be the associated range of motives related to the Other-role in the assignment of purpose or 'sentiment'. Such motives might be regarded as a reservoir of potential interpretations that could be dipped into by perceivers to provide meanings to be imputed to the actions of pupils in relation to their perceived Other-roles. So ground might be said to embrace the notion of identity and a related *reservoir of motives* (a concept suggested here and implicit in Schutz and Luckmann, 1974, to convey the notion of a store or pool of motives which may be dipped into by formulators of Other).

In fact it might be said that the existing power of the concept identity (in its usage as underlying theme for persons) is in its capacity to act as a reservoir from which motives of Other can be drawn at will in the prediction of future action and the empathic understanding of present actions. Whatever the 'actual' figure of an event or incident which is immediately apparent to the onlooker, Other's motives or purposes can always be supplied from the 'motivational reservoir' of ground and its supply of typical motives suitable for either the abnormal or normal Other-role already assigned as the 'pivotal category'. The meanings operated will arise from some relationship between figure (or surface appearances) and ground (or deep structure). This investigation of school careers attempts to explore the nature of such figure-ground relationships that teachers appear to employ as they engage in their classroom interpretation of pupils.

In seems that the present usage of 'motivational reservoir' is based upon similar concerns to that of Turner in his attempt to conceptualize processes of role-taking and also, of course, arises out of the Schutzian analysis of typification which provided an earlier focus for this study. This synthesis is seen to be a profitable and conceptually convenient merging of two otherwise separate lines of sociological analysis since the conceptual strength of Schutz in exploring typification has not seemed ever to develop the capacity to move very far into the *dynamics* of person formulation in action; Turner has quite separately provided a most useful conceptual framework for attempting an analysis of person formulation in outlining the dynamics of role-taking. The present notion of motivational reservoir seems to be, in effect, equivalent to Turner's references to an actor's orientation. The ground of a pupil's pivotal identity provides a motivational reservoir which is 'susceptible to interpretation' and 'directed towards the ends associated with the other-role'. While the trans-contextual or enduring ground (i.e. pivotal identity), is equivalent perhaps to Turner's notion that in imputing Other-role, the most likely outcome of interpretations of Other behaviour is to find 'a set of interpretations of his behaviour which will allow it to be seen as pertaining to a single role'.

The view expressed here is of a *ground* (as deep structure) which informs *figure* (or surface manifestation) appearances in the interpretation of such action. Ground is in a different temporal plane to figure. It is in an extended time-scale and so carries with it elements of previous figures. It is probable that all figures are immediately *neutral* in meaning until the ground is located.

Quite literally the surface figure is empty of meaning without its ground base.[10] However, once casting Other in either abnormal or normal trans-episodic roles, there is a secure ground or base upon which to construct an interpretation of the present figure. There is in the location of ground, an immediate access to either a normal or abnormal motivational reservoir which provides the meanings to displace the otherwise surface neutrality of figure, the equivalent to the ethnomethodological notion of identifying the underlying theme. In fact, the typification ground of Other *is* in effect the underlying theme. So the casting of the pupil in normal or abnormal Other-roles provides access to the ground of the motivational reservoir.

Turner has expressed a view on casting Other-roles which seems to anticipate this present figure-ground distinction:

> The unity of a role cannot consist simply in the *bracketing* of a set of specific behaviours, since the same behaviour can be indicative of different roles under different circumstances (p. 28).

The surface figure of the 'same behaviour' can thus, by invoking different grounds as 'different roles', be transformed into different frameworks of meaning.

Relating to the views of Smith discussed earlier (in formulating a case of mental illness), it can be seen how the formulating of a person in ground provides us with the transportable (in time and in situation) identity so as to make sense of Other:

— when ambiguity of identity suggests a variety of alternative accounts of Other are possible;
— when otherwise the *present* event would have no continuity with *past* events (of Other in previous settings) and so would be neutral (or ambiguous) in meaning just as they are for Schutz's 'Stranger' (Schutz, 1971) or when approaching Other or such an event for the first time (as a newcomer or new teacher) and when it would not be possible to 'see' in the figure the underlying ground which in-group members were already operating.

It is perhaps worth drawing distinctions from the present analysis of figure-ground and similar accounts previously employed in the social sciences. The present usage is to allow an analysis of the dynamics of past-present, current-ongoing, static-dynamic aspects of identity formulation. As such it is perhaps different from the psychology of perception (which examines predominantly static stimuli), and the ethnomethodology of theme (which tends to operate *within* episodes, i.e. at the micro level of intra-thematic minutae).

Thus the present approach is broader than the ethnomethodological in encompassing a longer-time scale. But as with much ethnomethodological analysis there is a shared similar concern for uncovering underlying 'structure' in the dynamics of figure-ground formulation. The present interest is in Other formulation at figure and ground level and how it proceeds as an ongoing 'practical accomplishment'.

In the psychology of figure-ground analysis, temporal parameters are often limited to short time-scales, such as can be found within experimental settings of a laboratory and, at most, limited to the episodic. The enduring elements are more usually defined out by the parameters of the prevailing methodologies dominant within the discipline itself. The sociological equivalent to figure-ground in ethnomethodology (i.e. the *ongoing* 'accomplishment' of theme) is more usually defined out methodologically in research by the absence of longitudinal analysis and the tendency to focus upon the immediate, or at least actors', methods of accomplishing the immediate construction of reality.

The interpretative framework being used assumes that *ground* is what gives meaning to *figure* in ongoing processes of Other formulation, and that perhaps all perceptions remain mere shallow descriptions until they can be given some sense of underlying pattern or theme. This underlying theme then acts as a foundation for uncovering deeper meanings.

This discussion has given some attention to the concept of documentary method, extended to include the process by which actors seek out and create meaning in relation to *situations* and to *persons*. It is suggested that such deeper structures implied by the notion of ground, whether episodic or trans-episodic, may be the elements of the interpretative framework actually used by actors to construct meanings — the imputed situated meanings of Other actors. Turner has seen similar processes in role-taking. Other's actions are thought to make sense when it is possible to make an interpretation which implies that the actor is adopting some role which is governing his conduct. The central reliance upon role interpretation suggests elements of both role-casting (in the invoking of boundaries), and the imputation of motives. It is a process which may be *episodic*, employing the search for episodic theme, or *trans-episodic*, employing the established ground of pivotal identity as a base for constructing the theme for persons underlying a present figure. Indeed, it may well even be a genuinely interactive process of the episodic and trans-episodic impinging upon each other. But the major implication is that without access to trans-episodic meanings of identity or the deep structure underlying the events of an episode, the meanings of an otherwise 'surface' or episodic figure would be problematic to the actor.

This implication would, in effect, be equivalent to Durkheim's notion of anomie (Durkheim, 1933) when the foundations of social action become problematic to actors. The concept has indeed been used by McHugh to relate to the micro-sociological manifestations of 'normlessness', as when an actor is unable to discover an underlying theme or meaning in a situation. The documentary method then can be seen to be quite critically related, at the level of the individual actor, to the concept anomie. In the analysis of the following case studies of deviant pupils, it can be seen how the difficulties faced by teachers in making sense of their actions on occasions lead to situations which are close to 'anomie'. At such times the ambiguity of meanings defies interpretation through either the figure or the ground phenomena to make sense of classroom episodes.

Notes

1 This expression is used in the sense that it is used by C. Wright Mills (1940) in making reference to a sociological account of action in 'delimited societal situations'.

2 'Normal space' is used in the sense employed by Erikson (1966), p. 19.

3 It can be seen, of course, that a temporal dimension has already appeared in this analysis. The earlier reference to a pathological model in the imputation of a deviant identity recognizes an enduring or semi-permanent construction of social reality. Once adopted by the typifier it seems to form a baseline of meaning from which formulation proceeds. In routine operation it is in effect treating Other, through employing notions of identity, as a semi-permanent phenomenon conceptually continuing through time, except for those occasions or episodes when it is otherwise apparently suspended.

4 This would in effect be a form of criterion-referenced categorization in which the surface features of events become the raw material outsiders have to rely upon as they engage in the process of formulation. However, insiders to the social world are able to engage in more sophisticated processes of relativity, using norm-referenced forms of categorization in relation to the known underlying qualities of the present population and in relation to Others experienced in the past.

5 The focus is upon past and present inter-relationships in formulation across trans-episodic boundaries.

6 This long term 'assembly' is the essence of the phenomenological approach to the interpretation of social reality. Reality is indeed constructed! For example, deviant pupils may, for more than 90 per cent of the time, be engaging in non-deviant actions. To maintain a view of Other as deviant in spite of this is accomplished by sustaining a continuing construction of Other from one episode to the next which retains features that usually lie beyond the immediate episode.

7 This idea corresponds closely with a view of trans-episodic role which is taken up in later chapters in the notion of pivotal identity and the perception of ground.

8 In approaching each observational situation afresh, as though it were independent of previous or preceding constructions of reality, researchers inevitably focus upon the figure phenomena which appear in current episodes. This usually leads to a neglect of the long-term longitudinal frame of reference that may in practice be naturalistically employed by teachers who are continually present within the same social setting. As researchers are only occasional visitors to the situation of ongoing social action they inevitably approach observation not from a frame of reference of 'natural' continuity but from a preoccupation with the immediate as figure.

9 Here I adopt Lofland's concept of pivotal category; the dominant category is Other's identity.

10 This assertion suggests that the more dominant social reality is the trans-episodic and that naturalistically teachers inhabit a trans-episodic world. Current events in real time are interpreted in relation to the trans-episodic.

Part II

Critical Cases in Emergence and Maintenance of Careers in Early Schooling

---

Gavin — A Deviant Pupil, School A

Alan — A Deviant Pupil, School B

James — A Normal Pupil, School A

Louise — A Normal Pupil, School A

Sally — A Normal Pupil, School B

Dawn — A Normal Pupil, School B

The career of each pupil is examined over the first four years of schooling, exploring the emergence, maintenance and modifications recognized in a variety of early school identities. Each case can be understood and appreciated in its own terms. The reader may accordingly wish to be selective in following through the individual careers. The two deviant pupils are discussed at some length. Alan's case is especially long as he is both enigmatic and changeable, experiencing continual reformulation over the first four years of his early school career and at times is seen to shift between a deviant and a normal identity.

Chapter 9

Episodes in the Emergence of a Deviant Career: Gavin (School A)

Having outlined a framework for exploring the interpretation of identities within the processes of relativity and emergence, this framework is now used to analyze each of the case studies. For the first case there is an opportunity to consider the emergence of a deviant identity: Gavin is a pupil who for much of his school career is seen as deviant. His early school career can be followed, examining the emergence and ongoing construction of his deviant identity beginning with his first week in school.

Year One: First Episodes in the Emergence of a Deviant Identity

Week One

The record of Gavin's school career begins with his teacher's comments on their first encounter. It seems his teacher, Miss Bennett, is engaged in a search for what McHugh has called an underlying theme and immediately suspects a possible deviant identity:

> I don't know what's hit me really. The first day I'd all these weepy shy kids. I thought ... what ... non-descripts. And then the second day I got Gavin. Gavin's a bit of a misfit really. It's very strange but from the minute his mum brought him in.... Sort of a way out kid in the sense that he punches everybody else, scribbles all over their books, locks the toilet doors.

This account suggests a rapid move from an *episodic* framework of formulation to the more fundamental identity of trans-episodic Other role formulation. The teacher is already presenting a view of how *he is*. The formulation is in enduring *personal* rather than merely in short-lived *episodic* terms (in which the focus would have been on the unique properties of a specific encounter). Formulation has already moved beyond 'acts' to 'dispositions' (Jones and Davis, 1965). For his teacher the issue is not so much what he did on that occasion but the more generalized concern about what he *does*. In the imputation of theme a continuity of identity is suggested. It seems too, that the search for understanding him has already resulted in the formulation of a provisional motivational base which is now in use as Miss Bennett discusses how she has attempted to deal with him so far:

> I've given him a shake today. Because he punched three children who came and told me. But Gavin doesn't *even* seem to respond to that.

This statement seems to be a confirmation that the teacher is going beyond the exploration of underlying theme as an episodic searching for a pupil construction and appears already to be touching a deeper structure — an underlying and enduring identity with its accompanying motivational base.

As the teacher goes on to recount another classroom incident she works out the probable meaning of the event by seeing it in ground terms. She transposes[1] the framework of formulation from the present episode to a trans-episodic motivational base. The present episode (figure) is seen as a sign of an *underlying* condition (ground):

> He wanders as well. We thought he'd run off yesterday. And he hadn't. He was just having a look round. But he couldn't see that we would be concerned because he wasn't with *us*. I think he's just been used to complete freedom.

At this point, the teacher is forming a *trans-episodic* view of the pupil. Other is being constructed as though the key to unlocking meaning in current events is to be found in an enduring personal identity. The associated motivational base gives the teacher something to work on. She can assume the motivational base may also be present in other future dealings with the pupil and so it appears to give her a means of strategy formulation. In the teacher's dealings with the pupil, the emerging ground or deep structure suggests a clue to his motivation and the teacher's strategy can now be formulated accordingly. In effect, she can act upon it. It seems the teacher is already dipping into a motivational reservoir:

> I understand that and have been making allowances ... I have been trying to talk him out of it.

At this point, all formulation is firmly within the abnormal model which seems to have been adopted as a provisional base for formulation. Other is not formulated as though the figure phenomena of each episode will provide the cues for constructing meaning. It seems to be assumed that these will be found in deviant ground which is carried forward into successive dealings as a trans-episodic formulation.

The pupil appears to have rapidly acquired a pivotal identity within the first week of school and it is even suggested in Miss Bennett's first encounter with him. Presumably the first observation of a deviant occurrence in any pupil will allow the encounter to be seen as a mere chance or episodic occurrence and so it may be viewed from a framework of normal identity as the 'baseline of meaning'. But as deviance persists then the ground of formulation will perhaps switch to deviant or abnormal in the manner outlined by Hargreaves (1975) when speculation, elaboration and stabilization increasingly confirm the baseline identity.[2] In this case it seems the pupil never operated upon normal ground since the moment he came through the door the normal ground was discarded (provisionally at least).

Week Two

Week two provides a continuing account of ground emergence. Miss Bennett recounts a classroom episode involving Gavin. The incident, although potentially deviant, is recognized by the teacher as ambiguous. It could allow either a 'normal' or a 'deviant' interpretation. The teacher in fact begins a 'normal' construction, attempting to understand it within its own episodic parameters but then sees beyond it to a 'deeper structure' or trans-episodic identity and its associated motivational baseline:

> I'm sure he's totally selfish! He's got no concept whatsoever of sharing or helping or cooperating ... unless he can see an end for himself. None at all! One day I asked him to tidy some cards when we were late going out to play. And he said: 'No, I don't want to!' And afterwards, he walked out. And then he turned and stopped and looked at me. Walked back and put the cards away! Now I thought: Wey Hey! I've done it. This is it. But it wasn't! Everything since has indicated it's something more.

At the time of the incident Miss Bennett attempted to 'normalize' the classroom action by treating it as a mere episodic phenomenon which might quickly pass. But the ground of abnormality quickly returns: 'everything since has indicated it's something more than that'. Although the teacher attempted to operate a 'normal' *episodic theme* at the time of the incident she has since formed the view that a deeper structure or *trans-episodic* identity is more appropriate for unpacking the meaning. In this formulation can be seen signs of the teacher recognizing that the emerging deviant identity will probably be an appropriate framework to search for theme in future episodes.[3] Its enduring form or identity-maintaining features are emerging.

In such incidents, the teacher attempts to operate a normal model but the realization that there is 'something more' quickly invokes a return of the abnormal model.[4] Presumably *at the time* the teacher is not in a position to 'know'. She is only able to hope or guess.[5] The 'professionalism' and openness of interpretative categories is apparent at this point in the teacher's repeated attempts to abandon the abnormal model. But retrospectively Miss Bennett is able to recognize from her *present standpoint* that effectively the abnormal model still operated: 'everything since has indicated it's something more than that'.

Miss Bennett goes on to recount another incident. Again there are signs of the 'professional optimism'.[6] She first confirms that Gavin is still a 'nuisance' but that on one occasion, when in the playground, he presented an appearance of normality when she, as his class teacher, was with him on playground duty:

> Punching other children in the playground. That's continued ...
> Throwing sand in their faces. Again ... generally making a nuisance of himself. Now funnily enough, when I was on playground duty he didn't! I don't know if that's because he knew me.

Miss Bennett is still looking for a normal construction. In this case apparently assuming a member's rule of interpretation that a person will tend to adopt a 'normal' identity when with someone whom one knows. This would then allow by implication that any deviation could be a short-lived or episodic phenomenon until he gets to know people. The deviance might therefore be due only to the pupil's temporary role as a stranger. Once again it seems the teacher is attempting to invoke a normal model.

The next incident amplifies the attempt further:

> One time this week, Charlotte took the story. I had to do something for Mrs. Russell. And when I went back over, Gavin said he was going to the toilet. And he'd got his coat. Now that was because it was with somebody different and he thought he could get away with it.

In spite of the teacher's recognition of abnormal model as a possible framework for formulation the continuing attempt to look for normal interpretations proceeds. Miss Bennett mentions a deviant incident where the pupil had to be smacked and sees signs of possible normality emerging following the deviant incident:

> but in the afternoon he was better ... since then his behaviour hasn't been quite so unruly.

Miss Bennett is now attempting to look for a normal baseline. The 'professional optimism' is noticeable as the teacher seems to switch to normal monitoring. (Note at this early phase the fluidity of Other formulation as the teacher moves between *abnormal* and *normal* models and between *episodic* and *trans-episodic* constructions. Figure and ground construction moves between deviant and normal interpretations).

However, the abnormal model is still present in the ground framework of Miss Bennett's formulation. She recounts an incident in which after working on a picture Gavin 'didn't want to take his picture home *again*'. Although the drawing had apparently been important to him, especially as 'he wanted to do those ships', Miss Bennett is surprised by the fact that 'he *still* didn't take it home ... and that's funny'. Apparently this figure instance is seen as a surface indication of a fundamental and basically abnormal ground. For this teacher, then, by the end of week two there are strong indications of a potential deviant ground even though she apparently remains professionally optimistic — keeping her categories 'open' and so allowing many potential deviant incidents to be neutralized,[7] in being seen as mere episodic occurrences contingent upon the features of the setting or the relationships with particular others.

At the same time another teacher, Mrs. Russell, is also formulating Gavin as potentially deviant. The fact that this pupil and another potential deviant is allocated to her own table at lunchtime alerts her to a potential abnormal model: 'They are the two that stand out'. This assessment, of course, could simply indicate a recognition of some marginality within the normal 'range' (Erikson, 1966) of identities and interactions within a typical pupil distribution and may not necessarily imply a categorization of this pupil as significantly an outsider *across* the boundary into abnormality. But Mrs. Russell immediately invokes a tentative abnormal ground: 'I was probably planted with them'. It suggests a recognition that other teachers were probably operating an interpersonal boundary — that these were not random allocations but from a more deliberate and confident Other-role identification by her colleagues. So the recognition of 'deep structure' and ground identity become the teacher's *own* methods of interpreting other teachers' perceptions of this pupil. There is an indication of an inter-subjective world of formulators.

Mrs. Russell's continuing speculative construction of pupil Other-role is assisted in a direction of figure-ground congruency by her recalling a meeting with the parents of the new intake pupils at which Gavin's mother 'was the only one who didn't respond and had nothing to say'. Mrs. Russell sees this passivity as possibly significant as a clue to the pupil's own identity: 'I would imagine the way *she* is will explain why Gavin is like he is'.

Here is an indication of the micro-sociology of home-school relations. It is suggested that a process of congruency is expected in the identities of members of the same family as the teacher assembles what she recognizes as an underlying baseline which links both pupil and parent.

The Dynamics of Emergence — Episodic and Trans-Episodic Constructions

Week Three

As week three begins there is an emerging trans-episodic deviant ground in the formulation of this pupil but with an attempt to interpret some individual episodes by continuing to use a normal framework. At this point there seems to be some confusion within the school as to whether deviance is to be treated as a *trans-episodic* or merely an *episodic* phenomenon.

As week three begins teachers are now given some significant information which 'completes' their assembling picture. Gavin's mother informs them of his past history in nursery schools and so provides some clarity to the teachers' formulation of ground:

> He's quite happy as long as he's with adults on a one-to-one but he just doesn't mix with other children at all. This is obviously the reason.

The motivational base is now clarified for Miss Bennett. It is perhaps in effect a firming up or elaboration of the model, i.e. abnormality is confirmed. What was previously only suspected is now apparently given greater validity by the exchange of typification between parents and teachers:

> He's an outdoor kid. And suddenly here was I in a classroom! And obviously he felt threatened[8] or enclosed and not happy! Now I hinted at that last week. So I was right.

Miss Bennett has now incorporated his mother's ground (mother acting as 'typification carrier') into her own formulation base. She uses it to explain her own current dealings with him. The deviant Other-role recognized in the placement of an interpersonal boundary is now being elaborated by Gavin's class teacher. Apparently she was never quite sure whether her difficulties with Gavin were due to her own inadequacy or inexperience as a teacher or whether the pupil really was deviant. Now it's resolved:

> I couldn't put my finger on it. I was worried in case it was something to do with us. Before that I didn't know what was the matter. I couldn't put my finger on it.

It seems that Miss Bennett's experience of trying to make sense of the pupil created a sense of potential anomie[9] in her difficulty in identifying an underlying Other-role to this pupil. Of course it would only be partial anomie as the teacher was able to postulate one of two possible themes: *either* 'something to do with us', *or* his underlying abnormal baseline. There was enough ambiguity for it to be one or the other. There was always a *potential* theme rather than a complete absence of theme.

Nevertheless, although there is a very clear deviant ground held by Miss Bennett in her formulatory frame of reference with this pupil, it is not operating statically. There is a shifting towards alternative interpretation[10] as an emerging potential for normality is recognized: 'still doesn't really mix well but whereas last week.... But this week ... a lot more cooperation'. Miss Bennett, it seems, is still attempting to invoke a normal frame of perception. After observing his 'manoeuvres',[11] many of which were beyond the normal boundary or boundaries, he can be seen to be possibly moving towards the normal world. Perhaps in 'distance' he is still only slightly closer to the normal world, but maybe the important thing for the teacher is the *direction* of movement. At this point, alternative methodologies using a static research framework may miss what is *emerging*. Although in *categorial* terms this pupil is obviously still seen to be an outsider beyond the normal boundary and therefore is seen to be presenting a deviant identity, if we adopt, as the teacher has, an open perspective, it can be seen that while the pupil is yet deviant he appears at the same time to be moving in the direction of normality. The teacher's *own* framework is dynamic. Even the ground formulation is a shifting one.[12] Although the underlying category is clear, it nevertheless is not treated by the teacher as an entirely static phenomenon.

An episodic framework is next used in interpreting a deviant incident which is formulated *within* its own episodic boundaries. It is presented as a self-contained episode rather than as a mere exemplar of a phenomenon which is connected with a trans-episodic deviant ground:

> He doesn't know Mrs. Hope. And he was very badly behaved. And yet in the classroom he'd been excellent that morning.

Miss Bennett seems to interpret this naughtiness as mere episodic deviance (Lofland, 1969). It has an underlying theme of potential normality.[13] This incident appears on the surface to be deviant but it is situationally neutralized[14] by the teacher's formulation of it. It is seen to be contingent upon the current interpersonal setting and not on an underlying deviant (ground) identity. There is an apparent neutralizing process in Miss Bennett's imputing a normal motive: 'he wasn't being purposefully naughty'.

The teacher is apparently drawing a motive from *within* the boundaries[15] of the episode and not from *beyond* its boundaries.[16] It seems to be interpretable from the construction of an episodic theme. In interpreting this episode, the teacher does not draw from a trans-episodic formulation of pupil identity as ground, nor its associated motivational reservoir.

In the next account, the teacher again ascribes Gavin's misbehaviour to motives within the boundaries as the deviance is blamed on another pupil — a bigger deviant case! The motive for Gavin's behaviour is imputed from *within* the episodic boundaries and not from a trans-episodic reservoir:

> It was partly his fault on Tuesday that Gavin started 'playing up'. Gavin didn't quite know what he'd done but he did it again just to please this kid.

Here the teacher invokes only an episodic theme for interpreting Gavin's actions and imputes a non-deviant motive of apparent innocence. This is a case of formulating in apparently suspended ground terms and relying solely upon the figure properties of the episode. The trans-episodic ground of deviance is suspended — the figure is apparently isolated from the construction of the continuing social reality of identity and so is formulated without ground as though bracketed within its own episodic boundaries. The pupil's own deviant ground then does not seem to intrude upon the interpretation of the incident. It is *insulated* from ground and the incident is apparently seen only in figure terms — as an event of mere episodic deviance. Consequently, the search for meaning proceeds at an episodic level — in relation to the identifiable features of the situation itself. It is the search for episodic theme which on this occasion yields meaning rather than the trans-episodic meanings of deviant ground and its motivational reservoir.

During the interview, there is a reference to a current deviant incident happening at that very moment; Miss Bennett has to leave the research interview for a short time, to dismiss the class at the end of the day. As she returns she announces her witnessing of the anticipated deviant incident:

> Just been horrible again. But nowhere near what he was before! At least we've got it down to that.

The teacher uses trans-episodic deviant ground in this incident. The basic abnormal ground still persists but nevertheless is seen within a dynamic framework. He is firmly within the deviant category but moving in a normal direction. Miss Bennett seems able to neutralize the impact of deviant ground or achieve an episodically structured normality as she implies in her continuing account of this incident:

> He was playing up. So I just insisted and put it [his coat] on for him! He is OK. Once you've told him!

The teacher is here drawing upon a motivational reservoir for formulating her episodic strategy. Her formulating of the pupil's Other-role is not then episodic but trans-episodic, that is in relation to the motivational reservoir and ground identity and not to the episodic dimensions of the situation alone. An important aspect of the process of social interaction is the *definition of the situation* (Thomas, 1931; Waller, 1932; Stebbins, 1969). The teacher may define the situation in episodic or in trans-episodic terms. It may be interpreted as an episodically-bounded setting or as a situation in continuity with an enduring trans-episodic reality as found in the notions of identity, ground and motivational reservoir.

Further Movement Towards Normality

For the next few weeks Gavin's career is seen to be on the move and shifting in a direction of normality. The headteacher, Mrs. Russell, remarks upon,

> how little the staff had noticed him this last couple of weeks.

For the headteacher, a significant reference point in the turning of the career is the visit of his mother to the school. It seems to be, and is recognized as a point of emergence in what is perceived to be a communal[17] redefinition of the situation.

> It was our attitude to him resulting from his mother coming up as well
> as their attitude at home. Mother began to relax at home about it. I
> think there are so many things that rub off after you've had a parent in
> to talk.

The parental visit seems to become an important reference point for the headteacher. A landmark perhaps not just in direction but in a shared *congruency* of direction as a redefinition of meanings results for everyone: 'It's a slight change of attitude all round'.

This 'slight change of attitude' is an aspect of formulation that is often neglected in labelling theory accounts of deviance. The *direction* of deviance in Other-role is often seen to be a one-way movement towards the abnormal role, and away from a perceived occupancy of normal role. Here, however, there appears to be a recognition of the social processes involved in the communal attempts both to neutralize his deviance and to mobilize his Other-role in a normal direction:

> Even though you were doing the best for Gavin and you were caring for
> him, and looking to see where you could praise him, instead of having
> to tell him off, the very fact that mother's been in and you've therefore
> learned a little bit more about him alters your attitude immediately'.

From Deviant to Divergent Model?

At this point in his career, teachers review the perceived changes in his identity. He is seen to be moving away from a deviant identity to a more modified ground position:

> Just went bananas the first week. He was screaming and shouting and
> not waiting his turn. Now he tends to wait a bit more.

It is as though he was a complete outsider in the first week but now there is a more modified abnormality. In this instance it is possible that the category may now be more appropriately seen as *divergent* rather than distinctly deviant or *pathological* — that now a quantitative rather than a qualitative 'boundary' operates. The abnormal model may still provide the baseline information but he is seen to be more moderate, as seen in the following comment in the same week:

> Needs settling a lot more than the others. But he does respond a bit.
> You don't have to blow your top any more to get a reaction from him.

This modification of behaviour also provides a clearer indication of boundary. The implication is that he was clearly beyond a significant boundary requiring the class teacher, Miss Bennett, to adopt a different strategy with him: to 'blow your top'. The strategy now required is the same qualitatively as with the other pupils but merely requires more of it.

The discussion above provides an empirical illustration of the boundary between *divergent* and deviant or *pathological* formulation. In this case there is no longer the qualitative distinction recognized between Gavin and other pupils in which a qualitatively different motivational base might be seen to operate, so prompting the use of a different strategy. Now it is merely a quantitative distinction. The same strategy operates as for other pupils but quantitatively adapted.[18] He: 'needs settling a lot more than the others'.

In this week there is a further confirmation of the movement towards normality: 'He's definitely sort of settled down and become anonymous'. This comment suggests the pupil is now incorporated into the normal world of the classroom in the perception of Miss Bennett. It is possible the pupil is simultaneously perceived differently by other teachers and that the pupil may be experiencing different careers with different teachers at the same point in time.

Deviant Identity Continues — Abnormal Pathological Restored

Week Eight

The potential normality is shortlived. In the next episode, which comes a month later, a figure observation is the entry point for another teacher's, Mrs. Bradley's, interpretation, but is transposed into a ground formulation revealing the continuing deviant identity underlying the pupil's use of bad language:

> For a 4-year-old child to come out with 'Miss Bennett is a bugger'.
> Would you ever've thought of anything?

Here, of course, the deviation is interpreted as simply a matter of rule-breaking — crossing a critical boundary: 'would you ever've thought of anything'. It also shows the element of 'career timetable' (Roth, 1963) which may be a background to interaction and formulation — the 'moving perspective' within which pupils are 'measured' — the age-referent yardstick.

In this week there is also an indication of how deviant ground is by now an ever-present feature of pupil identity for other teachers — even in apparently 'normal' figure incidents or episodes:

> Gavin, the little boy who can be aggressive, was playing a sort of pretend fighting game. But he wasn't actually hurting anybody. It was under control.

Next a suggestion of pupil identity in a temporal unit lying somewhere between the episodic and the trans-episodic. A unit of time extending beyond the short-lived classroom encounter — the *extended episode*:

> he was in an awkward mood all throughout dinner. But he was in an awkward mood all that day.

The deviant incident, then, is seen as part of an underlying theme extending for an entire day. But since theme rather than ground is invoked we may treat it as an episodic form of social construction — but in extended form: the *extended episode*.

Further Episodes in a Deviant Career

From this point there are numerous deviant episodes reported by the class teacher, but which are not worth repeating here. Reference will be made only to those examples which offer particular insights into the dynamics of formulation as the pupil is interpreted through varying kinds of classroom episode. Some are formulated at figure level only (as episodic phenomena) and some at ground level (interpreted in terms of an underlying deviant ground, even in spite of the appearance of normal 'figure' within the occasional episode of normality).

For example: 'he was hitting somebody with that card but it was only imaginative'. Here a potential deviant figure is neutralized by insulating it from a ground-based deviant construction and placing it firmly as an interpretation located within its own episodic boundaries. Episodic theme is used to give meaning to the pupil on this occasion.

Or, for example, when Miss Bennett, after giving him some help, had insisted he work on the model-making activity in a particular manner, a normal figure with deviant ground:

> I didn't think he would. I thought as soon as I let go he'd go back and be doing that again, thinking he wouldn't do it my way. But I think he sees reason sometimes.

This normal episodic figure interpretation is seen to have an underlying deviant trans-episodic baseline. The deviant ground is further maintained by formulating it more precisely to take account of such instances of episodic normality while still retaining deviant trans-episodic baseline. The occurrence of instances of episodic normality does not threaten the deviant ground. Another example of the teacher looking beyond a normal figure to recognize a potential deviant ground can be seen this time as the teacher relives some 'routine' video sequences of Gavin in the classroom. Miss Bennett gives an action replay of the sequence and interprets a quite normal episode on video-tape by recognizing that its meaning cannot be taken merely at its apparent surface level:

He fluctuates so much. That's his cooperative self. When you have a day like that it's wonderful. And it can change within half an hour. There you would say he had a very good relationship with me. He was warm. Coming to me for doing what I said. But then … but then …

— a clear account of the potential ambiguity recognized between any normal figure and the abnormal ground in the teacher's construction of reality. The teacher recognizes that a 'normal' surface perception will always rest upon a deeper ground formulation. Social reality is also seen to be a shifting or dynamic phenomenon. It 'can change within half an hour'.

Final week: Processes of Transition to Year Two

This is the point at which ground enters into a more long-term structuring of pupil career as the cohort are allocated to the teacher in the next year group. The headteacher, Mrs. Russell, recognized the presence of underlying ground and used it to ensure his location on the right class list for next year's allocations: 'Mrs. Hope has dealt with town children and this is why we've put Gavin with her'.

It seems ground operates at a level of organizational 'structuring', and not just in the spontaneous flow of classroom life. It would be possible to view this attitude perhaps as a further move towards the reification of a deviant pupil identity (as might Sharp and Green, 1975, p. 218) and the construction of an organizational frame for formulation. However, such would be an erroneous and mischievous interpretation. The teacher's own account, and certainly the researcher's sense of 'shared' understandings at the time (and since) suggest not! There seems rather to be an attempt to shift ground in a positive direction. Mrs. Hope is seen as one who will give this pupil a chance to start afresh and without undue 'societal reaction'. This strategy indicates an intention to adopt a 'professional' stance in dealings with Gavin by setting up opportunities for minimizing rather than amplifying the deviant ground.

Year Two: Episodes in the Emergence of a Deviant Identity

Gavin begins year two with another teacher, Mrs. Hope. Once again it is possible to examine processes in the emergence of his identity. As might be expected the early formulations are less clearly formulated from a baseline of firm ground, but of course the teacher's knowledge of Gavin through staffroom culture inevitably means his reputation will have preceded him. Early encounters at first seem to be seen as neutral episodes which are entirely groundless or are interpreted in figure terms with a provisional ground not yet emerged.

Week One

Formulation begins, in fact, with such ambiguities: 'He was very aggressive'. This statement seems at first to be a groundless formulation — a mere neutral episodic formulation suggesting no more than an instance of episodic deviance. But it is expressed in conjunction with a suggestion of underlying abnormality: 'Mum knows he's got some kind of problem'.

This comment suggests pathological connotations and that a possible provisional ground may be emerging in the new teacher's formulation of Gavin. The tentativeness is indicated at this point in the absence of a firm ground, as though Mrs. Hope is prepared to wait and see.

Week Three

The uncertainty of ground is implied at this point: 'The last week he wasn't too bad'. It seems as though Mrs. Hope recognizes the within-school culturally sustained deviant identity but is suspending judgment at this point.[19]

Week Five

Two weeks later the ground is more firmly acknowledged. The teacher at this point recognizes a potential 'reality' of deviant identity as formulatory ground. She is now apparently operating a suspected motivational reservoir and constructs her strategy in relation to it:

> He came in with a face like thunder. So I thought we've got to start off as we plan to, so if he's naughty at all he must be treated as such.

Mrs. Hope is formulating the figure observations of this episode in association with an underlying propensity for this pupil to be deviant. In recognizing his 'face like thunder' she is apparently choosing to treat it as not a mere episodic figure but as an indication of the suspended deviant ground which she seems to have resisted so far. At this point in exploring an episode, the teacher is treating its theme as something which is possibly to be found beyond that of the mere figure phenomena of surface appearances.

Mrs. Hope next outlines a deviant incident in which once again she is formulating boundaries, both contextual, spatial and interpersonal:

> He started off by kicking. So I said: Right. He had to miss a playtime. Because this happened outside, I said if he couldn't behave himself in the playground then he couldn't play with the other children.

Here, Mrs. Hope defines the incident and punishment in terms of its interpersonal boundaries. The whole event is contextualized even further by being prefixed with the context of 'it happened outside'. Perhaps the teacher is either operating, or trying to formulate, a contextual ground of Other in context A and in context B, and attempting, perhaps, to deny, or at least to resist, the core typification of deviance. In this way it is possible to insulate some aspects of ground as safe from deviant categorization.

This teacher has already recognized the predominant deviance of his identity.

She uses it for strategy formulation and even confronts Gavin with the likely interactional consequences of such an identity:

> I had him on his own. I didn't say it in front of the rest of the children. I told him if he's naughty the children won't like you.

Quite clearly, then, within a few weeks, the underlying deviance is so firmly formulated that the pupil himself can be confronted with it in direct negotiation and Mrs. Hope has it incorporated within her plans for further action:[20]

> I wanted to be blunt with him so he knew where he stood. So that if he was naughty and the punishment had to be quick and sharp then I didn't have to do all the explaining again to him why I'd done it.

The teacher is quite 'professional'. There is a recognition of an underlying deviant ground and its likely surfacing in future deviant incidents but an intention to act so as to anticipate and so modify some aspects of the 'societal reaction'.

In continuing through this account of Gavin's second year in school, comment will only be offered on those occurrences that are non-standard. That is, where formulation is not a straightforward construction of either a normal figure resting upon a deviant ground, a deviant figure upon a deviant ground, or a formulation at deviant ground level only. Such 'standard' formulations occur so often that little would be gained by repeating them.

Classroom Episodes in a Deviant Career

Week Seven

In week seven the predictive value of deviant ground now seems less certain. Mrs. Hope comments on a divergence from expected deviance during observed episodes:

> Gavin's expression was quite a lively one. Not his usual glowering one when anybody disagrees with him.

This comment suggests that perhaps ground formulations can be *segmentally* differentiated — according to the typical context of their application. In this case the teacher is surprised at the non-occurrence of something which was expected in a situation of some frustration. She sees it in terms of its continuities with similar situations and the usual ground which might be expected to operate.

Teacher Strategies in Relation to Deviant Pupil

It can be seen how the underlying deviant identity is always present. It guides Mrs. Hope's overall classroom strategy: 'I do observe him most of the time to see if I can keep him out of trouble'. Labelling theory accounts have demonstrated how an initial labelling may lead to both an increase in awareness and a selective subsequent monitoring of the 'victim' and so lead to a greater tendency to notice the deviant behaviour! Here, however, the very same process of closer monitoring is operated within a very different avowed framework — 'to keep him out of trouble'. It should be recognized that the operation of deviant ground is not a straightforward matter promoting processes of labelling. It has frequently been demonstrated in these case studies how the use of deviance can alert a teacher to implement advanced precautions to prevent deviant episodes occurring or assisting pupils in the renegotiation of what would otherwise constitute surface appearances of deviance.

Teacher Strategies in Negotiating Action in Relation to Deviant and Normal Pupils

An incident now occurs with a deviant baseline and yet an ambiguously normal theme. Other pupils have, on this occasion, to be treated as deviant in the presence of Gavin:

> I think he was quite pleased to see that I'd drawn the attention to the other children that he can be kind. That he's not always the naughty boy.

Gavin's Other-role here is formulated predominantly from a deviant ground but it surfaces in Mrs. Hope's quite deliberate use of it to impose a normal theme in interpreting and acting in this episode. It is the other pupils in this situation who are episodically given deviant Other-roles. But these are seen to rest upon grounds of normal identities:

> It wasn't really serious. I would probably've not made such a big issue out of it.

The teacher's strategy on this occasion is to act in an exaggerated way to both surface figures — the 'normal' behaviour of Gavin and the deviant actions of the others. However, it is the *underlying theme* of the episode which carries the 'real' meaning. The meaning for the teacher, and for the reader, is that the whole episode is founded upon the trans-episodic deviant ground of Gavin!

Societal Reactions in School: Further Negotiations in a Deviant Identity

Mrs. Hope recounts a situation in which while her own and the other teacher's common ground formulation treats Gavin as deviant, they do not share a common interpretation of the present episode. The pupil was accused of deviance involving children from other classes and so the teacher here is pressured into responding when she seems to prefer a strategy of under-reaction. An indication then, of how 'societal reaction' may in some contexts be itself a complex process of negotiation within organisational settings:

Yesterday, when he was very naughty and had evidently been aggressive all dinnertime. Even though I hadn't seen it I took him to the teachers whose children were concerned in it. And let them deal with it. I have discussed it with staff. And I said if we're going to punish him, can we be consistent.

Further Episodes in a Deviant Career

There is, next, a further indication that ground is always recognized to be not far from the 'surface'. The persisting deviant ground is seen to be an ever-present phenomenon, even when the figure appearances in an episode are 'normal':

Today he's been good. But I think this afternoon he'll probably be naughty because he had to stay in because the dinner nannies can't control him.

Some fluidity in moving quickly from normal to deviant episode is recognized and can even be predicted in these situated formulations of likely frustration or provocation.

Next there is a confusion of motives and a disputation of formulations from different standpoints:

Caught him hitting a child this morning. But it was in play. And the child immediately turned round and looked at me.

In spite of Mrs. Hope holding a deviant identity as pivotal ground, the perception of the figure phenomena of this episode is to interpret it as normal. Yet she recognizes that the other child's perception as an onlooker to this episode is of both deviant ground and figure. The teacher engages in a neutralising motive:[21] 'it was just his way of playing'. However, the child who is an onlooker is not in a position to make such sophisticated figure/ground distinctions: 'it was only actually tickling — very rough tickling anyway — and it would appear to a child to be like a hit'.

There is also a recognition of *personal* ground in the inter-subjectivity of the social world of the school:

when he's had a naughty period like he has just this past week he is talked about because then it affects children in other classes.

Social constructions of reality, then, can *precede* an episode in the notion of ground or identity — as a reputation that goes before. It travels ahead and sets the perceptual parameters in advance.

Week Nineteen

At this point a significant stage is reached in Gavin's deviant career. He is now to be referred to the School Psychological Service:

The reason he's being referred is because of his attitude to other children
... Mrs. Russell thought after the last time, it was the third time he'd
had a go at this particular girl that it was wise to refer him in case a
situation did arise ...'

Mrs. Hope's concerns are quite obviously to prevent a further physical attack.
This situation corresponds with the traditional rule-breaking concept of deviance,
perhaps even marking the very boundaries of reasonable or containable deviance.
It does seem, however, that it is the person formulation and not the rule-breaking
that governs the theme of referral: the dispositional properties of Gavin which
reside in his pivotal identity as 'his attitude'. So far the underlying deviance of
pupils has usually been regarded as a person-formulation phenomenon. But on
this occasion the rule of 'violence' seems to operate as a significant boundary
point. Teacher strategies are formulated so as to structure pupil actions in order
to prevent him reaching this point. The problem now becomes one of rule-
transgression. The pupil is manoeuvring on the very outer limits[22] of the social
boundaries and so becomes a critical issue for the group life of the school.

Mrs. Hope attempts to interpret the unpredictable outbreaks of deviance by
invoking the underlying motivational reservoir:

I don't think he really understands that it will hurt them.

While in relation to the incidents themselves (which pass very quickly) there
is little sign of person formulation by the teacher, there is nevertheless a reflective
formulation post hoc and encompassing all such events through the ground
formulation of a general propensity to be deviant. Mrs. Hope draws upon, and
founds her formulation and strategies upon, the general baseline of deviant
ground.

The trans-episodic formulation is grounded in an observation of a recent
incident:

This morning I was watching him. And he was hitting two children
over the head with cards. He was trying to hit them as hard as he could.
I think this is the sort of thing he would do. With anything he had in his
hand.

It seems the deviance is seen to reside not in his motive (it is almost neutralized
here as an unwitting deviant action) but in the social processes of relativity,
indicating his *perceptual* distance from 'normal' interpretations of reality. He is
seen as operating from a different standpoint from other children. Gavin operates
from an underlying abnormal baseline.

Towards Normalization?

During the period of referral to the educational psychologist there was a *phase* of
normality but deviant ground soon returns:

I don't know what has happened but for a week he was quite good. And today he's back to normal. He's had a go at strangling one of the boys.

Mrs. Hope recognizes the persisting baseline of deviant ground. It is now the occasional normal phase which needs explaining! For a period of about a week there is apparently a *suspended* deviant ground.[23]

Return to a Deviant Identity

It seems that the pupil is passing through a distinct phase. Mrs. Hope is certainly actively engaged in searching for its underlying theme and an appropriate strategy to allow her to relate to it:

He's sitting on a table next to mine at the moment, working on his own. It isn't really the solution but it's the only one I can use at the moment, where I can watch him and keep him under control without him hurting any of the other children until I find out really what I can do with him.

It seems then:

— *theme* is sought for;
— the rule-breaking deviance is the *final boundary* and source of concern;
— the *unpredictability* of outbreaks is another concern, especially as they concern rule-breaking at the outer boundaries;
— his *interactional boundaries* are being controlled so as to limit the inter-actional and spatial contexts of potential outbreaks (elements of the 'situation' the teacher can structure).

Deviance Amplification

There is now a continuing search for meaning because of what seems to be a newly appearing feature of the deviant ground: '[Mrs. Russell] is worried about his violence. And ... unpredictab[ility]. I can't see a build up to it'. This statement confirms the apparent rootless nature of the outbreaks of deviance which are not anchored in any ground that will allow the teacher to anticipate them. It seems to be a quasi-anomic phase in his career as teachers are no longer able to rely upon the ground of predictable relations in formulating their strategies with this pupil.

It seems that there is a phase of potential anomie now occurring for the teachers. The ground which might provide meaning cannot be discovered. Here the sociological processes are critical for the deviant career. While all 'normal' pupils are perceived to operate generally within the parameters of normality, and even deviant pupils usually within known and predictable parameters of 'abnor-mality' ('patrolling' the boundaries of group 'space' in a manner which is nomos producing for teachers) some abnormals provide a challenge to the nomic pro-cesses of construction of reality.

The educational psychologist is now called in because of the new unpredicta-bility and the now uncertain nature of ground:

> We thought the most important thing that we're finding it difficult to deal with was this unpredictable behaviour.

The same problem of formulating Other-role, within a process of rapidly changing boundaries, continues. Mrs. Hope recounts an incident which had apparently angered her to a point of upsetting her equilibrium while within minutes the pupil himself was back to 'normal' and yet she had remained very angry. It seems to present a substantial boundary confusion. His own role-taking and role-making boundaries change rapidly and his teacher couldn't keep up with the pace! It all confirms the *unpredictability* and the *rapidity* of change. Perhaps by the time the teacher has reformulated the situation and its appropriate theme it's already changed back! Mrs. Hope now sees a divided Self within Gavin:

> He's been lovely today. He's been his usual nice self. I think that's just normal. I think the other part is abnormal.

The teacher is now engaging in speculative or elaborative talk rather than con-fident formulation. It is a possible search for congruency between the deep and surface structures. She now decides to opt for the earlier stable ground for this pupil as a way of making sense. So the original ground is brought back in. She postulates the anomic outbreaks as separated from the general abnormal ground. Mrs. Hope reports a normal (almost ideal!) formulation from one of the other children:

> Elsa Rodgers came up and said: 'Gavin's been nice lately hasn't he?' She said: 'He hasn't been hitting anybody at all!' She said: 'He's been nice to everybody! So obviously this is happening away from me.'

The use of deviant ground here clearly demonstrates its embeddedness within the inter-subjective world of classroom 'culture'. It is present in the 'thinking-as-usual' or 'what everyone knows' of all members. Others, including other pupils, recognize these current episodic figures as worth commenting on precisely be-cause of their recognized incongruence with the deep structure of ground in a deviant baseline. The shared recognition of the deep structure of relations gives meaning to the pupil's remarking on it and the teacher's remarking on it in turn. The account shows also the teacher's recognition that the present 'ideal' phase has application across a variety of situations: 'this is happening away from me'.

However, it does leave one feeling quite bewildered at this point; his swings are confusing both to the researcher and to the teacher. One minute he's deviant enough to call in the the educational psychologist and the next he's *so* good — all in the same week!

At this point it is not clear what interpersonal boundaries are being invoked in the decision to refer the deviant pupil to the educational psychologist. Clearly there is increasing concern over him. In relation to the earlier movement *from* 'abnormal' *towards* 'normal' is it now a case of having changed direction? Is he now seen to be moving back further into abnormality?

There is, perhaps, no basis for knowing in which direction he is going. Nevertheless the teacher's own concern is increasing. A comment from Mrs. Russell, the headteacher, confirms this: 'She's become increasingly worried about him'. The educational psychologist referral now becomes clearer as the deviance is formulated in boundary terms: 'It was really because of the increasing number of physical attacks'. The *frequency* of attacks was increasing.

But also the rule-transgression reaches a further boundary: 'And the fact that they [the physical attacks] were beginning to be dangerous'. The nature of the attacks, then, had reached an outer boundary limit of tolerated acceptability.

Mrs. Russell indicates the precise temporal point at which the revised formulation occurred:

> It was at that point that Mrs. Hope and I felt there was a need to speak to the parents again and to ask for more help with Gavin from the psychological service.

Further Processes of Amplification

Week Twenty-nine

The reconstruction of Gavin's identity is now assisted by the educational psychologist's visit. The psychologist confirms Mrs. Russell's view of the underlying ground:

> She said it was as we thought: He relates well to adults but not to children. His problem is relating to children.

Perhaps the process of referral to an educational psychologist is always a situation which provides for a negotiation and exchange of the phenomena in deviant identity. Certain features of the pivotal ground may now perhaps take on additional legitimacy as they become 'officially' or 'professionally' verified. But the teachers seem to recognize psychologists as marginal to the definition of the situation. They recognize that it is their *own* construction of ground which carries weight here — 'it was as *we* thought'.

Mrs. Hope now seems to take on some of the 'professional' interpretation of *ground* from the psychologist:

> His attitude to other children is definitely an aggressive tone when he's playing. It was only through observing it while she [the educational psychologist] was doing it that I'd noticed it at as well.

The psychologist, then, is perhaps a professional purveyor of 'authentic' pupil identities as formulatory grounds. In this case, the referral leads the teacher to 'see' the 'real' ground that otherwise she would have missed. In these processes it can be recognized that the notion of 'career' is always rooted in the process of ground emergence.[24] The psychologist, perhaps, is consulted in the search for a ground — a 'professional' bearer of appropriate grounds. The 'professional' ground will perhaps begin to work because it provides a sound or secure base for strategy formation. In effect, the teacher is lost, as she admits. The teacher can relate with renewed conviction to a 'known' ground, which seems to be more or less what she 'knew' already. Since it is congruent with her existing interpretive framework it seems to lend firmness to its form.

Further Negotiations in a Deviant Career: Allocation to Next Year Group

Week Thirty-three

The ground is now used in allocating Gavin to the next teacher as pupils are moved on to their third year class:

> Mrs. Russell has decided to put him in with Mrs. Bradley next year.
> She's a formal teacher. She's very strict with children. The psychologist
> feels the stable situation that he'll get in the classroom will help him.

The formation of the pupil in ground terms allows allocation to his next year group by matching the ground against the proposed new teacher-pupil situation. This hypothesized total situation includes a formulation of Other teacher, the pupil in question, and the likely interactional context. Mrs. Bradley is a 'formal teacher' who is 'strict with children' and so might provide a 'stable situation' which is suggested as a strategy by the psychologist. For such grouping and allocation then, it seems a trans-contextualized or trans-episodic ground provides a baseline for strategy formation and is what the teachers work on.

Mrs. Hope then restates the pupil's significant boundary crossing which led to referral to the psychologist. This restatement is presented with the same apparent 'professionalism' as the teachers have often shown in relation to the labelling issues. The 'societal reaction' of the teachers has rarely seemed to have been of the sort that leads to 'victim' creation. It is important, then, not to operate a labelling perspective, naïvely regarding all societal reactions to rule-breaking as indications of victim creation. Here teachers show a remarkable under-reaction in their reluctance to exacerbate or amplify processes of core typification.

Week Thirty-seven

In one *segmental* aspect of Gavin's identity, he is now seen to be moving in a direction away from a deviant baseline:

> The relationship with children's beginning to develop. You can see it.
> And this is after a short period of time.

It seems one aspect of ground — relationships with other children — is moving away from the deviant base. As we come to the close of the pupil's second year there are signs of segmental modifications in ground.

Year Three: A New Teacher: Emergence of a Deviant Identity

Gavin now begins his third year of schooling. His new teacher, Mrs. Bradley, apparently recognizes his deviant identity *immediately* as a pivotal ground. In fact, of course, the teacher has been present in, or a party to, processes contributing to a continuing school or communal definition of pupil identity for the past two years.

The underlying deviant identity of this pupil is suggested by comparison in norm-matching with the others in the group who are apparently beyond the normal boundary: 'Everybody else has come in and settled down fine'. This evaluation, of course, may be seen *either* as a groundless formulation of mere episodic deviance *or* it may be recognized by the teacher as a sign of an under-lying deviant identity.

Teacher Strategies in Relation to a Deviant Pupil

The next comment suggests it is the deviant ground since it is already a basis for teacher action in strategy formulation:

> And this one I'm pegging down there, cause he's going to do his day's work the same as all the rest.

Not only is the deviant ground confirmed in the first week but a definition of interpersonal boundary is presented: on the one hand there is 'this one' (Gavin) and on the other there is 'all the rest'. The deviant motivational reservoir is already invoked in general strategy formulation and in imputing motives to the pupil in interpreting particular episodes.

Classroom Episodes in a Deviant Career

> Straight away he was out to make as much noise as he could possibly make.

Here, the motive seems to draw upon an underlying ground that perhaps extends beyond the immediate context. Mrs. Bradley goes on to show how the general strategy is formulated in this episode. Motivational reservoir comes into effect both in the episodic imputation of motive and the selection of strategy:

> In the line coming over [to the classroom which is an outside temporary building] he's making a commotion which I wanted to ignore, up to a certain point, not to set him off before he got through the door.

The same deviant ground can be seen in Mrs. Bradley's careful handling of the situation. It allows her to predict his reactions and even relate to them by under-reacting so as to avoid 'setting him off', as though appreciating a common-sense awareness of labelling implications. The ground is also seen as a recognized method by which the other pupils also relate to him:

> Kids are really frightened of him. And there was a dead hush in the class as soon as he came to the line this morning. And you could almost see they were shrinking away.

The interpersonal boundary, then, is not just in the teacher's frame of reference. It is lived through by the pupils too! It becomes a genuinely *social* process, a 'culture' of apparently 'shared' understandings. The ongoing social construction of reality is an inter-subjective process.

Week Five

The underlying continuity of his pivotal identity can be seen in a deviant episode: 'Had a set-to with my friend Gavin ... Had bashed a few of the children'. And so the persisting ground or long-term theme is anticipated:

> I had warned him that every time he started I'm going to start on him.
> So it's going to be more my side than his then.

The theme is seen to extend from the previous (i.e. *past*) warning to the *present* and on into the *future*.

A sense of 'social structure' can be seen in the teacher's further elaboration of the incident:

> You could see them sort of watching him and almost moving away from him cause they didn't want to have to be anywhere near him. And he's got to learn that it's going to be dealt out! For the sake of all the others.

A deviant ground is part of the 'social structure'. It is 'known' by the other pupils and by Mrs. Bradley in her use of 'social structure' as a framework to which to relate her strategy. It is further illustrated in another incident:

> And I just shook him. He was so surprised. And the children said to me: Oh but he used to be much worse than that.

The pupils recognized the social structure of deviant identity but here seen to be undergoing modification or neutralization over time. The 'social structure' extends to other teachers too:

> Mrs. Priestley happened to say to me: Mrs. Bradley, do you know Gavin's been ... So I said: Don't talk to me about Gavin today. I'm sick of him.

Week Six

The formulation of Gavin even within 'academic' episodes is linked to the trans-episodic deviant Other-role through the assumption of a common motivational reservoir:

It was obvious he didn't know 'b'. In the end I took him over (to the letter chart) and then he starts getting aggressive.

Here an event begins by being no more than episodic academic divergence but soon opens out into a deviant incident presumed to be resting upon a ground of deviant motivational reservoir. This occasion is perhaps a further indication that the base or ground is a fundamental aspect of the ongoing construction of core identity and that segmental roles (such as 'academic') are often subordinate to it.[25] The teacher recognizes that there is an underlying deviant reservoir of motives beneath apparently academic episodes:

You don't know how much he is just laying it on to be a bit of a nuisance. To get the attention.

So the deviant ground continues through the third year as a basis of teacher dealings with pupil in strategy formulation and also in the episodic search for theme. It is ground, of course, which brings continuity to interpersonal life. Ongoing processes are accomplished by maintaining notions of continuity which link *present* figure incidents with *past* and anticipated or taken-for-granted *future* episodes. The continuity is provided by ground. The ongoing processes of both emergence and relativity are seen to be accomplished by the teacher's carrying forward the enduring ground to future interpersonal dealings.

Week Ten

Although deviant ground continues, it has its variations in episodic expressions and so it is apparently seen to be phasic:

The only one really that I can say that there's a change for the worse is Gavin! He's just going through a bad patch again.

The recurrence of home-school boundaries shows up next in a 'parents' day' visit to the school. The home-school boundary is invoked even in precise episodic contexts. They bring a base for extracting theme:

He's quick enough. He looked round. His mummy wasn't there. Straight away! Belt everybody! It *does* spring from home. All his trouble springs from home.

A figure episode is seen to have direct continuity with the underlying deviant ground of both the pupil *and* his parents — the Other-role in its broadest sense. This suggests how perhaps at the primary level of schooling the formulation of pupils as Others quite naturally sees the entire family 'team' as part of the 'Other'. Not just the individual pupil but the entire primary group. It may be that ground and motivational reservoir do not have clear individual boundaries but merely blur into the group or perceived interactional network of the family as an extended 'Other'.

Week Eleven

The recognition of deviant ground is tested by a natural 'surprise' situation when Gavin spontaneously decides to sit next to Ellen:

> Mrs. Russell said: What on Earth! Fancy putting a child like that beside Ellen!

Here, a widely recognized underlying deviant identity is seen to make the seating incongruous within the processes of relativity engaged in by Mrs. Bradley. The underlying trans-episodic formulations and their appearance in this episodic theme indicate a presumed inter-subjective world is taken for granted by the school staff. The 'surprise' situation acts like a 'natural' piece of 'Garfinkling' to disturb and expose the social structure of the school. It might be suggested, then, that an essential feature of any 'common culture' would be the shared understandings and recognition of enduring personal grounds and an appreciation of their aptness for generating intra-episodic themes by the substitution or imputation of an assumed common 'deep structure' of taken-for-granted meanings.

Further Episodes in a Deviant Career: Processes of Normalization; Re-Emergence of Deviant Identity

Week Fifteen

Ground is seen to change from time to time: 'Discipline-wise he's a lot better than he was. More controlled'.

Week Seventeen

Although there were earlier signs of a normal orientation there are some occasional setbacks:

> He's been naughty again this week as regards knocking other children. A bit high. But sort him out. And then he said: Oh, it's me again! It's always me again!

Here the figure and the ground of both episodic incident and its enduring and underlying motivational base (and even the situational reaction of the pupil) can all be seen as deviant. It can be seen that deviance is not merely a rule-transgression incident but an *episode*. It is a genuinely *interactional* or ongoing unit extending over time. The pupil's reaction to a post rule-breaking incident is seen to be part of the total episode — the immediate episodic secondary deviation! All is seen as resting upon the underlying deviant ground and its motivational reservoir.

Gavin now seems to have changed direction from what seemed to be a normal orientation:

Yesterday I said to him: You know, I'm going to end up giving you a hard slap for answering back every time I speak to you. Because it's getting ... it is downright rude really. And of course he's allowed to do it at home. He must be.

This seems to confirm that the *direction* of movement is now oriented towards abnormality. The enduring continuity of the ground can also be seen — 'every time'. Also, it seems a 'deep structure' boundary has been crossed in the move from a normal to an abnormal base for operation. It is not just the rule-breaking of figure deviance but the motive too, since the pupil's actions are presumably seen to be intentional, making it a *boundary* (Erikson, 1966, p. 11) rather than a *rule* issue.

Academic Episodes in a Deviant Career

Week Twenty-two

There appears to be a quite frequent combination of academic and deviant Other-role, raising the question once again about the location of the interpersonal boundary between academic and deviant role. Obviously they do, and are seen to, interact. It was suggested earlier that academic roles are seen to be subordinate as sub-categories of the master status of deviant identities. In effect, deviant Other-roles are core typifications, pivotal categories (Lofland, 1969) and master statuses (Hughes, 1945).

On this occasion the potentially positive formulation of an academic episode is negated by the underlying ground of deviant motivational reservoir, the more dominant element in the construction:

He did a beautiful drawing. It's a beautiful vase. You see, there's plenty of ability. It's just unfortunate that he's been handled so badly, really from the start, by parents who haven't shown the right interest in him.

This assessment is an ideal-normal academic formulation of Gavin with an underlying deviant ground as pivotal identity. Here can be seen the role-taking and making of Turner (1962) with Other formulation proceeding at many levels simultaneously: Other's basic ground identity as a person together with many segmental role formulations additional to this master status. On this occasion the additional segmental formulation is of Other in an academic role, or more precisely of Other as artist.

Mrs. Bradley then sees a significant change in the pupil:

Just was careering round. Talking away as always and really not paying a bit of attention. And he just was as wild as could be. And I just said: Go out! Just like that! And he went. Which any other time, back along, he would not have gone.

Here can be seen signs of a continuing process of some apparent movement towards normality. The deviant incident is itself seen as a continuation of pivotal identity with the teacher drawing from deviant motivational reservoir to give it meaning: 'as always' and 'as could be'. However, the significance for the teacher is in the negotiated definition of the situation reached with Gavin in the deviant incident. It is this part of the episode which is seen by the teacher to indicate an improvement. It is worth making intra-episodic distinctions in formulation as teachers themselves apparently do in the distinction between: the deviant act and the negotiation of the post-deviant outcome.

On this occasion the post-deviant outcome itself develops into a second deviant incident. While sitting outside the room as he was supposed to: 'he let out such a scream'. In later examples Mrs. Bradley makes reference to many instances of quite normal post-deviant outcomes. However, the continuity of the pivotal category of his trans-episodic deviant identity is clear:

> There's times when I feel he's always the one. I mean, all right you could pick him out every time you went in there for somebody who's talking when you've said 'be quiet' or 'don't do this' or 'don't do that'. And you can guarantee that our friend will be doing it, to a certain extent. But with a child like him there's a certain amount that you have to ignore because it's more than he is capable of doing. He can't do everything when he's told. So you have to make an awful lot of allowances for him in the classroom really.

Here, there is a strange duality or ambiguity about the formulation:

1 A clear statement of a deviant ground seen in its enduring quality.
2 A clearly formulated strategy generated by and contingent upon, the deviant ground: 'you have to make allowances ... an awful lot of allowances'.
3 Yet at the same time an implication that other teachers might easily over-react or fail to employ the same strategy and so, in effect, move into a Labelling position.

This point is significant for interpreting classroom formulation. It shows the sophistication and complexity of the processes underpinning the *actual* interpretive work accomplished by teachers and also shows the naïvety of a simplistic labelling approach.

The above reveals too, how necessary it is to employ a methodology that will allow researchers to uncover the depths of the social construction of 'reality'. Unless a researcher is able to dig deep and probe the meanings of the participants themselves then it is never possible to know whether, even in situations which appear 'normal', the teacher is in fact soft pedalling to reduce the negative effects of labelling in a deliberate under-reaction founded upon a deeper structure interpretation of deviant ground which is at the time inaccessible to a researcher. There is always a methodological problem of discovering what ground of pupil perception a formulation actually rests upon.

The next account reveals staffroom 'culture' as a guardian and source of 'what everyone knows'. The extent of inter-subjectivity is seen in three teachers expressing in unison during an interview in the staffroom: 'We've always said it started at home. Because of the lack of attention' This unanimity confirms the pivotal nature of pupil identity and both its perceived causal and motivational structure. Additionally, it shows the 'structure' and 'culture' of staffroom knowledge ('we') and its continuity over time ('always').

End of Year Review and Differentiation of Teaching Groups

Week Thirty-six

The end of the year sorting of pupils for allocation to next teaching groups leads to the following comment:

> 'He is in no way being written off as a finished case because he's finishing this school. There will be continued involvement when he goes to the junior school'

Here is a sense of continuity in pupil identity. It is also accompanied by a future-oriented strategy. The psychologist's advice is indicated:

> She feels that 'firm handling and avoidance of occasions where trouble is likely to occur and a reduction of attention for inappropriate behaviour wherever possible' and that they should be 'contacted if the aggressive behaviour becomes serious again'.

Once again it can be seen how the labelling theory approach might easily lead to an over-simplification. The ground formulation can be used positively as well as negatively. Labelling, of course, is often regarded as negative. But the ground can be used positively to *avoid* deviant figure incidents occurring and in the formation of strategy to stimulate the direction of movement. The 'social structure' of pupil identity formulation is neither inherently negative or positive. It may be employed from an avowed 'professional stance' to reduce deviant outcomes in the direction not of amplification but of reduction.

Mrs. Bradley indicates a perhaps not uncommon view of the outcome of the relationship with the educational psychologist: 'Didn't reveal anything additional. It was really confirming what we'd found so far'.

It is, perhaps, quite obvious that referral to an educational psychologist involves teachers first recognizing the suspected ground of pupil identity. In order for a pupil to be referred, an *abnormal* ground must be identified or suspected. Consequently, psychologists will only confirm the ground and so in effect will not be offering anything fundamentally different to what is already known. It is, after all, the teachers who are the ones who are engaged in the more fundamental process of ground formulation and moreover have been engaged in the processes of its emergence over some considerable time. Psychologists, even if they observe pupils, can only observe *figure* incidents or episodes after they have been armed with a suspected or presumed abnormal *ground* formulation.

Finally, the next year's teacher allocation:

> For Gavin it was a question of who was the better disciplinarian. So he's actually going with Mrs. Marshall.

The underlying ground formulation of the pupil is matched against the type formulation of teachers. The inter-relation of the two forms the basis of pupil allocation strategy, drawing upon the 'social structure' of the school, and the processes of taking account of 'what everyone knows' about the pupil and about the teachers so as to attempt a 'social structuring' of pupil identity.

In fact it might be said that the continuing ground formulation over the last three years has been a carrier of socially structured pupil identity in the making. In the *dynamic* and *process* elements of what is called 'social structure' there is a *continuing* sense of an inter-subjective world. It is perhaps accomplished through individuals making real or reifying their perceptions of themes which are in turn seen to have continuities with phenomena recognized as *beyond the boundaries* of the mere episodic and so imbued with enduring *trans-episodic* or 'structural' characteristics.

Transition to Year Four: A New Teacher: Episodes in Emergence of a Deviant Identity

The pupil at this point goes on to a new school across the campus — the junior school department of the now reorganized all-through primary — and so now has a new teacher. The school had previously operated as a quite separate unit. Most of the staff would not know Gavin. The new year begins with an opportunity for teachers to start their formulation from a normal base. Their first impressions can be seen when the two first year junior teachers are initially introduced to the pupils at the end of the pupils' third year in the infant school and there is opportunity for them to engage in preliminary formulation:

He's totally egocentric that lad. Totally. Nothing else exists outside of Gavin in his little world. That was the impression I got this morning.

It is not clear what base is in operation here. The new teacher, Mr. Lindsay, could perhaps be adopting a normal base at their first meeting. This pupil is obviously seen to be divergent but as yet with no indication of whether the divergence is seen to be beyond a significant boundary. The account refers to only *one* facet of Other as a segmental role.

It seems that the interpretation of Gavin is back at the starting point of formulation, not the *total* formulation of Other-role which tends to emerge later but the apparent piecing together of fragments.[26] On this occasion there is Other-role specificity: he is typified in terms of 'egocentrism' and nothing else. Over the last two years there has almost been an absence of individual trait identification as teachers appear to be predominantly concerned with the *total* formulation of Other rather than with segmental role constructions.

However, it soon becomes clear that this present figure formulation is related to an emerging ground arising from Mr. Lindsay's previous dealings with the pupil in sports activity:

I've met the lad before and he's a type that if he's not completely involved in the game, and if he's not the centrepiece of the game he doesn't want to know. And that's the impression I got this morning.

The teacher was talking to him and he was having this conversation with this other child about giving him back his cars or something. And that was the main object of his life at that moment!

It seems a normal ground may be in operation at this point but with signs of some *continuity* being recognized by the teacher from past dealings, and suggesting some divergence from the normal. There have already been formulations that indicate location towards the extremity of the normal parameters: '*totally egocentric*', 'if not *completely* involved'. Now an episodic formulation suggests some detachment from the mainstream of classroom life when his conversation with another child becomes 'the main object of his life at that moment!'

It seems type emergence may be underway. The *present* figure or episodic formulation is apparently connected to previous ground constructions. The 'structuring' of opportunities for preliminary formulation is apparently assisted by staff interchange between junior and infant departments. The present formulation is a mere continuation of a process that is already underway.

With Mrs. Marshall, who is encountering him for the first time, there is a mere episodic formulation from her initial impressions in a figure incident. The focus is upon acts not dispositions:

He was one that was organizing the line outside here. He was quite full of himself.

In this case there is the sort of construction more appropriately described as mere 'person talk' rather than 'person formulation'. It simply focuses upon 'acts' rather than upon 'dispositions'. The framework of formulation is that of discovering within the boundaries of the episode itself the Other-role apparent in the person's actions at a particular moment. It is presented as a figure description with no apparent underlying ground or dispositional formulation offered at this point. In such constructions it may be that a token normality is presumed. The information available about the pupil at first is merely of the episodic or figure kind in 'acts'. Only when the pupil's actions suggest something 'significant' about his underlying or trans-episodic identity requiring the introduction of a more appropriate baseline will the formulation switch to that of dispositional or ground identity search. Perhaps all pupils are given the benefit of the doubt at first and assumed to be 'normal' and so operating from a normal identity. In the present case it seems a normal model is provisionally adopted but only in suspended form and so hardly used or drawn upon to make sense of the surface events.

The headteacher of the school indicates something of the exchange of ground constructions between the two schools:

We looked at him very carefully, deciding whether or not a man would be a good influence or whether or not he needed the more womanly approach.

It seems Mrs. Russell is recognizing that there was a pivotal category or dispositional ground identity to be acknowledged in the school's organizational processing of Gavin's career. The structuring of this pupil identity was of critical importance and not to be merely allowed to go through in an undifferentiated form as other 'normal' pupils might:

> I don't believe in prejudging to be quite honest. He comes in here. He has a fresh start. But having said that we must obviously bear in mind things that have been learnt in the past as well.

This seems to represent a professional and quite appropriate use of the ground (a ground that in the case of this pupil is part of the culture or 'folklore' of the school). The school appears to be acting upon the knowledge of ground with an avowed aim of positively assisting its normalization, or at least so as to not knowingly exacerbate the ground in a more deviant direction. It seems that for most pupils (the majority of 'normals'), there is a 'fresh start'. But for those with a deviant identity, or for special cases, there will be a careful attention to their individual placement.

The nature of this placement process is further explored:

> It's very difficult to say how we decided 'cause we were working on feelings. But we felt in the end that the steady influence of Mrs. Marshall would probably suit a child of his temperament better than the more flamboyant approach of Mr. Lindsay. It was thinking of the security aspect and that sort of thing.

Here is suggested the exploratory nature of the process of prediction and projection — certainly not the 'closed' process that might arise from a reification of categories. Nevertheless, the social control aspect of formulation is important on this occasion (as it is also recognized to be in the work of Sharp and Green) and yet here it refers more to *classroom* control than the *macro-control* which seems to be the real concern of Sharp and Green. At least for this situation and for these purposes the abnormal pupils are treated at an *individualized* level of formulation.

Mrs. Marshall has been assigned this pupil and so the potential deviant ground that might have been carried over to Mr. Lindsay, from his earlier contacts with the infant school, is prevented or avoided. It seems in Mrs. Marshall's first account that the pupil starts his career in an open category without a ground or baseline:

> He straight away wanted to start with a packed lunch on the very first day.

There is no indication here of basic ground underlying this episode. It is apparently just treated as a neutral episodic formulation without ground. The formulation is apparently without a baseline. It appears the decision about whether to use normal or abnormal model is held in suspension.

This suspension, however, is more apparent than is really the case! Clearly a deviant ground is only temporarily suspended. There is a well-formed reputation for this pupil which Mrs. Marshall next admits she is aware of in her previous contact with school and staffroom culture:

> *The* Gavin! He was the one, as I told you, that I noticed straight away when I went for the first time for the infants.

Her first encounter with Gavin had resulted in a 'scanning' process which may have alerted the teacher to the potential abnormality. Although he may not have been formulated in pivotal category terms at that time, the potential for the deeper structure of dispositional identity may have been at least recognized at the time of the visit a week before.

The emerging ground of deviant identity is recognizable in the social processes of relativity. Interpersonal differentiation or boundary construction in the teacher's construction of reality is apparent in the recounting of the following incident:

> Yesterday, when we were actually sitting in their hall, Gavin was the one who couldn't keep his tongue still. And he was the one, of course, who was racing ahead.

The potential deviant identity is already becoming well-formed as can be seen in Mrs. Marshall's strategy:

> He came to stand next to me because I didn't want him chatting as we walked through the area. And he was fairly noisy until we got into the quiet room.

Mrs. Marshall still seems to be unsure of Gavin. Although there may be signs of an emerging deviant baseline, it is as yet tentative and the motivational reservoir has not yet been opened. A sign perhaps that the basic category is provisional and so will not yet allow the generation of motives:

> He didn't seem worried about the place at all. But then I'm not quite sure whether children who have a lot to say for themselves really are little mice underneath. And it's all just a front. That's something I'll find out as I get to know Gavin.

Year Four Career Begins

The transition from infant to junior departments has so far been the focus of attention. The initial formulation arising from the preliminary visits made by the pupils has shown the beginnings of type construction. Year Four now begins with the first interviews arising from the first teaching encounters. It is interesting to recognize that in advance of the year's beginning there is already a provisional or tentative differentiation of perceived Other-role in the formulation of this pupil emerging.

It is clear that formulation has already been influenced by school or staff-room culture, although it would be mischievous to regard this as anything other than 'professional'. The information supplied could not be withheld without running the risk of failing to 'warn' of the dangers adequately.

> Well, I was warned about Gavin. About his odd ways. And about his family background. And I was hoping that I could forget about what had been said to me and just try and start afresh.

An equally 'professional' stance was apparent in Mrs. Marshall who receives the ground information. She seems ready to underplay her reaction to it.

It seems that pre-interactional exchange between teachers provides an outlining of ground and alerts other teachers to the likely model to be used in ground formulation. This has two elements: first, the obvious 'professional' alerting to the pupil's identity so as to form appropriate strategies, perhaps adopting 'incorporative' strategies (Reynolds and Sullivan, 1979) — either to attempt to normalize or to contain; second, the dangers of selective perception and labelling in reaction to received ground.

There is also an as yet unexplored issue in ground exchange. Since the ground is likely to be communicated in the form of a 'framework' or a connected 'network' of ideas, then it is likely to be presented and received as a coherent *whole*. This appears to be so in the present case: — 'his odd ways', 'his family background' — and so has an in-built causal structure. It might be expected that receivers of information in ground exchanges might encounter congruency or dissonance problems (Festinger, 1957; Jones and Davis, 1965) if their existing frameworks seem inappropriate to the incoming data.

A later comment in this interview seems to be an opening up of the reservoir of motives:

> Yesterday he started whistling. And I really think that he knew it wouldn't be approved of. But he did it so that I would make some comment about it.

The motives appear to derive from a recognition of possible meanings to be found beyond the episode. Could this be the first dip into the motivational reservoir? In the formulation of this episode the theme operated by the teacher is of deviant actions. Whether the formulation takes in frameworks which arise from beyond the boundaries of the episode is not clear. Perhaps it at least indicates to the teacher that she can now adopt the 'suspended' provisional model of deviant ground. It can now be set down and used.

Teacher Strategies in Relation to Deviant Ground

Week Two

The quite predictable processes of relativity often noted in early formulation seem to be occurring here. The boundary differentiation between 'normal' and 'abnormal' pupils seems to be being resolved. What at first appeared to be a pupil beyond the boundary now seems to be a less divergent case than was feared:

> Definitely this week I feel happier about having him in here with these children. He does annoy the others a lot. But I try and reason with him.

The distinction between 'these children' and 'him' is now less marked but nevertheless is still present.

Week Three

The continuing deviant ground is well-formed and provides a foundation for Mrs. Marshall's use of strategies:

> I probably wouldn't do this with every child. Quite often, just so that he gets on and he's busy, when he comes to the front of the line, if he's got a problem we solve it. Or if it's just something that needs to be marked I mark it quickly.

By now the teacher has formulated a strategy which happens to be ground-based. It shows, perhaps, what the 'professional' nature of teacher knowledge consists of: using the knowledge of *pupils* and of the *situation* in order to deal appropriately with each pupil. Far from the negative effects of labelling, and the reification and anonymization often seen to be incorporated within labelling processes, it is clear that here the teacher is engaging in a highly individualized construction of Gavin in attempting to avoid deviance.[27] The minimizing of deviant outcomes seems to be a common ground-based strategy operated by teachers.

Routine Episodes: Groundless Figures

Week Four

The next example is drawn from the sampling of classroom processes. Using the method of time-sampling, a randomly selected moment becomes the focus of attention and provides an opportunity to observe the teacher's formulation as it perhaps occurs in the routine flow of classroom life. On this occasion, as might be expected (since deviant pupils conform for most of the time), it picks out an apparently 'normal' episode for Gavin:

> He was working. He just had his head down. He was sitting on his own and he was just getting on. And I just saw the back of his head. And that was it.

This is an observation of the routine events that *may* be operating between the 'high points' of formulation which teachers bring to research interviews. It is unnatural, of course, to require teachers to notice a child when they otherwise might not have done so, but it does give an indication that the deviant ground is in suspension. The formulation is merely episodic. The figure construction is in fact unremarkably normal: 'just had his head down', 'just getting on', 'and that was it'. Either everything was normal or there was no real dispositional formulation at all — just the groundless description referred to earlier.

An Extreme Boundary

The following week an extreme boundary seems to be reached with this pupil:

> Yesterday he was a nuisance in a story. And I was sort of telling him off.
> And he puts his fingers in his ears. You see he doesn't want to listen.
> I've never had a child do that sort of thing. Usually you can tell them off
> and they accept it. I've never had a child mutter underneath his breath.

Mrs. Marshall is now firmly operating the deviant ground and its motivational reservoir. At first, apparently, she uses a tentative construction by recognizing his divergence from expected pupil role: 'puts his fingers in his ears', and 'doesn't want to listen'. Then she recognizes significant processes of relativity in the extreme boundary crossing: 'I've never had a child mutter underneath his breath', 'he's the only one that's ever done it'.

Gavin is seen to be the most extreme case in the teacher's professional career: 'I've been teaching for quite a long while now and I've worked in some difficult areas'. There couldn't be a more extreme case apparently. The extent of deviance is further clarified: 'You could really write a book about somebody like Gavin'.

The puzzling nature of the pupil's pivotal identity which is only revealed gradually as individual figure incidents are pieced together:

> It's going to take me much longer to work out what he's like. 'Cause
> each week something else happens. He hadn't done this fingers in ears
> business until yesterday.

From Academic to Deviant Episodes:
Normal Figure to Abnormal Ground

In some respects, however, he has a normal career. In his academic Other role: 'He's usually very good in story'. Perhaps a segmentalized normality of ground is seen here. The ground is confirmed or used in the recounting of a specific episode:

> We were reading *The Fantastic Mr. Fox* [by Roald Dahl]. And it verges
> on being a little rude in places. And they really enjoy it. And *he* does.

How then does the deviant ground of the pupil's pivotal identity relate to academic ground? Perhaps after all the clue or key is to be found in the motivational reservoir. Academic grounds appear to have only narrowly academic constructs such as 'ability' dimensions in their motivation. A pupil is, for example, 'able' or 'capable'. But the *manner* of operation of this academic capacity is seen to reside perhaps within the general motivational reservoir of the pupil and his Other-role identity. This can be seen in the way in which the same episode develops:

And he just spoilt it for himself. Another child would not have chatted.
Because he knew that he wanted to listen to the story. But Gavin doesn't
seem as though he can help it really.

The underlying deviant ground and its motivational reservoir is seen to intrude
upon a generally academic setting. This is consistent with the earlier view that
segmental roles are subordinate to a more general formulation of pivotal identity,
master status or core typification of Other-role. It seems there may be a fundamental ground or identity upon which are constructed segmental roles having
a narrower or limited area of ground operation yet resting ultimately upon the
same basic ground and reservoir.

Societal Reactions in School

There is next an indication of role-engulfment in the career of Gavin's deviant
identity. It is noticeable in the teacher's account of something equivalent to
Kounin's (1970) 'ripple effect'[28] as the deviant ground pervades the entire school
culture:

> The dinner ladies in this school fell out with the dinner ladies over there
> because of Gavin. Because he'd got into the infants' playground. And he
> was strangling some of the infants. There was a bit of a to-do about it.

The negotiated deviant outcome also reveals the extent of deviant ground:

> He had to go and see Mr. Lindsay at that point. And [Mr. Lindsay]
> didn't really know him then. Just told him he hadn't to go do it any
> more. And he'd got to be very good for the rest of the day.

It is as though she is saying that at the time the extent of deviant ground was not
known by Mr. Lindsay, the other teacher. His strategy, or rather 'tactic' (Woods,
1980), was therefore more moderate than suited the pupil's later-to-be-revealed
deviant ground i.e. 'he just told him'. Perhaps Mr. Lindsay had treated the pupil
as a 'normal' child, as though the incident or episode were founded upon a
normal ground. Clearly the pupil is known to be inherently deviant. At the time,
the apparent normality of the pupil seemed to warrant a strategy based upon a
presumed normal base. Later, however, this apparently appropriate treatment
was to become noticeably inappropriate and indicated the extent of his deviation
from the normal:

> A lot of children, if they'd had to go to one of the teachers from the
> other end, it really would've frightened them. But it doesn't seem to
> bother Gavin.

Thus, a significant interpersonal boundary is suggested, but perhaps the qualitative distinction between Gavin and 'a lot of children' at this point indicates only a
divergent model.

A Continuing Deviant Identity

The Other-role of deviant ground is an ever-present feature of classroom life:

> It's enough for Gavin to get something down. And he's got so many other things to think about anyway cause he has real problems with his writing.

In academic contexts the deviant ground can be present. It intrudes upon teacher action such as in the selection of tasks for pupils or the allocation of special duties: 'So he's got many other things to think about. I wouldn't ask Gavin at all'. This comment reveals how on some occasions the non–occurrence of a phenomenon may also be being influenced by deviant formulation as an underlying episodic theme beneath a perceived figure. Here the non-selection of the pupil is founded upon the recognition of deviant ground. It is important to recognize that *'non-events'* can also be founded upon deviant ground. Things that *don't* happen, where they are the result of conscious choice on the part of the teacher, can have figure properties and so be in effect resting upon or founded upon deviant ground!

An Ultimate Boundary

Gavin is now seen to reach a far outpost[29] in reaching a boundary point in the social world of this classroom:

> Wednesday morning when he came back to me from Mrs. Gordon he wasn't wanting to get on with his work at all. And he's standing right in front of me having a set to with Alistair Conran. So I just about burst a blood vessel. And I don't think I've ever shouted as loud as that. You tend not to in this kind of set-up because there are so many people working. And I sent him to go and sit down and get on with his work.

This indicates both the extremity of pupil behaviour *and* of the teacher's *reaction* to it. Mrs. Marshall has '[n]ever shouted as loud as that'. Labelling theory treats 'societal reaction' as critical in processes of deviance. Here it can also be seen that the teacher's own recognition of societal reaction becomes a phenomenological measure in her own acknowledgment of the interpersonal boundary. Her own outer boundary point is apparently reached as she constructs her action.

The outer boundary is further conveyed as the negotiated outcome of the event appears:

> And of course all this muttering and chuntering under his breath. So I marched across to him. And it's the first set-to that I've had with him. And I wasn't losing control. I knew what I was doing. But he really did make me mad that day.

Here there is a *temporal* boundary in the societal reaction. It is the *first time* he has ever reached such an extreme position in the social world of this teacher's classroom.

It can now be seen how the earlier deviant incident was after all resting upon a deviant ground and therefore also upon its underlying motivational reservoir:

> The fight with Alistair Conran was the last straw. Because he's all the time he wants to come to me and tell me things. But I can't stand all day listening to him. And even when we're just sitting round and discussing things he interrupts the whole time. And most of the time I've learnt to sort of switch off.

It seems the deviant ground (the prevailing identity) persists across everything ('all the time') and knows no limits ('even when we're discussing') and endures permanently ('the whole time'). It generates a teacher strategy to ignore him. It is as though there is a permanent scanning mechanism set not to react or to 'sort of switch off' for 'most of the time'

It is important to recognize how such an incident has its *emergent* framework — a dynamic framework in which it builds over time:

> It was like that that particular morning as we talked first about the work. A lot of noise and sort of shouting across to me. And then he was coming with his work. And there was a line of children.

This comment represents an account of the situated episode in its emergent processes. Against this the deviant high point occurred:

> And that's when there was all this to-do. It wasn't a sort of punchy fight. But they were writhing round together. And perhaps I wasn't in a very good mood that day anyway. Perhaps there was something wrong. But I really was mad with him. I think it's the maddest that I've ever been with him.

Societal Reactions

This event is such a high point in the pupil's fourth year career that it leads to a different sort of societal reaction. This time the *boundaries of reaction* are extended. Until now they have been intra-school processes. Now they are to become extra-school again as they have in the past:

> I'm not happy at all about him. I haven't really moaned to anybody. I felt that he was a problem. I feel as though we should be able to do something. And I've racked my brains and I just can't think of anything.

The deviant ground is once again not only present but seems to have reached a threshold point which triggers the teacher's renewed search for a means of orienting the pupil towards normality. Once again there is an implied interpersonal boundary as though the teacher has exhausted her own supply of 'recipe knowledge'. Although she is an experienced teacher, Mrs. Marshall has 'never known anyone like him' and has 'racked her brains' and yet 'can't think of anything'.

Academic and Deviant Identities: Processes of Figure and Ground

The underlying processes of person formulation (in ground) seem to pervade all contexts of Other-role construction. First in an academic context:

> He absolutely loathes reading. I've practically turned myself inside out
> to try and find a book that he'll like. And it's virtually impossible.

The formulation of the pupil in an academic role is in terms of the underlying baseline. It seems that even in relation to segmental formulations of Other in an academic role that the teacher is dipping into the underlying motivational reservoir which relates to the pivotal identity. The pupil's Other-role, even in academic contexts, is seen to rest upon the core typification which is the ultimate ground of pupil identity.[30]

Normal Episodes: Surface and Deep Structure

In addition to the deviant episodes there are, of course, many 'normal' episodes appearing in Gavin's career. It is important not to overlook them. Nor, by concentrating on the present ground-figure interest, should the impression be given that teachers 'have it in' for deviant pupils by constantly labelling them and resurrecting their deviant ground, even when they are seemingly engaged in 'normal' episodes.

Nevertheless, it does seem that whenever a 'normal' episode is at 'surface' perceived to be going on the teacher is still likely to be separating 'surface' and 'deep structure'. There is a simultaneous process of formulating the underlying base of pupil action. The following incident brought up by the time sampling indicates this as Mrs. Marshall recounts her observation of how Gavin appeared at the particular moment:

> Happily involved I would say. Gavin was very involved this morning.
> He was very involved. He was concentrating quite a lot on what he was
> doing. There wasn't any sign of aggro from what I could hear. There
> was no aggression at all today. It wasn't characteristic for those two. It
> was a quiet moment.

It is viewed then as an uncharacteristically normal episode. The teacher is operating from an 'abnormal model'. The fact that abnormal model is firmly present is indicated by the perceived boundaries containing the 'normal' episode:

> It doesn't surprise me because of the nature of what they were doing.
> That's what made it uncharacteristic. 'Cause at that moment I wouldn't
> have been surprised if say Gavin had been sort of bellowing across the
> table at Alan. Which he tends to do. But it was a quiet moment.

The episode is apparently contained within or bounded by the parameters of the activity. Previous normal episodes have been bounded *interpersonally* by *who* was present at the time, but this one is bounded by the *activity*. The boundaries are seen by the teacher to indicate that specific patterns might be expected (resting upon a motivational base). Although a 'normal' moment, it is seen to be resting upon a deviant baseline of meaning. The abnormal model is still in play.

Several normal figure episodes follow. After some probing it reveals they are figure formulations which are insulated from deviant ground. It is perhaps worth emphasizing once again that deviant pupils experience many normal episodes or figure formulations, maybe even more normal than deviant ones in each day. However, it is not the *number* that matters nor the *ratio* of normal to abnormal — such are mere surface considerations. It is the figure-ground phenomenon or deep structure that is critical. The deviant ground is seen to be a continually present phenomenon. However many normal figures arise there is a prevailing deviant ground. The deep structure appears always to be the key to understanding social action and not the surface formulations. What lies beneath the surface is a more significant social reality and yet it is not 'visible' by observation. It is nevertheless critical for processes of person formulation. It can be seen how the ethnographic and participant observation range of methodologies are the only likely means of getting at the 'deep structure' as a level or layer of social reality which is accessible only through the participants themselves and which seems to be being operated all the time.

Week Twenty-three

The emergent and temporal location of formulations can be seen:

> Has had a good week up to today. Been in a lot of bother since nine o'clock this morning. Been a bit cheeky and one thing and another, and since I spoke to Mrs. Russell about him [concerning the educational psychologist] he's been smashing all this week! And I thought: What have I done, I've got this chap to come in and he's being no trouble. He's been different to the other kids but better for him. But he's started again today.

Here are indications of a normal figure lasting some time. It is an extended episode: 'he has had a good week'. But it rests upon a deviant ground; the educational psychologist has been sent for. Yet the teacher was now about to rethink the nature of this ground in the light of the extended normal episode. Perhaps at this point the teacher was now recognizing that since the deep structure of social reality would not be visible to an outsider then her own 'professional' credibility might be in question. Here it is possible to recognize processes of the *negotiation* of ground formulations. They occur at an interpersonal level of negotiation between intra-school and extra-school formulators.

The phase in question, however, appears to be at an end:

> 'one thing and another' (refers to deviance continuity);
> 'he's started again today' (the return to abnormality).

There is an enduring sense of interpersonal boundary. Even the 'normal' episode is seen to rest upon a deviant ground in that 'he's been different to the other kids but better for him'. So the normality of the 'normal' episode is remarkable precisely because of its contrast to the deviant ground.

Renegotiating a Deviant Identity

The educational psychologist institutes a behaviour modification approach to dealing with the pupil. Its effects may be more in terms of influencing teacher perception than in pupil modification however:

> It's got things much more in perspective for me as well. Being able to look at this with him.

It has now become redirected as an *interactional* and *negotiable* aspect of classroom life. But Mrs. Marshall's sense of the prevailing deviant ground leads her to expect failure:

> I was still very pessimistic about the whole thing. And so I asked [the psychologist] if he would come in half way through and see what was happening. 'Cause I was expecting it not to work.

The whole thing is *instituted* by a recognition of deviant ground and is *implemented* with the teacher's recognition of prevailing deviant ground: 'I was expecting it not to work'.

However, Mrs. Marshall's optimism seems to recover in the implementation's own momentum:

> It's working up to a certain degree. And I'm presuming that once the month has gone by he'll come and look and suggest whether we carry on or what else we should do.

There is some slight movement *towards* normality now recognized. The teacher is now beginning to see that a modification of identity may be possible.

Perhaps in this can be seen an element of sociological processes. A distinction might be made between *manifest* and *latent* processes (Merton, 1957); the psychologist's method of behaviour modification has its overt function but the pay-off in practice is perhaps in a possible latent function of regenerating the teacher's motivation and her orientation-set of optimism.

End of Year Review

As he comes to the end of his fourth year:

> We seem to be curbing his temper a little bit. But he's still a very strange lad really.

The continuing deviant identity is evidenced both in his continuing contact with the psychologist and also in the reaction that very morning following a visit to the educational psychologist:

He's been threatened with other schools and this sort of thing! But he came back this morning all smiles. Any other child would've come back looking very serious and cheesed off. But he came running in. He came back as though nothing had happened.

The teacher is perhaps dipping into his deviant motivational reservoir to interpret the meanings to be attributed to Gavin's actions in this episode when he was 'all smiles', 'came running in' and 'as though nothing had happened'.

There is a clear statement of the interpersonal boundary point between Gavin and the normal child apparent in 'any other child would've come back looking very serious and cheesed off'. The prevailing deviant ground provides an underlying structure to the situation and a baseline of meaning for interpreting this figure or episode.

The same issues of relativity are seen in the interpersonal boundary which shows itself in his interactional dealings with other pupils in the classroom. As Mrs. Marshall reviews his movements in seating arrangements over the year:

Gavin's been everywhere 'cause he doesn't get on with anybody. So quite a lot of the time he was on his own or sitting next to me. So he's probably the most moved boy in my group.

There is a suggestion here of a communal 'societal reaction' by pupils too: an indication in classroom culture[31] of a possible 'shared' community of formulators who recognize, and construct their own actions in relation to, his deviant identity.

The pupil comes to the end of his fourth year and the end of this monitoring of the course of his early school career. In doing so it has indicated some of the key processes of Other-role construction as they operate in classroom life. It has become evident that a recognition of both *episodic* and *trans-episodic* formulations of Other are critical. This suggests distinctions between the 'surface' and 'deep structure' of social action implied within the concepts of 'figure' and 'ground' which provide the means for recognizing interpretations of Other in the ongoing and dynamic social processes of schools and classrooms.

Notes

1 The musical concept of transposition provides an appropriate metaphor. The interpretation begins from the figure representations of the phenomena which are immediately apparent but the final construction is accomplished by substituting a reformulated version which better fits the known definition of the situation. In effect the interpreter starts from what is provided in the home key but 'reads' the situation in another.

2 It may be that what is suggested is a sharper distinction than is made by Hargreaves in the emergence of deviant identity. Rather than the process of 'elaboration' which suggests a quantitative accumulation of 'evidence' of deviance it seems here the crucial issue is of a qualitative leap. A decision to use a deviant baseline in the construction of reality. This is perhaps equivalent to the point of type stabilization recognized by Hargreaves.

3   The framework of formulation switches from current episodes to the trans-episodic and the enduring or ongoing phenomenon of Other identity.
4   Although it is tempting to revert to more standard sociological terminology and refer to this as a deviant rather than abnormal model, there is a preference for retaining the term abnormal. It encompasses a wider range of phenomena than deviance. It includes divergence as well as retaining the central focus upon relativity in boundary operation and so locates the analysis within sociological processes and separates it from rule-based studies of deviance. This book focuses upon ongoing identity or person categorization and not on the analysis of societal reactions in isolated deviant incidents.
5   The teacher is now in the elaborative, exploratory and testing phase of Hargreaves.
6   'Professional optimism' is meant in the sense of giving a child the benefit of any doubt in the construction of reality, by crediting a child with a normal identity and retaining the possibility for as long as possible that ultimately the child is normal.
7   The idea of neutralization corresponds with Lofland's concept of episodic deviance. It is a short-lived phenomenon and is to be understood merely in surface terms. It has no underlying origins in deep structure. The surface episode is in effect seen to be 'insulated' from a deep structure of deviant ground.
8   The teacher is moving between ground and present episode in constructing a definition of the situation. It suggests she is still open to either episodic or trans-episodic constructions at this point.
9   Anomie is used here in the general sense employed by Durkheim (1933) referring to situations of normlessness when the constraining norms of collective life are no longer apparent to actors. Here it is also used in the specific sense of McHugh (1968), following Durkheim, to refer to the empirical properties of anomic situations when it is not possible for those trying to interpret the action to impute a theme so as to make sense of the events.
10   Formulation is not a simple linear process as might be suggested by Hargreaves *et al.*, 1975.
11   This idea is employed by Erikson in suggesting that in the social diversity of collective life individuals are 'deployed across the range of group space' and deviants in particular 'patrol its boundaries' (Erikson, 1966, p. 19).
12   It might, of course, be expected that in the course of certain episodic encounters, in spite of recognized underlying trans-episodic ground, the teacher may nevertheless make a normal construction at certain times. It will be possible later to explore the dynamics of the teachers' moving in and out of normal and abnormal frameworks in the course of the ongoing processes of interaction. But here the movement is *within* the abnormal framework. There now appears to be a shifting ground.
13   This 'underlying normalcy' appears to be so, at least for this episode, as a discrete temporal unit. It may be that teachers at times suspend deviant ground for the duration not only of a single episode but for what is seen to be a normal phase lasting for longer than an individual event or episode but for an entire morning.
14   This absence of deep structure when the situation is formulated without the apparent deviant ground might be termed ground suspension. The episode is formulated in isolation from Other's trans-episodic identity. It is, in effect, an isolated episode which is 'insulated' from the underlying reality. It is important to make a distinction between the absence of ground in a 'neutral' as distinct from an 'insulated' episode. A neutral episode is when construction is in episodic terms during the early process of formulation before ground has emerged. An insulated episode occurs in a career beyond the point of ground emergence once

the underlying identity has been recognized but when it is temporarily suspended as an interpretive framework for the duration of an episode.

15 Drawing the motive for misbehaviour from *within* the boundaries seems to be implicit in the concept of episodic deviance (Lofland, 1969).

16 Where the motive for deviance emanates is the key to identifying episodic and trans-episodic formulation. The motive search goes on either within the episodic boundaries or beyond in the trans-episodic.

17 Such communal definitions are perhaps more likely to occur in primary schools — a very different 'context' to that of most secondary schools.

18 The pupil is apparently at the extreme end of the 'normal range' for 'settling down' and may even be operating close to an outer zone of the classroom world, suggesting his arrival at a significant boundary marking entry into the category of abnormality. There may even be two boundaries separating the 'normal' from those beyond its boundaries; the first marks the point of entry into divergence and the second into a pathological or deviant category. If so it would suggest a 'natural' career progression towards normalization might involve a shift from pathological into divergent before acquiring a normal identity:

Figure 9.1: Career progression from pathological to normal

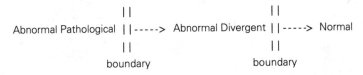

19 In the inter-subjectivity of staffroom culture it will be impossible for teachers to ignore the deviant reputation of a pupil. Although at this point the emergence of deviant ground has not yet surfaced it seems as though the teacher is delaying the first recognition of deviant identity at this point. The formulation is not genuinely neutral but from a suspended ground.

20 Once again it might be regarded as a quite 'professional' and 'sensitive' strategy. There appear to be no grounds for trivializing the teacher's motive at this point in the manner of some researchers with an overconcern for signs of reification and labelling!

21 This 'neutralizing motive' is one of the 'techniques of neutralization' recognized by Sykes and Matza (1957) and referred to by Scott and Lyman (1968). This example corresponds with the particular technique of 'denial of injury'.

22 The pupil is also engaged in acts which 'patrol' the boundaries of 'group space' (Erikson, p. 19).

23 Gavin's deviancy is suspended in the sense that it is insulated from surface events. For this period it does not provide the baseline from which to interpret the pupil's actions which are now seen to operate from motives to be found within the boundaries of insulated episodes.

24 Other accounts of 'career' (Goffman, 1968) have also recognized this. Perhaps the recipe for 'successful' dealings with psychologists, either in contexts of education or in relation to mental illness, is simply to recognize the 'truth' (the real ground). Once ground is acknowledged the client is then on the road to 'recovery' (in psychiatry) or to 'tackling the problem' (in educational psychology).

25 This aspect is perhaps equivalent to a negative halo effect. It has similar properties of a master status (Hughes, 1945) which dominates, and spills over into, the construction of all other aspects of the person.

26 The assembling of fragments in the construction of an identity is in effect a

'characteristics model' (Hargreaves, 1977) in which individual traits of Other are identified. This gradual piecing together of separate segments of Other's identity is apparent in the tentative early formulation of pupils. It seems to operate without a clear baseline but rests upon the provisional assignment of a normal identity to Other.

27 It is the individualized formulation of pupil which acts as a baseline for constructing action.

28 Within the 'group life' of educational settings deviance may have an impact beyond the immediate setting of its initial occurrence (Kounin, 1970).

29 As though 'marking the outer edges of group life' (Erikson, p. 13).

30 This interpretation would be understandable if teachers constructed pupils as a *gestalt*. Presumably teachers have a tendency to see pupils as wholes rather than as a collection of individual traits or segmental typifications.

31 This reaction corresponds with Erikson's (1966) interpretation of deviance within collective settings. Each individual is seen to participate in the 'confrontations' which occur in marking out the boundaries of group life.

Chapter 10

Episodes in the Emergence of a Deviant Career: Alan (School B)

There is now an opportunity to look at some of the dynamic processes in the emergence of pupil identity in the second school, School B, and explore the critical case of a pupil who, for much of his time, was recognized as diverging considerably from the norms of his school, his cohort and his peer group. Alan's career is traced through four years of continuous monitoring of his school career and its formulation by the teachers. This chapter provides an opportunity to check out some of the processes already identified in School A and to explore any equivalent processes in a different social setting. It should be emphasized, of course, that this research is not primarily concerned with the verification of a generalizable theory but is attempting merely to generate a conceptual framework for exploring the parameters within which the interpersonal processes of Other formulation appear to proceed in primary schools. The following account, then, is of a critical case in School B considering processes of emergence, maintenance and change over the first four years of schooling.

Year One: Review of Emergence of a Deviant Identity in Pre-School Career

At the point of entry to the research, some teachers were already acquainted with this pupil from his pre-school days in the nursery school attached to the primary school. Consequently, as he enters the infant school, some teachers have already begun to form a view of him. For different teachers the processes in his formulation are at different temporal points in the construction of his identity.

Week One

The first account indicates some reluctance for this pupil to conform to the expectations of participating in the activities of his group. It is seen in comments from a nursery teacher, Mrs. King, who has already had over a year's contact with him when the research monitoring begins. His career therefore extends back in time and the teacher is able to review the emergent development through retrospective reconstruction:

Initially it was a battle to get him to join a group at all. So I had to leave him on his own.

There is much to indicate potential deviance is in operation in the teacher's formulation. This is apparent in the teacher's implicit meanings. Her account suggests a confrontation situation. It was: 'a battle to get him to join a group at all'. Both 'battle' and 'at all' convey quite extreme constructions.

Negotiating an Identity

The pupil's identity is seen to have emerged in a process of negotiation and exchange. As his mother and Mrs. King discuss Alan:

His mother said that he's self-conscious. She said even when it's just me and him he's self-conscious. He won't run *even* in front of her.

Each party then, parent and teacher apparently, exchanges dispositional ground. Each brings to the situation a contextualized ground of Other-with-mum or Other-at-school. Apparently the *contextual* range of ground is being extended and a firmer view of ground constructed. It would seem that it is not just that parents act as 'typification carriers' (discussed earlier) but they appear to operate as *ground carriers*, a more critical process. Although formulatory ground will have a particular identifiable form to its originator, it can nevertheless be *added* to or *fused* with received ground from other formulators. As ground knowledge of Other across different contexts becomes acquired then the *predictive* value of ground may perhaps be seen to increase. The teacher now has a formulatory ground as a base for predicting Other in a wider range of contexts. It might be assumed that in the event of the two contextualized grounds appearing incongruent then perhaps processes akin to those outlined in cognitive dissonance theory (Festinger, 1957) might occur. In the present context, however, the compatibility of grounds apparently leads the teacher merely to incorporate his mother's ground within her own. As *compatible* or *congruent* ground they are fused together. (There will later be a negotiation of *incongruent* ground in the formulation of this pupil.)

In the present case, where his mother's formulation is *congruent* with that of the teacher, the received ground may even be viewed by the teacher as more significant than her own construction. Since it relates to the pupil as an Other within a primary group context rather than in interaction with herself as 'stranger' it may perhaps be assumed to relate not just to another *context* but to an interpersonal context of greater formulatory significance in revealing the pupil's 'real' identity. Since Alan's mother is perhaps viewed as the most significant of Others for formulating the pupil in his unique individuality, then her view of underlying dispositional characteristics is likely to be seen to have greater value in uncovering the real Alan. It seems the teacher does see significance here: 'He won't run even in front of her'. The parent's ground is not merely received by the teacher and added to her own but perhaps superseded by it. After all, here is a significant piece of information. The process may well be not merely a simple addition but even a *weighted* addition.

Mrs. King next indicates the developmental or emergent changes which occurred in Alan over the nursery phase:

His behaviour was more controlled by the end. I wouldn't say he's perfect. But he's not too bad.

The final phase suggests an orientation towards normality is now recognized. It is not clear whether the ground being employed at this point is normal or abnormal. But there is certainly an orientation towards normality indicated.

Yet there is also a sign of some abnormal ground even though it may be highly specific in its reference to only one facet or segment of his identity: 'I think he's the only one who uses baby talk. Or he did before the holiday'. Here, the recognition of an interpersonal boundary is suggested as processes of 'relativity' (Mead, 1934) lead to marking this pupil off from others and identifying him as one who is clearly segmentally operating from an abnormal base.

Teacher Exchange in Reconstruction of Pre-School Identity

Another observer, the headteacher Mrs. Strang, has had only occasional knowledge of this pupil from the past and at the point of entry to the primary school finds it difficult to remember much about him at all:

I find it very, very difficult thing to recall anything particularly sort of noteworthy[1] about him

— a suggestion of some anonymity in the formulation of this pupil. Perhaps the headteacher's comment is a sign of groundlessness or even that the pupil is informulable. It could also indicate that pupils are processed in teachers' 'memory' as ground and not as individual figures. It may be that ground generates recall of figure incidents from 'memory'. The difficulty of recall may suggest a groundlessness in person formulation up to this point for the headteacher, with no enduring dispositional formulation.

There is an exchange with Mrs. King to recover the unrecalled ground:

She said: Well, he used to *sit* when we were having music. And I can remember this. He was one of these children who would come over and just wouldn't do anything at all. Didn't ever want to join in at all. And she said that this was fairly typical of him throughout his time in the nursery.

Here, then, is a teacher-teacher exchange of ground. Perhaps school or staffroom culture as a realm, of 'what everyone knows' is experienced as a range of dispositional or ground knowledge. It is certainly communicated to the headteacher as ground: 'she said that this was fairly typical of him throughout his time'. It is apparently seen as an indication of enduring identity, also as a situated or contextual ground. As in the earlier exchange of ground, it involves addition of *contextual range* to the dispositional knowledge of Other. Once again, there is some indication of *significance* ('throughout his time') and therefore of some

Figure 10.1: Additive ground formulation

$$\text{Ground 1} \quad + \quad \text{Ground 2} \dashrightarrow \quad \underline{\text{Episodic}}$$
$$\uparrow$$
$$\text{Act}$$
$$\downarrow$$
$$\underline{\text{Prediction}}$$

permanence in his identity rather than the mere transience of the episodic. Teacher exchange is of pupil's *trans-episodic* identity.

This trans-episodic identity forms part of the working knowledge of the teachers, as it is then used to predict the pupil in the current context of starting school:

> You would think, perhaps, that he might have had some problems adjusting to school on his first day. But in fact he hasn't.

A reference was made earlier to the likely predictive value of *additive* ground formulation across contexts. Here it is actually working. The headteacher applies the contextually extended ground to predict Alan's actions in an emerging situation as seen in Figure 10.1. Since Ground 1 is a negative it leads to the prediction of a negative act. However, the expected outcome is inconsistent with the perceived actual outcome. In fact, the outcome is interpreted apparently as a neutral episodic figure or groundless episode:

> He's just come in ever so quietly and just watches the rest of the group. He doesn't take any initiative. And certainly doesn't make himself noticed. But neither does he cause any bother with crying or anything.

At the end of week one there are signs of a *potential* deviant ground emerging but as yet it is only tentative and person-specific in relation to particular teachers and their knowledge of Alan in specific contexts.

A New Teacher: Beginning of Infant School Career

Alan's class teacher, Mrs. Thompson, who begins from having no previous knowledge of the pupil, seems now to be formulating an aspect of dispositional ground: 'He is still solitary. He doesn't play with any of the others'. Here there is perhaps a suspicion of deviant ground as processes of relativity and indications of interpersonal differentiation become apparent.

For the class teacher the suspicions of a more fundamental and deviant identity are obviously now growing:

> I think there was one morning or one afternoon we had a terrible sulking do with him because he wanted a piece of a toy that somebody else had. Not only had. It was a construction toy. It was in the middle of their construction so they couldn't take it away for him. But he wanted it! And when they said 'No' he went into a sulk on the carpet. Hands

over head and head between knees. And that was at half-past one. And at half-past three he was still sulking! Which I thought was unusual.

This is presumably another link in the chain that may lead the teacher into a use of abnormal model. In this example, too, can be seen a reference to a category of formulation parameters that so far has not been given attention in this research but which could well be an important dimension in the phenomenology of the formulation process recognized as critical to teachers themselves.

Physical Gesture: 'hands over head and head between knees'. (It is to be remembered that 'gesture' is a significant element of the SI account of Self-Other interaction indicating aspects of Other's intended presentation of his Self, although its physical manifestations have often received less attention in research in this tradition.)

Temporality: 'at half past three he was still sulking!' The significance of temporality is recognized by the teacher: in emergent terms it seems this is the point 'which I thought was unusual'. As it crosses a temporal boundary it reaches the point of being 'unusual'. The longer the sulking goes on the less it can be seen as episodically arising from a 'surface' phenomenon and so the more it must be seen in terms of a 'deeper' structure as personal or dispositional identity rather than episodic theme.

Mrs. Thompson continues:

> I picked him up a few times and transported him to various parts of the classroom where he could sulk in peace. But he didn't come out of it at all. I tried talking to him and that just made him worse. So we left him! He didn't even go out to play!

As the account continues it seems that the teacher is apparently testing out the situation for mere situational or episodic divergence rather than the more fundamental dispositional deviance attributable to a pivotal deviant identity. She is perhaps attempting to neutralize the situation as though its 'form' were bounded or contained within episodic parameters and so potentially neutralizable as episodically generated divergence which might be reconstructed as the properties of the episode itself are changed:

> 'Picked him up a few times',
> 'Transported him to various parts of the classroom',
> 'Tried talking to him'.

Again the *sequences* in the formulation of a deviant identity can be seen. First there is the teacher's response (Social reaction 1) to the pupil's presumed or suggested deviance. Then there is the perceived pupil response (Social reaction 2) to the teacher's response. An episode then apparently has its own recognizable internal sequences of emergence.

Elaboration and Verification of Deviant Identity

The pupil's response to all these *episodic* strategies seems to suggest to the teacher that the problem was not mere *episodic* divergence: 'he didn't come out of it *at all*' and '*he didn't even* go out to play'. Here can be seen how a teacher strategy may perhaps operate as a means of checking out whether the motive to be imputed resides in ground or is episodically bounded. (A more specific or situated notion of strategy than that used by many of the writers in Woods, 1980). There is an implicit boundary apparently operating behind all this, as though a 'normal' pupil would soon, perhaps, have come out of the episodic divergence and would certainly have gone out to play. It leads onto a further statement of apparent deviant identity as the formulatory ground on this occasion:

> Just because somebody had that piece of toy and he wanted it. He seems very, very stubborn. I've never met anyone who seems quite as stubborn as him.

Here the deviant ground is clearly formulated. There is an apparent recognition of an extremity of deviation: 'very, very stubborn'. The extent of deviation is perhaps further seen as extreme because it is triggered by what after all is merely a *routine* classroom incident. It was: 'just because somebody had that piece of toy'. Here too are processes of relativity (Mead) in the formulation of interpersonal boundary. The teacher has: 'never met anyone who seems quite as stubborn'. It is at this point that the final deviant ground emergence can be seen. It seems to emerge together with the motivational reservoir. This presumably 'normal' trigger indicated above ('just because somebody had that piece of toy') seems to lead to the suspension of any normal motivational reservoir. The teacher's apparent testing out of the incident, as though it may be a possible case of episodic contingency generated by the properties of the context itself, has no doubt led to the conclusion that a theme of apparent episodic divergence or mere contingent deviation arising from an otherwise normal setting cannot apply. She has apparently used this as a hypothesis and it has not worked. Consequently, it seems the teacher now has to presume personal ground as explanation for this episode rather then episodic theme. The model is confirmed; it now makes sense. The deviant ground has to be the explanation. The motivational reservoir now provides meaning. (The answer lies in the dispositional properties of the *person* and not in the *act* or its episodic or contextual properties.)

Processes of Figure and Ground in Interpretation of Classroom Episodes

Mrs. Thompson recounts her earlier mistaken use of normal model (and its assumption of normal motivational ground reservoir) in the interpretation of an earlier episode:

> We went in the hall for dancing and he didn't want to dance. So I took hold of his hand and I was dancing with him. I thought perhaps it was just he needed reassurance. But no. When I looked down he was scream-

ing his head off at me. He thought I hadn't heard him. I've never had any child shout as loudly.

Here, then, is the use of the figure-ground formulation framework in action. In perceiving this figure phenomenon (of Alan not wanting to dance), the teacher immediately formulated this divergent encounter in *episodic* terms. She apparently operates an implicit normal baseline and assumes the occurrence to be no more than a situated episode to be understood or interpreted from wihin its own episodic parameters. Consequently she selects the pupil motive *not* from a dispositional *deviant* ground and its associated motivational reservoir, but presumes a *normal* motivational reservoir and therefore looks for an explanation *within* the episode itself. Apparently she would look for the answer in a search for episodic theme (or what in attribution theory might be seen as formulating in terms of act rather than disposition).

Figure-Ground Formulation and Generating Strategies

Having formulated her strategy on the assumption of *episodic* theme ('I thought perhaps it was just he needed reassurance [in that situation]') which proves to be ineffective as a strategy, it seems that the teacher must now look to *trans-episodic* frameworks for generating a strategy. This then is perhaps the point when the deviant dispositional identity begins to be consolidated in the formulation process.

Perhaps an alternative view for the teacher at this point would be to assume an incorrect, inaccurate or inappropriate interpretation in the episodic formulation itself or in its consequent strategy. This is where teacher differences are likely to show; presumably different teachers might construct the situation differently. While Mrs. Thompson appears to have presumed deviant identity as ground it may be that in formulation another teacher, Mrs. Strang for example, might have continued an episodic search and so attempted to impute an alternative episodic theme.

In the present case, Mrs. Thompson seems clearly to have adopted deviant ground. In interpersonal terms the pupil is formulated as a uniquely different sort of person. He is regarded as being beyond a qualitative boundary: the teacher has 'never had any child shout as loudly'. In consequence either the episode would have to be regarded as an extreme situation or the pupil was himself to be regarded as an extreme case. Mrs. Thompson's interpretive work now leads to a selection from motivational reservoir: 'He was really mad that I was asking him to do it when he'd told me he didn't want to'. Here the teacher is perhaps drawing upon the apparent dispositional identity in operation and its generating motivational base.

Having adopted a deviant ground in the formulation of this pupil, the teacher now uses a ground-based strategy in her dealings with him:

So rather than leave him out I changed the whole dancing lesson. And we had some games. Which he would join in. And he did join in that kind of game. But he wasn't going to hop or skip or jump.

Here it seems the contingently selected strategy in its implementation in turn confirms the ground: 'he did join in'. But, as in the earlier activity, 'he wasn't going to hop or skip or jump'.

It is notable how this situation seems to operate within a *developmental* or emergent framework. The Other, then, is apparently not formulated as a permanent outsider but as one who has 'not yet' moved into the boundaries of normality:

> Interviewer: Why was he ready to join in Farmer's in the Dell but not the other [activity]?
>
> Teacher: I don't know at all. One's a group activity and the other's an individual. He doesn't seem ready yet to do any individual activity'.

It seems the teacher is operating an episodic theme linked with emerging dispositional identity; an *episodic theme* diagnoses the situation as either a group or an individual activity — the social or perceptual boundaries operated in the formulation of this episode; an *emerging dispositional identity* is indicated in that he doesn't seem ready yet to do an individual activity. It is apparent that dispositional identity is now *emerging*:[2] 'doesn't *seem* ready yet'.

Although Alan is acquiring a deviant identity as formulatory ground (for the moment at least), there are nevertheless normal or non-deviant episodes experienced too. The pupil had shown some reluctance to join the other children with Mrs. Prentiss and so Mrs. Strang bided her time to coax him into going:

> He quite readily took my hand. Which I think is a sign as well. As I held out my hand to him he put his hand in mine and went with me. No bother at all. And just with this sort of look around the corner he went and joined people that he already knew. And stayed there.

There is, of course, a persisting deviant identity here. It is noticeable in the teacher's reference to 'no bother at all' — an apparent figure formulation of episodic normality[3] viewed from a deviant baseline. The deviant ground is apparently present as an underlying theme at a deep structural level within the episode. The underlying pupil resistance is still displayed in the perceived figure appearances of pupil's actions: 'just with this sort of look round the corner'. This suggests a motivational base rooted in something beyond the present episode as figure and therefore in dispositional identity of ground.

Processes of Negotiation and Amplification in a Deviant Identity: Further Episodes in Emergence

Alan now reaches what seems to be a critical point in his school career. There is a dispute over his readiness for staying to dinner. It becomes a point of negotiation and interpersonal exchange of formulations in respect of constructing pupil identity:

His mother wants him to stay at school for his dinner. And at the beginning of this week I said to Mrs. Knight that I didn't want to be contrary about this but that I'm sure he would be very, very unhappy if he had to spend lunchtime with us as well as the other parts of the day.

In this account there is an attempted exchange of deviant identity. Or rather a negotiation of formulatory ground. The teacher presents a formulation of the pupil as abnormal but his parent is seen as not being prepared to receive it. The strength of the teacher's ground formulation (however temporally or emergently based) is seen in its generation of strategy:

Even though the beginning of his coping with school may not be very obvious to us at the moment, I don't want those undermined by him having to take on other responsibilities that he's not ready for.

Here, the sense of at least an emergent if only temporary deviant ground is presented. The negotiation proceeds from a basis of totally opposing formulations:

She professes to be absolutely amazed that he has this shyness. I'm calling it shyness to her at the moment. She says he talks to people at home. Well, really I'm doubtful about this. He doesn't seem to have the vocabulary there at the moment.

It results in a formulation non-exchange. Presumably Mrs. Strang operates from a 'common-sense' theory (Heider, 1958) of perceived cognitive dissonance as the received ground is so incongruent with her own ground that she cannot accept it. (The transposing of ground across the interpersonal or socio-spatial boundary between teacher and parent seems to generate a problem of relativity that will not permit an exchange. The teacher cannot accomplish it. A comparison might be noted here with an earlier example of ground exchange with Alan's parent and also with Gavin in School A, where there was also an exchange over his identity this early on in his career *but* in which the exchange of typifications are *added* together. The compatibility of data between the 'ground carrier' and the teachers permitted it. Here, however, the two sets of data are recognized to be dissonant).

Mrs. Strang acknowledges her own formulation of the deviant ground at this point in his school career:

He worries me very much. I mentioned this to her. That for children like Alan it's important that he feels secure within the group. And it can't be very helpful to him to be *brought* in on his own. To then have to join in with the group as a latecomer.

Mrs. Strang is aware of possible peer group consequences arising from the interaction between parents' actions and the underlying disposition of pupil's abnormality recognizable in the use of boundary differentiation. She employs a category — 'children like Alan' — to refer to the potential deviant identity of this pupil as distinct from others.

A New Teacher: Episodes in Emergence of a Deviant Identity

Week One

A new teacher, Mrs. Gill, takes over the class at the start of the second term. She is new to the school and to the profession. The pupil apparently begins as a groundlessly formulated Other with this teacher:

> I don't really know him. He seems to have got lost in the general classroom situation.

Certainly no abnormality is suggested but there are perhaps signs of the enigmatic disposition that has previously been known by other teachers. As Mrs. Gill goes on, there are indications of something which may turn out later to have been the beginnings of the emergence of abnormal ground in formulation: 'He's a funny little chap'. However, this construction of the pupil's identity suggests formulation from at least a tacit normal base.

Week Two

As the pupil moves into his second week there is a tentative dispositional ground as a baseline for formulation:

> He's very quiet with me. I've never really had a good talk to him yet. The other boys I've managed to break through. But Alan, he easily gets upset.

Here, perhaps, are the beginnings of interpersonal boundary differentiation since 'the other boys' and Alan prove interactionally different. Also Alan's motivational base is now emerging: 'easily gets upset'. His trans-episodic identity and motivational baseline is beginning to be known. As yet, perhaps, it does not constitute a firm ground. Such apparent deviation may even turn out to be no more than a normal base with a segmentally specific 'trait' related to contexts of getting 'upset'.

It must be recognized that if person formulation does proceed in its early phase by the formulation of both a ground base and an associated segmental role formulation appended, then there is always a problem methodologically in recognizing whether a particular trait is a *general* or a *segmental* ground phenomenon. If the teacher offers an observation which is a segmental formulation then the ground upon which it rests will not be visible. There appears to be no method by which it can be determined empirically whether the latent ground is normal or abnormal. The present case is itself an instance. The present indication of inter-personal boundary appearing in the recognition of a difference between Alan and the others may suggest either a mere segmental typification or a more general ground.

It may be, of course, that teachers are, like the observer, in the very same position. Perhaps they too can only operate tentatively at this phase of formulation. Indeed, Mrs. Gill's tentativeness can be seen in the next comment:

Or at least that's the impression I get. And I've not been able to get to know him as much as I would like to yet.

The sense both of provisionality and of continuing emergence is evident in this preliminary phase of early formulation.

Week Four

The continuing sense of emerging dispositional ground is apparent:

he's a funny child. He tends to keep away from people. He always seems to be by himself.

Suspicions of dispositional ground seem to be behind the teacher's continuation of the account:

I just don't know him any better at all. I try to ask him what he likes doing at school best. You try and get the conversation going by asking what he likes to paint. But he seems to go into himself.

Here, the teacher is apparently coming up against the boundary between *episodic* and *personal* abnormality. Since there appears to be an expectation of some positive movement over time in 'getting a conversation going' then the absence of any movement (by inference) may well be interpreted as dispositional property of the pupil. However the teacher's expectations are meeting with little success: 'I just don't know him any better at all'.

Mrs. Gill appears to be operating an episodic strategy: 'I try to get the conversation going'. It seems the teacher may be operating on the assumption of the pupil's reluctance being an episodic phenomenon and which, at the moment at least, is seen to have causes that lie not in the dispositional properties of the person but in the episodic setting. Teacher strategy, then, is episodically selected and implemented. However, this point must be where the episodic and the dispositional identity personal boundaries meet. After operating the episodic strategy it seems the pupil response does not correspond with the teacher's assumption of an episodic motivational structure: 'but he seems to go into himself'. At this point, the teacher begins to organize ground-based formulations.

Mrs. Gill further explores or elaborates the ground theme and relates it to what are seen to be its manifestations in typical incidents:

I've got the feeling he's probably not mixed with children before because of his whole reaction to me. He is the cause of many a squabble between him, Kevin and Paul. And it's always him that sort of gets left out or punched or hurt or whatever. I think it's probably because he's not mixed with children before and not quite sure how to share things and how to react to them.

In *interactional* terms ('not mixed' and 'gets left out') the teacher acknowledges an interpersonal boundary and in *motivational* terms the pupil is recognized to be perhaps a 'stranger' to the world of other pupils ('not quite sure how to share and how to react to them'). Here is an indication of the normal/abnormal boundary, but perhaps even more important is the teacher's casting of Alan in a role of deviant trigger ('he is the cause of many a squabble') and also the butt of deviance ('always him that gets left out or punched or hurt'). Alan is significantly associated with deviance. However, it is at this point perhaps merely a suggestion that the pupil is not intentionally deviant but is seen as an unwitting element in the flotsam and jetsam of classroom life associated with deviance through 'drift' (Matza, 1964). His deviation is seen to be more evident in his dispositional difference from others than in his intentional rule-breaking. This point is perhaps the critical one in personal or in motivational terms. No matter how unwittingly, he is clearly on the deviant side of the boundary. His deviance is manifest in the processes of relativity of the classroom — in his difference from others (his Other-role) rather than in his rule-breaking.

Further Episodes in Emergence: Elaboration of a Deviant Identity

The teacher now moves further into anonymity in apparently adopting a ground formulation. She moves further from the episodic use of ground to the trans-episodic use in talking through a videotaped sequence of classroom action:

> [That's typical of him] to slightly turn away or fully turn his back on you. [Being] stubborn more than anything I think. Not particularly shyness. Because I don't think somebody can be as shy as that to get to the stage of turning away.

Mrs. Gill suggests that the pupil's actions indicate something beyond what would otherwise be 'normal' shyness. She seems to imply that episodic shyness due to the particular features of the setting might have led to one thing but here the pupil has done something else! Certainly, the pupil seems to have gone beyond normality to the boundary point of abnormality. The episodic theme is formulated by imputing personal ground: 'is stubborn more than anything ... not particularly shyness'.

Mrs. Gill then moves on to make a finer distinction which would mark the boundary between normality and abnormality:

> I think a shy person would cower more. They'd probably hold their head down and hunch their shoulder[s] up. I would think that was more a child's reaction to shyness than turning away. I think it's stubbornness. And probably lack of manners being taught at home more than anything. He's certainly a stubborn little monkey when he wants to be.
>
> [It's] very hard to get him to do anything he doesn't want to do.

It can be seen here how motives applied by teachers can have either a contextual or a non-contextual (trans-contextual) focus. This must be recognized as separate from *episodic* and *trans-episodic* distinctions in formulation. Motives, then, can have *more* or *less* sharpness or specificity. In the above account, the first quotation is a contextual motive and the second a trans-contextual. The second is both a *trans-contextual* and a *trans-episodic* motive combining space (a generalized context) and time (an enduring phenomenon from one episode to the next).

Deviance Amplification: Episodes in Anomie

Next an indication of the pupil's enduring abnormality and also of the significance of boundary between episodic and trans-episodic forms of construction:

> He really is strange. I don't understand him at all. I don't know whether
> it is shyness or just sheer awkwardness. Sometimes I think it's shyness.

Mrs. Gill faces a dilemma: whether to treat Alan's behaviour as 'shyness' or as 'sheer awkwardness'. It is not clear whether the problem is seen in the pupil's own inconsistency or in the teacher's changing interpretation from one episode to another. The enigmatic pupil presumably is so because the teacher cannot formulate him on secure ground. Therefore the motivational base apparently cannot be predicted with any accuracy. It has its episodic fluidity. Presumably then, as the teacher encounters the pupil in different episodes, each figure appears to have no direct relationship to ground or perhaps the mismatch between *predicted* and *actual* ground leads to the suspicion of groundlessness.

Here, of course, there is a relationship with the notion of anomie (McHugh, 1968). When experiencing classroom episodes, teachers have to be able to see a theme in order to make sense of it. Although dispositional ground does not always provide theme, it may assist the search for it. Since ground seems to provide access to a motivational reservoir both for present understanding and future prediction of pupils, its absence inhibits the episodic search for theme. If a pupil in an episodic encounter defies analysis from the failure to discover a theme from within the parameters of the episode itself, then it is necessary to fall back on trans-episodic or person formulation. Without a secure ground, nothing else makes sense! Here the teacher still seems to be searching for the secure and stable ground of 'deep structure'.

The following account conveys once again Mrs. Gill's continuing sense of anomie:

> I don't know what to do about him. I don't think anybody does. No
> sign of breakthrough at all. No sign of him wanting to communicate or
> wanting to be with other children or mixing with other children. None
> at all.

This seems to confirm the inherent abnormality of the pupil and the teacher's continuing experience of anomie with him. It seems the pupil's enduring position beyond the boundaries of normality and his apparent interactional strategy of not 'mixing with other children' confirms not only his difference from other pupils in the normal distribution but his location at the outer limits: 'None at all'.

End of Year Review: The Beginnings of Normalization?

Week Eighteen

A few weeks later there are signs of change in the pupil as he now appears to be becoming more responsive and communicative:

> He's started to talk more openly recently to me. He doesn't come and complain and tell tales as much as he used to. And that at one time was the only time he did communicate with me. But just generally I've had quite a couple of decent conversations with him since we came back after half-term.

The possible new facet of his identity is formulated tentatively but yet is seen as an emerging phenomenon. Any change in identity is likely to be recognized as just segmental rather than a fundamental change of motivational baseline. It is perhaps significant that it is formulated in ground terms and not merely as an episodic occurrence within its own temporal boundaries. Indeed, no episodic motivations are offered.

Week Twenty

The emergence of ground is now seen more definitely. A new phase appears to be under way:

> It's certainly all the time now. He's talking. Whereas it was spasmodic before. But every day now. This last week he's been fabulous. It's every day he comes in and tells me something. And he's always talking to me.

A general reformulation is apparent as the pupil is seen to go through a change. It is not a total retyping but early signs of an emerging new identity. A new boundary is crossed as some segments of ground are revised and seen to be enduring phenomena: 'all the time' and 'certainly'. The previous occurrences were seen as a transition: 'it was spasmodic before'. The new ground is consolidated as the pupil is now: 'always talking to me'. This has perhaps been a point of crossing into normality. It certainly seems a possible interpretation as Mrs. Gill now begins to look tentatively in a different motivational reservoir:

> I'm not sure whether it's stubbornness or insecurity now. Now over the last few weeks ... he's developed. And it's continuing this development of him talking to me. It's marvellous. Every day brings something new. And he's always wanting to express himself.

The pupil seems to have moved across significant boundaries and is in the process of demonstrating further movement:

'every day brings something new',
'he's developed',
'it's continuing this development of him talking to me'.

Further Normalization: Processes of Relativity; Retrospective Reinterpretation

In addition, there is a sign of a fading interpersonal boundary. In interactional terms, Alan is no longer seen to be apart from the rest. Still more important is that the teacher is now apparently in the process of re-applying motive search to earlier ground: 'I'm not sure whether it's stubbornness or insecurity now.' Whether the earlier motive is now being reformulated or a new one substituted is not possible to detect, but most certainly in the present context the pupil is seen to be crossing a motivational and therefore a *model* boundary: from abnormal to normal!

Mrs. Gill goes deeper, suggesting deviance when it occurs can now be viewed merely as an *episodic* phenomenon and therefore operating from a different base of normality and not a reversion to a ground of earlier deviant identity:

> I suppose if I talk to him and he stops ... you could class it as stubbornness. That he doesn't want to communicate. But I never looked on it lately as stubbornness on his part. More shyness, perhaps, in the situation he's put in. That he doesn't want to talk.

She is here apparently stating the boundaries which operate in the typical episodes which now derive from the new ground. It can be seen how the boundaries are now expressed less in personal terms of pupil formulation but rather in terms of contextual or *situational* parameters, confirming the suggestion of apparent model change as there is now a move *away* from dispositional identity to a framework of episodic formulation.[4] The imputations of divergence now move from the personal to the episodic. This is followed by a commentary reviewing Alan over the year. It confirms the present retyping:

> Last two, three weeks he started to volunteer information in the hall. In the midst of the whole school group. That's the difference in his confidence. I find that he's very often the leader in a small group. He'll take the leadership role. Which he never would before!

It seems that the retyping[5] is viewed within a developmental framework, apparently providing a tentative causal texture to their recognition of pupil change:

> He sometimes gets a little bit weepy if children have knocked his model down. And that's reverting to his older babyish self. Because he was a little bit babyish when he came in. I think it's just a gradual process of maturing in school.

It seems the new ground is given a meta-legitimacy by casting it within a developmental framework, as though no further explanation were needed. Any divergence is now apparently interpretable and containable within episodic terms. The newly apparent normal ground is retained.

The first year ends, then, with a confident reformulation of Alan as a normal pupil. The ground appears to have shifted. There is now optimism about his remaining career. Its course will now be examined as he moves into year two and begins with a new teacher again.

Year Two

Alan begins his second year apparently well on the way to normalization. It seems the abnormal model has now largely been abandoned.

In the continually changing career of this pupil a more detailed account is necessary to convey the ongoing and emerging features of his early school identity than was the case with Gavin, the deviant pupil in School A. Alan seems to be more puzzling to teachers and so his case illustrates the 'accomplishment' involved in constructing his identity or interpreting the ambiguity of his actions within episodes. He seems to experience so much more change and reformulation than Gavin, who experiences a relatively stable deviant identity throughout his early school career.

A New Teacher: Episodes in the Emergence of Identity — Normal or Deviant?

Week One

Mrs. Byrne, the new teacher, gives her view of Alan. Her comment may be scrutinized for an indication at this point of whether the pupil is perceived from an abnormal or a normal base:

> He's always moaning about something in the classroom. He whines a lot as well. If he's built something and somebody else touches it or knocks it down, blimey you'd think there'd been a murder. Cause there's great screams!! It's Alan. Somebody's knocked something down. And he really cries. He sobs his heart out over it. He gets very upset over it. And it's difficult to make him see reason.

It is not possible to know whether an underlying pivotal ground identity is in operation here. However, it is clear that already the pupil is in some respects out-of-the-ordinary and seen to be close to the outer boundaries of normality:

> 'great scream',
> 'you'd think there'd been a murder',
> 'he really cries',
> 'gets very upset',
> 'it's difficult to make him see reason'.

The last formulation suggests a motive boundary. It indicates more than anything the potential abnormality, as the pupil is seen to be operating from a motive outside the boundaries of what by implication might apply to normal pupils: beyond 'reason'. The real issue is whether the teacher's formulation is pointing to a potential deviant ground or to a mere episodically contingent deviation.

Week Two

In the emergence of deviant identity there is now a further revelation:

> Whiny still. He seems to be worse this week than he was before. But I think he's just generally feeling that way out. He's always whined if he can't have his own way.

This could be a reformulation of pivotal category as there is seen to be a reversion to a possible deviant identity as ground: 'worse this week than he was before'. It is not clear whether this is the emergence of a new ground or whether the teacher is viewing it more cautiously as episodic divergence. There is perhaps a hint at the episodic in the possible episodic motive: 'I think he's just generally feeling that way out'. It seems the teacher is here invoking a typical episodic theme: 'always whined if he can't have his own way'. This seems to be a formulation at the level of the typical episode: the mid-position between general ground and figure episode. It is recognized as a general pattern but limited to specific contexts or settings.

Mrs. Byrne next moves from this level of generality in its typicality to a specific figure instance:

> Like this morning. Everybody got their milk. Except five people. And he was crying his eyes out 'cause he thought he wasn't going to get any. He will whine on and on and on about things. But if you don't stand for it he doesn't go on. He changes.

It is apparently viewed as an episodic figure instance of a more general phenomenon: 'He will whine on and on about things', which in turn seems to generate a teacher strategy.

The exploratory processes of formulation persist as the teacher continually seems to move between episodic and trans-episodic forms in her attempt to construct reality:

> He was quiet at the beginning. And rather sullen. He didn't whine as much. But now that he's coming out of himself more and talking more he's whining. It becomes more apparent. Maybe it was as bad before but he just seems more apparent this last week or so.

An emerging ground is indicated. The teacher appears to be reformulating and is uncertain whether a new ground is forming ('he's whining') or whether it only *appears* new since previously it was hidden by the pupil's conduct ('whereas now he's coming out of himself more'). It seems the teacher senses a new boundary is being crossed but is aware it may be too soon to formulate with any trans-episodic generality: 'he just seems more apparent this last week or so'.

Mrs. Byrne next relates an episodic figure observation of the pupil experiencing a seemingly significant interpersonal boundary:

> He got some counters out for his money yesterday and he was counting them. And then Matthew was doing his number. So he went and took some of his money. And he started crying and carrying on. And you've got to keep explaining to him that he has to share. He's still very possessive over everything!

It seems here that the teacher recognizes a potential abnormality. It is suggested in this account that what seems to be interpreted as a quite 'normal' action on the part of the other pupil is seen to lead to an apparently 'abnormal' figure response from Alan. This is not a mere episodic but a ground formulation apparently operating from an abnormal model. The other pupil is interpreted through a framework of *episodic* normality while Alan is viewed from a trans-episodic framework of abnormal ground.

This account shows how the very same event may be seen both in episodic and in trans-episodic terms. Different individuals in the *same* context are being viewed either from an episodic or a trans-episodic frame. In the same incident or event, for one component of interpersonal relativity (the formulation of Alan) the present figure is perceived in relation to a *continuous ground*. For another pupil (Matthew) the incident is seen as *episodic*. It is important to recognize the interpersonal relativity of emergence or emergent processes.

Elaboration of an Emerging Deviant Identity: Processes of Relativity

Week Seven

The processes of emergence now continue by an apparent clarification of the interpersonal boundary between the normal and abnormal pupils:

> Most of the children you always find smiling. Everywhere they are. But Alan, whereas you sometimes think it's unusual to see some of the children unhappy, it's unusual if you see Alan smiling.

It is clear that the teacher is now operating a different formulatory ground and therefore an abnormal model has been adopted for Alan. Mrs. Byrne now offers a further statement of dispositional or underlying deviant ground:

> He cries at nothing. Nothing at all. He's been like that since I first came. And he's still the same.

This tendency to cry is illustrated by a figure observation from a recent classroom episode:

Yesterday they were changing library books. So I said: Get a partner. And he's no sooner realized he hadn't got a partner before he was sitting on the floor with his head down crying. Really crying. Little situations like that. It takes a long time to make him see that its not the end of the world.

The deviation from the normal is apparently now seen as quite extreme: 'really crying'. After outlining figure observation, the teacher moved immediately back into ground for its interpretation. This provides a basis for interpreting the pupil's general motivation: 'it takes a long time to make him see that it's not the end of the world'. It seems to become the basis for a strategy formulation too.

The Beginnings of Normalization?

Week Nine

Two weeks later, in the next account there is an indication of developing normality:

He's suddenly coming out of himself. Yesterday I was surprised because after the holiday we were talking all about what each other'd been doing. And about four times just in that one session his hand was up and he was wanting to speak. It wasn't just a look and one word answer. He talked quite freely about what he'd been doing. And that's just suddenly.

An episode has begun that indicates processes of change are perhaps under way. It has 'suddenly' appeared in this emergent episode. Episodic figure and motive illustrate a suspected change of ground. The suggested episodic theme: 'it wasn't just a look and one word answer' suggests the teacher regards it as significant. She is obviously searching for underlying pattern as she invokes previous images and then rejects them. It seems a genuine searching process is under way as the teacher is actively constructing as much in terms of what the episode was *not* as what it actually *was*.

This is what theme search is all about. The teacher is not just constructing a supposed episodic theme but also providing the background of its structure. The discovery of an episodic theme is perhaps more likely to involve searching and processes of accomplishment, since each episode is potentially unique and for-the-moment, therefore previous themes are unlikely to apply. They are less enduring than ground — indeed episodic!

Further Normalization: Processes of Relativity

Week Eleven

The pupil's career, although deviant, now seems to continue in an apparently normal direction:

They're all quite sociable except for Alan Knight. But he's getting better. There's been a vast improvement just lately.

A fundamental difference still persists between Alan and the others. This suggests an abnormal model may still be in use. However, there is a process of limited or perhaps segmentalized normal orientation going on: 'vast improvement just lately'. This apparent normality is further outlined:

He's becoming much more sociable and wanting one-to-one attention from me. Very interested to do more work and show me now. He's taken a sudden turn. He's interested in showing off what he's done if he gets praised for it to all the children now. Which wasn't Alan at all. He's even started giggling. Very unlike him.

This may perhaps be complete normalization. The teacher now engages in biographical Other matching,[6] a contrast with former ground 'which wasn't Alan at all'. The move into the normal phase is so marked it reaches a significant boundary: 'even started giggling'.

Further Normalization: Processes of Relativity and Negotiation

Week Fifteen

Normalization continues:

He's changed a tremendous amount. Even his mother's remarked. He's more eager to come to school.

This seems to be a remarkable change. A total revision of ground is seen as justified by his mother's own formulation. New ground is apparently 'negotiated' by the fusion of two compatible grounds both in-school and out-of-school.
Another indication of normal ground:

He mixes a lot with other children. It's become very apparent. It seems such an obvious fact. 'Cause before he used to be very sullen. And now he's laughing with all the others. And going to others to play. Whereas before they would be going to him. And he wouldn't want to know most of the time.

Normalization continues. The interpersonal differentiation boundary has been dissolved. Whereas there was an *interactional* difference perceived before, it no longer applies, leading to a double dimension of normality. At the pupil level of Alan's construction of action there is no self-imposed boundary (the genuine sociological 'identity' of the pupil's presentation of Self) and at the teacher level of perception there is no longer a boundary of typical action and motive to distinguish Alan from other pupils. Boundaries have blurred and disappeared — the essence of a process of normalization.
The new ground is supported by new motivation:

He's becoming very affectionate. Which isn't like him. He likes to be round you. He likes to be noticed. Does little things *to* be noticed. Which he wasn't before at all. It was hardly noticeable before.

This new behaviour is a change which is most noticeable since it is a contrast with previous ground. The new ground now provides a source of understanding motivation. He is now seen to be operating from a new motivational reservoir: 'does little things *to* be noticed'. Since it is not apparently an *episodic* motive then it confirms the view that a new ground is now in play.

Reformulation: A Normal Identity

Finally a review of the total change. The move into normality:

> If I ask for anybody to do anything he's always there offering. And things like that. Which for *him* is a big improvement. It's quite surprising sometimes some of the things he does which you wouldn't think of from Alan. Not from the Alan I knew when I first came. Well, he didn't really know me. So he was maybe a bit dubious about the fact that he kept getting all these new teachers!

The process of normalization is apparently complete then. A statement of new ground which is now seen to be a widespread phenomenon: 'things like that'. In addition it is seen as specifiable in a typical episodic or boundary form: 'if I ask for anybody to do anything he's always there offering'. This is contrasted with earlier ground: 'the Alan I knew when I first came'. This earlier ground is now seen to have been temporally and interactionally contingent and bounded.

Again, the essential perception problem in the formulation of deviance can be seen: is it shortlived (an episodic phenomenon) or is it enduring (a dispositional or ground phenomenon of pivotal identity)? Unless there is absolute certainty, for open-minded teachers there will perhaps always be a potential episodic explanation of any untoward action or events attributable to the circumstances of the 'act'.

Retrospective Reconstruction

Normalization now seems to result in a reformulation of earlier deviance from the new standpoint:

> I expect at some time boys do go through a period of showing their personality over others. Over teacher. And he seemed so introverted at first. Now I feel he's becoming more normal. He's becoming overtly normal.

This is a straightforward statement of normality. The earlier deviance is now neutralized by being reviewed within a developmental framework. It is, in effect, recast within an episodic framework as a phenomenon now seen to have been no more than a developmental phase or an extended episode. What at the time may have been thought of as ground is now seen to have been a mere extended episode as he adjusted to life with a new teacher. Obviously, this episodic reformulation will always be a post hoc process reviewing earlier phenomena from a new standpoint in time. Episodic or phasic neutralization of deviance then is possible only when it can be seen how it turned out or what it turned into, — when it has come to its end. Deviance has no clear form until then.

Normalization and Submergence

The normalization seems to be further confirmed in the apparent submergence[7] of Alan in the social world of this classroom. The pupil no longer appears in interview talk (as though perhaps he is no longer of any concern to the teachers). In a period of six months there are only three interview references to Alan. One (week twenty) suggests either a mere difference of opinion between teachers about Alan's identity or perhaps a recognition of situated variations in pupil identity in relation to specific teachers:

> When we were talking in the group before Mrs. Williams said about Alan. She found him difficult when she has him to get him to concentrate and to do work and things. And I still haven't found that since then. He's not that way with me.

This comment hints at a possible disputing of segmentalized ground formulations within the inter-subjective world of the staffroom. The next (week thirty-one) sums up, in Mrs. Byrne's own words, the concept of *submergence* which is used later in relation to the 'normal' pupil case studies:

> I feel that it is only where there has been something unusual or different that I've mentioned anything. Because life, and everyday life of every child, and your relationship with that child, seem to run on a relatively even pattern.

— a statement of routine submergence within the parameters of normality.

The third reference to Alan in this period of six months is in the end of term review. Although the submergence during this time suggests a period of normality in his career there are still traces of abnormality:

> He still has his usual mannerisms. But they're not as pronounced as they were before. Which makes him more on a par with other children.

The pupil has become more normal; the implied traces of his abnormality no longer differentiate him from 'other children' so much. The *interpersonal* boundary and the *interactional* boundary once again are dissolved. (In Alan's case these two boundaries seem to go together). Mrs. Byrne continues with an account of how normalization is apparently socially structured by attempting to manage his responses by adopting a particular strategy:

You know that you have to wait quite a long time for him to reply or to join in. You know what's going to cause him to hang his head and withdraw. And so consequently you don't put him in that situation. You avoid it.

Is it really a normalization in pupil career or merely an interactionally structured avoidance of the abnormal? Since abnormal ground is still present as a basis of this teacher strategy, although the pupil's response is made normal, is there not a potential deviant ground behind these typical episodic figures?

Mrs. Byrne also indicates how extreme the earlier abnormality had been regarded. The boundary so dominated the formulation that it seemed to be beyond normalization:

He had something to cause my concern. Because I didn't think that with his attitudes and behaviour that he could ever get, or at that time get, into a situation, and a sense of ease with me sufficiently enough for him to learn.

Formulations have temporal projections; at the time of original formulation they extend some way into the future. To formulate is to anticipate, and begin to act upon, the Other's future career.

And so year two closes with Alan's career apparently having undergone a process of normalization — whether 'natural' or 'socially structured'. He now enters his third year in school.

Year Three: A New Teacher: Episodes in the Emergence of an Identity

Week Three

Alan gets a new teacher once again. Mrs. Wilson begins the school-year with no previous knowledge of him. Formulation apparently starts from a baseline of implicit normality:

Now he's a little lad who will follow things through. If he's on his own he'll work hard and long at a thing.

This comment seems to be a routine formulation of conformity to expectations, even though it is qualified and at this point, the teacher seems to be operating from a normal base. There is a recognition that potential abnormality may not be too far away:

Apparently he cries. Not cries, as much as he looks as though he's going to. His eyes fill up. It fits, unless he's misunderstood my intentions. There's been no reason that I could see. In fact the first time I said to him: What was wrong with his eyes? I didn't realize that they were in fact tears.

Here is an instance of a teacher acquiring a communal formulatory ground from negotiation with other teachers. Staffroom culture provides a basis for acquiring knowledge about pupil identity as ground. Here it seems the teacher is attempting to discover an underlying pattern to her observations. She tries out trans-episodic *communal* ground and apparently 'it fits'.

She also attempts to neutralize this by trying out an episodic form of alternative interpretation: 'unless he's misunderstood my intentions. There's been no reason that I could see'. She even has to reformulate her original figure observation itself since even the figure was not clear: 'In fact the first time I said to him: What was wrong with his eyes? I didn't realize that they were in fact tears'.

In this instance there is much *movement between perceptions*: between *mis-perceived* figure and *received* ground; between episodic theme and trans-episodic ground. A dynamic or ongoing process indeed. Mrs. Wilson continues the search for meaning by reverting to the emerging provisional ground framework of typical episode:

> We were going to do number cards again. So I wonder if they come when he feels as though he's being asked to do something that he can't do.

Again, there is an apparent mid-position in formulation between the episode and the more general ground. There appears to be a search within the generalized or *typical* episode. But finally the teacher goes on to express it as a possible segmentalized ground:

> His results weren't right. But then he sat ... on his own and he worked through and he did get the right answers. And he could think what he was doing. So I wonder if that's it. If he thinks to himself: I can't do this. A bit of timidity.

The teacher, throughout this sequence of classroom action, has moved through tentative figure, revised figure, episodic theme, communal/received ground, typical or generalized episodic theme, and finally a tentative and segmentalized form of ground. In the first week such movement is to be expected since it is a process of *searching* for patterns and underlying meaning. This searching occurs before a stable formulation base emerges — that is, until a firm ground appears.

Week Four

In week four a normal or perhaps even a normal-ideal segmentalized formulation:

> Alan Knight is remarkable. He swims all the time with his head under water. He got a certificate. He really is quite confident in the water. Does very well.

This seems to be a possible 'ideal' formulation: 'remarkable', 'very well'. Alan is interpreted from a *segmentalized ground* or *typical episodic setting* relating to speci-fiable contexts of action and interaction.

Next a figure instance is offered:

> On Friday of last week he almost made the distance they had to swim. Swim to the length of three posts it was. And he almost made it. I'm sure it was Alan 'cause we congratulated him in red group this morning.

This account is offered within the staffroom where other teachers confirm the normal/ideal formulation.

The event is quite unexpected to another teacher:

> I was quite surprised. [EF] I would've thought that he might have found a bit of difficulty coping with a new situation [SG].

The matching of an implicit episodic figure (EF) with segmental ground (SG) leads to surprise. Such 'surprise' situations demonstrate the importing of ground-based frameworks against which episodic figures are interpreted.

An Emerging Normal Identity?

Alan seems in some respects to be experiencing a normal career now. The abnormal ground from earlier in his school career is often used as a backcloth in matching with his former self. For example, the next account is a video–taped 'live' observation with a number of teachers present. The teacher interprets the present figure phenomenon by remarking on its divergence from an earlier abnormal ground:

> [On the video tape Alan makes a thumbs–up gesture and everyone in the staffroom remarks positively on a recognized change in him] Yes. In-dicating I suppose really his development of confidence. Because he was really an introverted child when he first came. He wouldn't hold his head up. Or look at you at all.

This figure observation is recognized by all as such a contrast with earlier ground. The comments in unison from everyone in the staffroom is quite a clear indication of a prevailing view within the 'thinking-as-usual' in staffroom culture.

Further Episodes in Normal Career: An Underlying Divergence?

The teacher next indicates a difference between Alan and another pupil. It is formulated first as an *episodic* difference but then perhaps becomes more than that:

> Alan is different to Paul. There was an incident the other day. Paul knew
> immediately he'd done wrong. And he more or less sprung up to me.
> And he said he was sorry. Now Alan will do wrong in a very quiet sort
> of way. And I wouldn't say he's as open in his actions as is Paul.

An interpersonal boundary appears. It may, of course, not be a significant boundary, but episodically a difference is noted. The intra-episodic sequence demonstrates a difference:

> 'Paul knew immediately',
> 'he sprung up to me',
> 'and said he was sorry'.

Is it significant that the formulation for Paul is merely episodic: 'he said he
was sorry'? Whereas for Alan the formulation is *trans-episodic* as though it were a
mere instance of a recurring pattern: 'Alan will do wrong in a very quiet sort of
way', 'wouldn't say he's as open' — as though the *figure* incident were less
noticeable than the *ground* for which it stood. Faced with an instance or event
involving two pupils, the teacher sees *figure* with one pupil, and *ground* with
another! This dichotomy suggests a significant element of the dynamics of
typification. Teachers, it seems, are able to see either figure or ground in the
same event. It can be seen either as a unique episode or as a recurring pattern.

End of Year Review: Indications of Normalization in a Deviant Career — Reconstruction and Reinterpretation of Reality

Week Thirty-five

As the analysis approaches the end of Alan's third year there is some reference to
his earlier career at the start of infant schooling, a 'natural' temporal context
within a three year time-scale. Knowledge of Other has ground elements extending three years back into the past. (It can be seen that ground 'naturally' has
extended dimensions to participants. It is a genuinely developmental or longitudinal view of Other which may remain untapped except by the use of methodologies that acknowledge such longitudinal frameworks):

> It took him such a long time to bring himself to even talk to people and
> to join in anything that was going on. He would just sit. Literally in his
> own little space with his head down. And he wouldn't take part in
> singing nursery rhymes or playing games for a long time.

The speaker reviews Alan's earlier deviance, in its general (trans-episodic) ground
form, and more specifically in its segmentalized form.

A Common-Sense Theory of Ground Formulation:
A Dynamic Perspective on the Negotiation of Reality

As the teacher explains what she has written about Alan in his report she revisits the earlier deviant ground:

> I've written Alan was extremely withdrawn during his first year in school (1) but has made remarkable progress. And has much to offer in group activities (2).

This recap is not just a revisit in the context of the third party talk of interviews but the communication to third parties in the next school. This is important because it indicates how the teacher recognizes that for future teachers to begin to formulate the pupil appropriately (from present teachers' standpoint) it is important to know the ground from which development has proceeded and been seen to proceed. They will need to know not just the appropriate ground but the *developmental* ground so as to recognize 'actual' development and the 'relative' evaluation of it. What is seen to matter is not just how the pupil is *now* viewed but what he has *become* and the distance over which he has travelled. The teacher is obviously offering a normalized ground (2) to neutralize or offset the statement of ground (1). This is a significant instance for understanding the *negotiation* of Others as it occurs within organizational settings. (Similar processes of career emergence may perhaps occur in other organizational contexts.)

The teacher goes on to give the ground formulation greater segmental specificity:

> [Alan] has much to offer in group activities. Particularly in Art and Craft. He's very talented at drawing and painting. He does things in minute detail and uses colour very nicely. And it's one of the things that I particularly used to build up his self-confidence. His talent at Art and Craft. Because once he knew he could do something, possibly better than other children, he became quite confident about doing that. And other children would say: Alan can draw cars, fairs or ... Alan can paint this.

After first outlining a general ground, this is translated by the teacher into specific segmental role instances. These are employed strategically by the teacher in her attempts to maintain the direction of normalization for Alan's career. Her own construction, and that of other pupils, is seen to produce a normalization of his career through segmentalized 'ideal' constructions and their continued negotiation in the world of the classroom.

The teacher finally sums up the developmental dimensions of ground:

> I think reading and number really you can say he's lost a year out of his infant school life. Or going on for a year.

Here, then, is a temporal and segmental construction in two specified segmental roles. Formulation is seen to be within a temporal or developmental framework with rates of emergence seen to be lagging behind other non-specified segmental roles. This account represents a powerful summing up of the *temporality* of infant school life and the particular place of 'development' (*direction* and *pace* of movement) within the temporal frame of the '*cultural* timetable' of infant school life.

Year Four

Alan now enters his fourth year of school and the final year of the investigation of early school careers in this research cohort. At this point there would have been a move into a 'new' school — the junior school, but because of school mergers the fourth year was within a changing or merging organizational situation: the combining of the infant and junior schools. The headteacher was attempting to redefine across the new school the ideologies and boundaries (interpersonal, curricular, and even typificational, I suspect!) as she took over what was to become the junior department of the new all-through primary school. The early phase of the merger involved an opening of 'spatial' boundaries as the former junior teachers began to operate in the teaching area which had previously been the I3 home base. Within this changing context, Alan's new teacher, Miss Tait, is a newcomer both to the school and to the profession and so perhaps is something of a 'stranger' to this social world, owing no allegiance to the ideologies of either of the two former 'schools' in the merging process.

A New Teacher: Episodes in Emergence of an Identity

Week One

Within what framework does the interpretation of Alan begin — from a normal or an abnormal base? It seems in the first interview, Miss Tait's interpretation begins without reference to ground. The first formulation account is mere episodic or figure formulation: 'At first, he was very reticent when I first met him'.

The teacher's next statement appears to move towards a ground formulation:

> The first thing you'd think about is the fact that his brother's in my class as well now. And physically they look very alike. But Alan tends to seem very much older. Because Andrew's so young.

How does the 'sibling phenomenon' (Hargreaves, 1975) become an element in the figure-ground processes? Does it perhaps provide a readymade figure-ground relationship, with each sibling acting as a covert ground for his or her pair as a permanently present interpretive framework within these early figure formulations?

In this case the teacher's use of the 'sibling phenomenon' permits the emergence of ground formulation. As an opener, she focuses on the dimension of development/maturation: 'Alan tends to seem very much older because Andrew's so young'.

Next we move onto a formulation of Alan himself:

He's at first a sort of bit sulky. But now he seems to be working ... he's working quite well.

It seems the teacher has noted a brief temporal resistance which quickly fades into a normal formulation.

Indications of a Normal Identity

As yet no ground of a trans-episodic kind has emerged. It seems about ready to emerge however:

I find him polite. He tends to be one of the ones that will do things when he's asked to do it. Reasonably straight away.

Here, then, is an apparently conformist pupil, who is expressed in segmental ground form after all. In week one there is a limited *trans-episodic* formulation. It seems at this point to be from an emerging normal base.

A Suspicion of Deviance?

Week Two

So far the formulation has apparently been normal. In the next account, however, Miss Tait now indicates a suspicion of potentially deviant ground which has become visible within a figure incident:

There was an incident with him. The other day he was playing with some dominoes. Big dominoes. Building some kind of structure. And another boy came along, just took over from him rather than kicked it down. And Alan went under a chair and cried. And then he came out and he went and sat somewhere else and sort of cried. And eventually went in to dinner and cheered up. But he obviously takes things very hard of that nature.

The teacher's formulation begins as an episodic observation from which she generates a trans-episodic construction of potential deviance, but it is seen as highly specific and segmentally role-related: 'he obviously takes things very hard of that nature'. It is generated from an episodic occurrence which is itself seen in divergent figure terms. Since the intruder is formulated in implied normal terms ('just took over from him rather then kicked it down' — he is seen to have merely done this rather than anything deviant) then Alan's response is obviously seen as out of all proportion to the 'surface structure' of the incident which acted as a trigger — a divergent or deviant response on the part of Alan, yet also more than that. In its *temporality* it is longer lasting than the normal. The teacher's use of 'eventually' suggests a struggle against time, and so not the 'normal' time-scale. (In the analysis of this incident it is the *apparent* meanings, rather than the teacher's explicit formulation of boundaries, that provide indications of normality and abnormality in this case. The deviance is continually *implied* rather than stated. At this point in the teacher's interpretation of Alan's career the account is less valid then and so must be regarded as merely exploratory).

Episodes in the Emergence of a Deviant Identity

On to an apparently more explicit deviant formulation:

> Sort of misbehaves. He's like Andrew [Alan's brother]. He's very stubborn. And if I ask him to do something he doesn't *want* to do he tends to ... Like I said: Will you put your book away. So he shut it. But he wanted to keep the page. Eventually, when I said: 'Oh, you could find the page again Alan', Alan put the book back. But it takes that amount of getting him to do it.

There is quite a mix of constructions offered here. Nevertheless, it seems overall, however, to be an account of deviance. It begins with rule-breaking deviation but is expressed in person formulation (ground) terms: 'sort of misbehaves'. Then using the 'sibling phenomenon', a further figure-ground interpretation: 'he's like Andrew. He's very stubborn'. The sibling relationship becomes a ground for the formulation of Alan's figure deviation. All of which is encompassed in suggesting potential deviance: 'very stubborn'. It is illustrated with a figure instance or episode of deviation. The deviance is seen to have two possible boundaries both *temporal* ('eventually ... put the book back') and *degree* ('takes that amount of getting him to do it'). It seems on this occasion that Alan has exceeded or crossed both boundaries of normality. Both boundaries are implied in this incident.

Week Three

Apparent signs of a continually emerging divergent ground, perhaps:

> Alan is still crying if people upset him. Always it seems to be to do with something that he thinks is his. Like if he's playing with Lego [bricks]. Somebody comes and breaks it. Which happens twenty times a day to other people. He doesn't retaliate but he cries quietly.

Here is a sense of a continuously emerging ground, ('still crying') as though as an emergent feature it may be open to modification before long. But then finally what seems to be the first statement of the normal/abnormal boundary. Here, for the first time, is the location of Alan on the abnormal side of a boundary as compared with the others who are on the normal side. His reaction is seen to be so different in an occurrence: 'which happens twenty times a day to other people'. A significant interpersonal distinction.

Signs of a Normal Orientation in a Deviant Identity

Nevertheless, in relation to the formulation of a deviant identity, there is a recognition of some movement towards normality:

> He's started coming to me a bit more to appeal for help rather than just cry. He'll come and tell me who did it. And if he's restored, he seems to buck up and carry on. And he seems to be a lot happier. He's started standing near me in assembly.

Here a definite movement is recognized. There is an underlying deviance, as in previous instances, but his response to the deviant situation is apparently perceived as more oriented towards the normal. In addition, there seems to be the reduction in the strength of interpersonal boundaries, at least as they operate between teacher and pupil.

Week Four

A time sampling observation generates a routine and apparently normal formulation:

> Alan was sitting with his book open and finishing a drawing. But he wasn't actually *doing* anything much. He was just sitting. Looking worried. Which again is fairly typical.

An account which captures the 'natural' moment and forces the teacher to interpret it. In terms of formulation, it is not 'natural' but in its attempt to capture the dynamics of everyday teacher-pupil relations (especially the 'lows' as well as the 'highs'), it comes close to the naturalness of situated typification across a range of classroom life, which other foci of interviewing tend to distort by encouraging an orientation towards the 'high' points in the teacher's reporting of classroom events.

In this case there is nothing very remarkable to report. It is formulated from an implicitly normal base, a routine but normal episode with normal episodic figures: 'sitting' and 'drawing'. In addition, there is an apparently abnormal figure not merely episodically divergent ('looking worried') but linked trans-episodically by the teacher to an implicit ground: 'is fairly typical'. In a randomly selected moment it is still evident that deviant ground is operating at a deeper structure level. This is noticeable not in what he was doing ('wasn't actually *doing* anything', therefore a routine normal formulation perhaps) but in the *manner* of doing it ('looking worried'). In so doing it has exposed or tapped the covert presence of an underlying deviant ground — at a randomly selected moment.

Beyond this, Miss Tait expands and invokes an earlier deviant ground:

> He does tend to scowl a lot. Which I think I noticed at the beginning. That was the main thing about him. He looked very sulky.

Here the deviant theme of the event is *episodically* transformed into a *trans-episodic* formulation by relating it to ground.

Dynamics of Deviance Formulation in Classroom Life

Now there is a move into the potential deviant ground:

> Alan still sulks. Last week he did get on fairly well. This week I've noticed him started sulking again.

The normal orientation is now seen perhaps as an episodic phenomenon, a temporary interruption. The reversion to previous ground continues: 'started sulking again'.

Miss Tait recounts figure formulations which are regarded as extensions of, or founded upon, deviant ground:

> We've had three incidents this morning where he's been crying because he couldn't see the television. And he wouldn't move himself! And he was told to move. He wouldn't move. He just sat there.

There seems to be an implied normal yardstick used for comparison here (of what any normal Other might do in the circumstances). The teacher applies episodic strategy as though the source of the problem were to be found within the parameters of the episode but again 'he wouldn't move'. The attempt to structure the situation and the pupil into normality fails — a double deviance. Both 'natural' and 'structured' responses are abnormal: 'he just sat there'. It is not clear whether Miss Tait is aware of some of the categories of deviance employed by teachers in this pupil's earlier career: 'just sat there'. This construction is reminiscent of such earlier deviant formulations though its direct continuities with 'what everyone knows' cannot be assumed.

The deviance in this case moves into a *temporal* mode. It becomes a deviant *response episode*:

> He just sat there. And then moaned. And then he turned away. And then he cried. He spent a long time. A good five minutes turned away quite deliberately from the television.

Four temporal references occur here, all presented in a sequential form. The response episode has a temporal framework. In some ways it is not unlike the notion of 'societal reaction' operated in labelling accounts of deviance. Here, however, it is the *deviant's* response rather than the *onlooker's* that is under scrutiny. (The present framework, nevertheless, would suggest that any account of 'reaction', whether of the deviant or the onlooker, should take an episodic view encompassing a dynamic or process interpretation of the entire episodic unit).

The above account by the teacher also indicates a deviant motivational base since a motive is seen to have no source within the episodic parameters but beyond these events. The pupil's action is seen to have slipped from an episodic response to a ground response. As the episode unfurls, its theme increases ground potential since it moves from the potentially transient or episodic (deviant response to contingent circumstances) to the more *enduring* bases of his behaviour, recognized in deviant ground and its motivational reservoir. (This point is where the temporal dimension of interpretation is critical. Ground is an ever-present phenomenon within or beneath any figure.)

The sequence of linked episodes or episodic chain continues:

> Then he was in the line and somebody pushed him. So he cried because
> so-and-so's pushed me out of the line. Again, nothing that any other
> people wouldn't've solved by either shoving them back or just standing
> there! Or going somewhere else. But Alan seems to draw a blank at
> doing something about things.

This formulation then confirms the view taken earlier in the analysis. Here is an overt statement of what was previously implied. While deviant ground was previously only noticeable in the teacher's apparent use of motivational reservoir, it is now overtly referred to. The teacher is claiming an interpersonal boundary of a fundamental (ground-based) kind: Alan is compared with what 'any other people' would do.

This event leads onto a more dynamic exploration of the ground-related basis of this deviant incident. She considers the changing form of ground over time:

> I think I've mentioned something about him going under the chair. And
> he would cry under the chair rather than cry in public. Maybe not sulky
> ... last time. I've decided it's sulking now perhaps! *Then* I think he was
> genuinely upset.

The use of a dynamic or ongoing perspective indicates how an earlier *figure* now becomes viewed from what seems to be a *reformulated ground*. This figure begins to change in meaning because of its redefined ground. Here we can see how the 'sociology' of figure-ground is crucial. Figure is a form which can be changed or reconstituted into more than one dimension of *meaning* when ground and the covert facets of formulation begin to operate as underlying elements in the social construction of reality. Miss Tait outlines the basis for her reformulation: 'I think it's the protracted nature of it that makes me term some of it sulking'. The temporal dimension is what is significant.

Miss Tait immediately elaborates an instance of this 'protracted sulking':

> Like yesterday. He and Sally had been making very intricate plasticine
> models which've been going for several days. Sally is getting a bit
> naughtier perhaps we could say. And I told all of them we were 'tidying
> up now'. And I'd specifically gone over to them and said to them that if
> they helped tidy up the floor *then* just before play then they could have
> ten or fifteen minutes when they came in to finish off. And if it wasn't
> done then it goes right away.

The ground, of course, once again can be seen to be an enduring phenomenon since it can be entered at any point on a moving time-scale: 'like yesterday'.

Yesterday's event is itself seen within episodic terms as the time scale or episodic unit over which the two pupils have 'been going for several days'. The other pupil in the episode is seen to be embarking on her *own* moving time-scale as she is shifting towards deviance — yet from a normal base.

The dynamics of interpersonal boundaries are even more evident as the account proceeds:

> Now they didn't [tidy up]. They carried on. So I sort of said one more time: 'Listen, you tidy up now and then you can have some more time.' They didn't! So I just took the whole thing and bunged it back in the plasticine. Which upset the pair of them. Sally sulked. Sort of sat with her arms folded and sort of stared at the wall during the initial time we had. Then she went off to story. She came back. She was perfectly normal. She'd obviously got over it. Alan just glowered. And he wouldn't do anything. He went and sat.

This is a fortuitous naturalistic coming together in the teacher's formulation of a 'normal' and a potential 'abnormal' pupil in one incident! It is even more interesting to note the reaction of 'sitting' or 'just sat' which for Alan had been his first sign of deviance at the start of his school career: his first divergence from the normal.

Here, we appear to have the same situation except that it is not in itself related to earlier constructions of deviant ground by the teacher. In fact her knowledge of Other extends only to the start of this fourth year. However, it is clear that the episode is seen in abnormal terms with the interpersonal boundary differentiation occurring between Alan and the normal pupil, Sally, whose reaction was short-lived and then 'She came back. She was perfectly normal'. However, Alan's reaction was longer lasting and apparently is seen to be operating from a different motivational base. He 'just glowered' and 'he went and sat'. It seems that the motivational basis of this episode quickly passes into a normal frame for Sally ('she'd obviously got over it') but for Alan the abnormal base continues ('he wouldn't do anything'). In this way, episodic emergence and transformation continues. For Sally the episode is over and another has begun. For Alan, however, the same episode continues:

> Sally went and I said: 'Well, you tidy up. You've lost your chance. If you don't tidy up now then the plasticine doesn't come out again for you two.' Sally went off. Sort of went off and tidied up. Alan just sat and sulked I think. Sort of very stony faced.

The differences in reaction can be summarized as follows: Sally has normalized her episode by moving on into another and *normal episode*. For Alan, however, clearly the incident continues into an *extended episode* (with its same underlying *deviant* theme and ground) which is seen to differentiate him from the normal pupil. In addition, he also crosses a further boundary in the *category* of deviance: he 'literally sulked'. The deviance at this point is apparently reified. It is recognized as a 'real' case of deviance and not just an episodic phenomenon. Clearly, the interpretive base here moves away from the episodic to the trans-episodic. The direction of formulation moves from episodic act as figure to dispositional properties of ground. In its deviation across the boundary into abnormality it is seen as extreme: 'very stony faced'. For the normal pupil, Sally, it was *temporary* divergence, merely a brief excursion and contained within episodic boundaries, while for Alan it was potentially trans-episodic! The teacher's comparison here brings out the 'normal' reaction of the 'normal' pupil and the 'deviant' reaction[8] of the 'deviant' pupil.

Next, an apparently routine and recurring form of deviance:

> Today he's done the same thing. I said: 'Alan you're not fiddling with whatever it was.' I said: 'Don't start that. I've told you to go and get your book out so you'll be ready. And packed away (1).' And he just looks at me and carries on (2). He does it with other teachers. I've noticed. Even Mrs. Williams.

A deviant figure is perceived within this episode. It is treated by the teacher's episodic strategy and so is potentially neutralized. But the pupil's response is again deviant. The second figure then is a response to the initial entry point. Since the opportunity to neutralize the event episodically is offered and rejected then the teacher apparently assumes an underlying theme that would reside in ground. Here too, there is an episodic primary and secondary deviation as episodes 1 and 2 are linked sequentially. In effect, this is an *episodic* version of processes of sequencing recognized as critical in the concepts of primary and secondary deviation. The difference is that here the second deviation itself confirms the ground whereas in the secondary deviation of Lemert (1967) the subsequent deviation results from a prior confirmed or presumed ground.[9] In this case the concept of *interactional Other* is also important. It provides the teacher with an additional check on the likely ground. If the Other with Teacher 1 is deviant and the Other with Teacher 2 is also deviant then the deviance must be independent of the teacher with whom the pupil is interacting. The deviance can be assumed to be a property of the pupil as trans-episodic ground and not a mere property of the episode. In this case there is a further check as the teacher recognizes different categories of interactional Other. The outer limits of its testing as dispositional deviance occurs with 'even Mrs. Williams', the deputy head.

Amplification Processes in a Deviant Career

Week Twelve

Signs that the deviance orientation is now accelerating:

> I think the only one is Alan. And he's getting worse. We had an incident this morning. I think it was just after you left. Where he'd written something rude about the female anatomy ... On a table. In pencil. And the other boy had said it was him. And I usually try not to jump down their throats unless I've actually seen it. But I said: 'I want the truth. Did you see it?' No. All the others were saying it must be him. And in the end when I'd said: 'Right, if you're not going to tell me you

can tell me by your actions. If it was you go and wash it off.' And he went off. And he washed it off.

In this case there is a clear indication of abnormal ground. It is expressed in interpersonal boundary terms: 'the only one is Alan'. A clear boundary between other pupils and Alan. In addition, as well as having been located on the abnormal side of the boundary, the negative direction of movement is seen to be continuing: 'he's getting worse'. On two dimensions (in *extent* and in ongoing *dynamics*) he is increasing in deviant ground. Although the pupil is operating from the abnormal side of the boundary, there are distinctions to be made about the kinds of deviance: its degree and its direction.)

The episodic corridor or chain continues:

> I'm sure it was him. 'Cause it was his writing. 'Cause the boy he was sitting next to writes nothing like him. But that was it. It may not be different. It's typical Knight intractableness, that once challenged they're a bit strange.

Here, a psychology of figure-ground is operated in differentiating Alan's writing from others. The handwriting is contextually used to eliminate the other boy and gives the teacher strong suspicions. Episodic theme is well-formed, especially since the whole episodic chain has pointed in this direction. But finally the teacher invokes a trans-episodic ground. The episode and its figure observations are linked trans-episodically with a ground beyond the boundaries of the episode itself. But more important still, the ground is not a mere *static* formulation but a *dynamic* one: it links a typical episodic chain or corridor. The present episodic chain is compared to conceptions of the typical episodic corridor[10] held in ground. It fits and so the teacher is convinced! Although everything so far has pointed in this direction, the typical episodic sequence is seen to be quite significant as a crunch point in the decision.

The incident is further probed:

Interviewer: Were you sure it was him?
Teacher: Oh yes. Now I feel that if Alan hadn't done it, first of all he would've cried and secondly there was no way he would've gone and washed it off. It's just the way he is. He cries if he's wrongly accused. If he's hurt. If somebody pinches his toys. If they mess up his work. He cries a lot at things and withdraws.

On this occasion, upon false accusation, the deviant pupil ground would have shown itself in an episodic figure: 'he would've cried'. That he didn't is seen as consistent with the view that teacher formulation of the current deviant episode is correct. More significant, though, is the *interactional corridor* or typical episodic chain, which is seen as critical: 'there was no way he would've gone and washed it off'. This is double or triple evidence. Perhaps it may be viewed as a ladder or series of stepped moves rather than a corridor. Although the teacher may have been wrong in the first formulation, the second step or rung is even more convincing. It is a stepped corridor.

Further probing:

> I don't know [why he did it]. He's doing it a lot. A lot of the boys have
> become more aware, I think, at the moment. Sexually aware. There's a
> lot of drawing of various bits of the body keeps going on. And he's
> done something before actually.

It is important to recognize the temporal dimensions of the previous account. It
has reference points further back in the past. Not only is there an *intra-episodic* but
also a *trans-episodic* chain. The incident is seen in relation to earlier episodes. (It
can be seen how the construction of reality is within temporal dimensions acting
backward and forward in time.) The trans-episodic formulation here also helps to
neutralize the incident. Alan is identified with 'a lot of the boys'. In this sense
then the pupil is on the normal side of the interpersonal boundary. There is a
reference to the beginning of the trans-episodic sequence, however: 'he'd done
something before actually'. A trans-episodic general theme or ground for all the
boys is established and a particular one for Alan.

This earlier incident is recounted:

> He'd drawn something. And it's: 'I can see the tits'. Or something like
> that. On a piece of paper which somebody else brought to me. And
> again Alan's handwriting is fairly clear. Because he has two very charac-
> teristic letters, Ws and Rs, which nobody else does like him.

The earlier incident was interpreted on the basis of calligraphic 'evidence'. The
segmental role formulation of Alan allows a resolution of the incident by invoking segmental ground since he 'has two very characteristic letters which nobody
else does like him'.

However, perhaps more important still is the more fundamental underlying
theme in both episodes. In the evidence which the interviewer elicited, the
deviance is not rule-breaking in terms of the sexual. In fact, it is hardly treated as
deviance: 'A lot of the boys have become more aware ... at the moment'. No
ground is invoked. It is more routine or episodic, almost a neutral formulation.
The only trans-episodic feature refers in the last quotation to a routine or
'normal' ground — his letters. Although there may be some divergence it is not
a boundary matter. In fact, the issue in the previous teacher's comments is the
deviant person formulation (the trans-episodic ground) invoking the deviant
ground interpretation, 'he cries a lot'. It is not the deviant incident (which is seen
to be a mere episodic matter) but his *reaction* to it which is critical. The more
usual labelling perspective is turned around. The *pupil* reaction to imputed
deviance is the issue and not the 'societal reaction' of others to the routine deviant
incident. The trans-episodic then dominates the episodic; deviant person formulation is a trans-episodic phenomenon.

The teacher indicates her intended 'neutralization' of the rule-breaking features of the episode:

> I don't want to make too much fuss about that either really. 'Cause I
> imagine it's something that now'll go on for the next however many
> year[s].

Figure 10.2: The sequence from rule-breaking to deviance

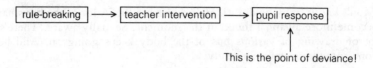

This is the point of deviance!

The rule-breaking element of deviation is quite clearly neutralized. What remains in this incident is the person formulation issue, the non-rule-breaking feature of the event.

End of Term Review: Summary Formulation in a Deviant Career

Week Fourteen

At this point the pupil reaches the end of the first term in his junior career. Clearly he is still viewed from an abnormal base:

> Still the main thing that strikes you about him is his sort of rather strange personality. Stubbornness comes out. Persistently will do things he's been told *not* to do. And if he's told not to do something he just generally stands still. Or sits still. And he sort of stares. And he does that with other teachers as well. So I don't think it's just me brings that out in him!

The teacher begins, almost with a psychological view of figure-ground, on the theme of abnormality and its pathological connotations: 'still the main thing that strikes you is his sort of rather strange personality'. The dominant perceptual frame is a dispositional ground model (perhaps a case of the 'psychological' figure being the 'sociological' ground').

> It would be at least a month, I think, into the term before I really noticed him. Particularly in that way. When it hit me. Because of something I did. Which was, I think, to shout at him for something. And he just stood there.

Again, it is the pupil's reaction to the deviant incident which is at issue, not the rule-breaking itself. The teacher recognizes an unusual pupil response to her own intervention following an apparent rule-breaking: 'he just stood there'. A figural representation of a typical incident is shown in Figure 10.2.

Final Interview: A Review of Earlier Deviant Ground

Six months later, in the final interview, the teachers provide a review of Alan's identity in his early school career.

Mrs. Strang: I can remember when we first started talking about this group that Alan Knight took up a lot of time. He was this strange boy who was very withdrawn when he first started school.

The extent of Alan's differentiation from other pupils is noted in this reference to his early deviant ground. He was: 'strange' and 'very withdrawn'. The abnormality was so prominent as to absorb 'a lot of time' in interview talk. The teacher's reference here once again gives some indication of the extent of this pupil's deviation from school norms.

Mrs. Strang continues:

He was this very strange boy. And during his four years with us has periodically displayed this tendency to be isolated from the group. He occasionally has great difficulties with his relationships.

A continuing differentiation as processes of relativity indicate a marking off of this pupil 'from the group'. The apparent sense of boundary and a recognition of abnormality which has persisted over his career and been 'periodically displayed'.

The account goes on:

He's temperamental. When he's at his most stable is a very interesting boy to work with. A very interesting boy to talk to. He has interesting things to say. Initiates conversations. Responds quite easily to an initiative from anyone else and makes contributions to group discussions and so on.

The general framework of formulation suggests a 'temperamental' and not a stable ground. The teacher appears to be suggesting a dual identity composed of two grounds. The pupil alternates or moves between them. This may perhaps be a special case of deviant ground — a case of deviance in the very deep structure of ground itself — in the lack of ground stability!

After outlining aspects of his 'normal' ground Mrs. Strang then outlines the other ground:

But if he's going through one of his more unstable periods really he's an extremely difficult boy to work with and withdraws into his silence. Or if it's insisted upon that he replies to something that's been said to him will blurt it out in a loud voice and: Well all right! I'll *speak* but I'm not doing it because I really want to! It's only because *you* want me to!

The deviant ground is seen to be contextually or episodically modifiable by teacher strategies up to a point. The ground even impinges upon the pupil's response to teacher strategy, i.e. 'it's only because *you* want me to!'

The pupil has a latent deviant career right to the end.

Mrs. Strang: Really a very unusual boy. I know that during the year [G.] had words with his parents. And it was his father

> that came to school. He found it very difficult to under-
> stand why it was that we were having problems with
> Alan in school.

This comment exemplifies the difficulty of negotiating an agreed base for proceeding with strategy formation because of the incompatible or competing
grounds of teachers and parents.

The significance of ground and the basis of its operational use by participants
in different settings is seen as critical by the headteacher. She recognizes
that a key element in the development of a pupil's career is perhaps the different
standpoints that can be taken in interpreting Self-Other interaction. This seems to
be implicit in her reference to a pupil's past career and the critical point of junior
transfer:

> I think that had he gone to a separate junior department this year, in his
> strange moods I would guess that a teacher who hadn't known about the
> difficulties he'd overcome during his career in school, they might have
> been saying: Well we need the psychologist in to look at him.

Here, the 'reciprocity of perspectives' (Schutz, 1963) is a critical issue, or is seen to
be so by the participants. It operates even as a member's method for constructing
accounts of other teachers. Other teachers are recognized as interpreters whose
views of the 'deep structure' of ground is likely to be problematic. Mrs. Strang
recognizes how different perceptions may arise from different standpoints and
also how figure appearances may lead to misinterpretation of ground: 'in his
strange moods I would guess that a teacher who hadn't known about the
difficulties he'd overcome ...' Beyond the formulation of deviant ground, the
new teachers would perhaps fail to take account of the *moving* ground or the
dynamics of ground movement over time (the developmental ground referred to
earlier). From the present teacher's standpoint the meaning of figure phenomena
in the observation of children rests upon the emergence of ground over time. To
a newcomer or stranger the lack of long-term ground is a critical problem as
there will be no access to the temporal emergence which provides a backcloth to
formulation for those teachers who have known him throughout his early school
career. In the context of in-group culture perhaps the most significant element in
operating ground is in recognizing its moving or *emergent* nature.

This emergence can be seen in Mrs. Strang's final comment reviewing
deviant ground over the final year:

> When Miss Tait finally asked his father to come it was when he was
> physically removing himself. In some instances by putting himself under
> the table. But he doesn't do that too often!

Here ground is seen as an emergent phenomenon. It is a moving phenomenon
gradually being revealed or becoming apparent over time. It 'exists' within an
ongoing temporal reality.

In this example there is also an acknowledgment of *spatial* differentiation
which is generally formulated ('he was physically removing himself') and *precise-*

ly illustrated ('in some instances by putting himself under the table!') The outer limits of the deviant category are identified.

This phenomenon is additionally viewed within a temporal framework which is both developmental or emergent and manifest in terms of its frequency or rate of occurrence. In *developmental* terms it is apparent in its increasing *emergence* to the teacher, Miss Tait, and is evident in the *frequency* of its occurrence: 'doesn't do that too often!'

Both space and time are apparently critical elements within the in-group 'world' or 'culture' of classroom life in early schooling (Hartley, 1987). This account of Alan's career has focused on the continuities between a *trans-contextual* process of pupil formulation and the *contextual* dynamics of its ongoing construction in situated classroom encounters. The case study has been explored by recognizing the apparently 'natural' dimensions of *'time'* and *'space'* and their sociological counterparts — the processes of *emergence* and *relativity*. In the case of Alan, a consideration of these processes has taken the analysis through a lengthy exposition of his career. In the course of its continuing emergence, his identity has been seen to indicate continuing movements of distance, direction, and pace. It can be seen, then, how the social construction of pupil identities is a complex and ongoing phenomenon, at times recognizing significant movements even across the apparently fundamental normal-abnormal boundary itself.

Notes

1 That the headteacher finds nothing conspicuous about him suggests that at this point in his career Alan's behaviour is not 'out-of-role'. His conformity makes it difficult for the teacher to talk about him. The reference to his not being noteworthy or out of the ordinary suggests a clue to teachers' strategies for noticing or formulating pupils. It is interesting that this 'naturalistic' acknowledgment by the teacher corresponds exactly with Warr and Knapper's (1968) theoretical account of the process of attribution.

2 It has *two* facets of emergence:

   — the appearance to the teacher — its arrival on the scene;
   — the developmental nature of Other — Other in context of likely development over time.

3 This interpretation extends Lofland's notion of episodic deviance (for otherwise normal Others) to the idea of an episodic formulation of normality for a deviant pupil. Episodic normality implies the temporary suspension of a pivotal identity as the baseline for the construction of a definition of the situation.

4 This instance of episodic formulation is different from the occasional or intermittent episodic formulation of insulated episodes found at certain points in both deviant and normal careers when there may be a temporary and isolated episode which is seen to be separated from the underlying baseline. By the end of year One, the teacher is now hypothesizing, testing out and using a fundamentally different model. Although some 'surface' behaviour may appear the same it is now suspected to have a different base.

5 Retyping in this context refers to a fundamental reformulation of pivotal identity or core typification rather than of changes in individual traits or segmental

typifications. It therefore indicates a major shift in the underlying baseline in the adoption of a different trans-episodic model.

6   Biographical Other matching is perhaps an empirical indicator of a reformulation having occurred. Alan is seen to be different in his baseline identity permitting a comparison with his former self.

7   Submergence is used to refer to the extreme degree of anonymization found in the formulation of 'normal' pupils and particularly noticeable in those who are considered ultra-normal. In classrooms there appear to be two major social processes at work: those of convergence and divergence in relation to social conformity. As pupils become convergent they can be seen to be norm-oriented. The more convergent they are perceived to be the more they experience anonymity in formulation as they become less noticeable or 'noteworthy' as individuals. This invisibility leads to pupils apparently submerging for long periods.

8   The emergence of deviance here is not unlike that in a 'deviant corridor' (Rubington and Weinberg, 1973) recognized in the interpretation of connected episodes. A sequence of events funnels the pupil into a deviant identity. Once the deviant identity has emerged through this corridor and 'become' his identity it is then adopted as a baseline for interpreting future events. The teacher's interpretation of the next event begins not in the perception of it as a unique episode but as something whose reality is linked with a deeper structure elsewhere. 'Today he's done the same thing' — a construction which sees beyond the current episode.

9   For Lemert it is the first deviation that is critical and which sets up the starting point for constructing reality, providing a baseline in the definition of the situation. Here it is the second deviation which acts retrospectively and confirms a provisional view of an earlier reality.

10 The episodic chain is viewed as a sequence of inter-connected episodes which are contingently linked together. These are seen as a series of contingently related predictable events. An intra-episodic structure or sequence is inferred from ground generating a string of predictable inter-connected figures.

Chapter 11

Social Processes in Primary Classrooms: An Interpretative Framework from a Study of Deviant Careers

This book has attempted to provide an account of processes of identity interpretation and imputation occurring in schools. It has especially sought to offer an account of the *dynamics* of such processes in the ongoing stream of classroom life. Consequently, particular attention has been given to:

1 the longitudinal and ongoing character of processes in formulation as these occur within the first four years of schooling and,
2 the moment-by-moment dynamics in formulation as episode follows episode in the fast flowing stream of classroom life.

Basic Elements: Figure-Ground

The analysis has centred upon the notion of figure-ground to provide a conceptual framework for exploring the dynamics of person formulation as a *process* involving a continual shifting between different elements of the identity constructed or imputed to Other. It has seemed appropriate to redeploy the notions of figure-ground from the psychology of perception into the sociological processes of 'taking the role of the Other'. In doing so this establishes theoretical continuities with the work of Garfinkel (1967) in 'documentary method' and McHugh (1968) in the use of emergent 'theme'. In the formulation of the children's school careers, the term *figure* was settled upon to refer to the essentially immediate episodic or fleeting appearances and manifestations of Other-role. The term *ground* referred to the enduring Other-roles that are seen to persist beyond the episodic, such as may be found in trans-episodic notions of 'identity'. The ground provides an enduring base upon which the identity of Other is seen to be founded and especially suggests a stock of typical motives that may be imputed by an onlooker from what has been referred to as a motivational reservoir.

Other-Role

Central to the analysis has been the notion of *relativity* in the placement of boundaries in interpersonal relations. As with Turner (1962) it is recognized that:

> The role becomes the point of reference for placing interpretations on specific actions, for anticipating that one line of action will follow upon another and for making evaluations of individual actions.

It is appropriate to recognize a conceptual continuity between 'core typification' (Hargreaves, 1977), 'role', 'identity', 'pivotal category' (Lofland, 1969) and 'career' in the ongoing construction of reality.

It seems the casting of Other within a framework of role is central to the whole process of formulation at both episodic and trans-episodic levels. In the interpretation of deviance, either in the recognition of isolated deviant incidents, or of enduring deviant identities, it is the perceived role which is critical. In the present analysis of deviance in primary schools, there has been an attempt to move away from the more usual notion of rule-transgression and its related 'societal reactions' which has been so prominent in previous literature presenting a process view of deviance (Becker, 1963; Lemert, 1967). It has been recognized in the course of this analysis that, unlike in the labelling tradition, it is the *role* rather than rule aspect which is critical to the perception of deviance in schools. Situations are apparently interpreted as either deviant or not deviant as a consequence of the teachers' interpretation of pupils' role-making or role-taking. Since any behaviour can always be potentially rule-breaking (according to context) then perhaps understandably it is the *role* that is critical. Rules are seen to come into play when *first* the player's *role* has been identified and therefore the set of rules which would apply, given his role as player in whatever game[1] is seen to operate in the emergent setting. The present framework is suggesting a move in a direction opposite to the general sociological trend to be found in Coulson (1972), who argues for a rejection of 'role', and Harré and Secord (1972), who advocate the adoption of a rule-based model of social interaction.

It seems that the central issue is how the teacher *formulates* the pupil, whether at the time he or she is seen to be in academic *role* or in deviant *role*. Whether the *context* of observation or interaction is defined[2] as academic is not itself important. What matters is whether the pupil is formulated to be operating *within* an academic or a deviant role at the time and therefore from a base which is deviant (pivotal ground) or which is academic (subordinate segmental ground). The dynamics of the process are evident in the teacher's casting of Other within a framework of role, the critical process. It has been seen how once ground emerges it tends to become regarded as a dominant Other-role, a core typification (Hargreaves, 1977) or pivotal category (Lofland, 1969). The emergence of a deviant ground influences the formulation of Other even in academic situations, recognizing a process which has also been identified by Turner (1962):

> the placement of any one of these boundaries for a fleeting instant or for a longer period limits the identification of other roles.

Episodes and Strategies

The critical boundary has proved to be that of the *episode* and those boundaries that are seen to surround it and so insulate it from, or permit its perceived continuities with, trans-episodic realities. In the study of deviant careers, a critical boundary is that between the *episode* and beyond, the boundary between episodic and trans-episodic phenomena. In the interpretation of children in schools, an important issue is whether the formulation of Other is contained within the apparent episode or whether trans-episodic dimensions are introduced. The critical boundary is between the episodic and the trans-episodic as recognized by those who perceive the 'incident'. It is the *phenomenological* boundary which is a critical element in the processes which underpin, and provide continuities in, 'societal reaction'.

An important dynamic element is the *exploratory* search for *theme* as teachers encounter a pupil in classroom episodes. A critical process is in perceiving whether the theme resides *within* the boundaries of the episode or *beyond* in trans-episodic identity. Teachers appear to move across and between these boundaries in the active process of searching.

An *episode* can be turned into a *trans-episodic event* by the introduction of the underlying personal or dispositional properties. It is *in* the episode that the underlying personal identity emerges and so makes it a *personal* rather than an *episodic* event. The parameters of such an event are then seen to be within trans-episodic notions of personal identity and not within the more limited boundaries of the episode itself.

In teachers' dealings with pupils some *motives* and *strategies* appear to be drawn from within the episode (seen as episodically limited) while others are drawn trans-episodically from ground. In the case of normal pupils, in the course of deviant episodes, it seems teachers are likely to employ episodic frameworks and strategies in their interpretation.[3] For those pupils categorized as deviant, however, they are likely to employ trans-episodic motives and strategies in the interpretation of deviant episodes.

As teachers begin to operate an episodic strategy they are assuming an episodic phenomenon which, for the moment at least, is seen to have a causal structure found not in the personal identity of the pupil but in the motivational parameters of the episodic setting. Teacher strategy, then, is episodically selected and implemented and additionally seems to mark the boundary where the episodic and the personal boundaries meet. For example, after operating an episodic strategy and encountering a response from the pupil that does not correspond with an assumption of an episodic motivational structure, the teacher begins to organize trans-episodic or ground based formulations.

The critical point for a teacher's selection of *strategy* seems to be its links with *figure* or *ground* in the construction of Other. It would seem that access to 'deep structure' and the constituent elements of ground (pace, direction, distance) all require in-group membership. The 'stranger' to the in-group culture (Schutz, 1971) would not be in a position to operate 'deep structure' in the interpretation of persons or events and so would be unable to select 'appropriate' strategies compatible with ground. Inevitably for a stranger, strategies would then be figure-based and related to an *immediate* search for *provisional ground* rather than the operation of a *dynamic emergent ground* which is part of the 'taken-for-granted' world of in-group culture. Perhaps the most significant element in operating ground is the recognition of its dynamic or *emergent* career.

A possible distinction to be made is that between episodically bounded strategies, and trans-episodic strategies. While in-group strategies will eventually derive from ground and so are trans-episodic in both *origin* and in *operation*, it is possible to use episodic strategies in an exploratory manner to check out, tease out or even test a suspected ground. The newcomer or 'stranger' to the in-group, however, can operate only episodically-bounded strategies.

Phases of Emergence

In the figure-ground construction of early careers, it seems that for most children the teachers begin formulation from an assumption of *total* normality. Total normality will operate immediately as the presumed or anticipated motivational base. Teachers appear to assume that a framework of normal motivation applies until this is proved to be inappropriate. However, such processes as 'pairing' of siblings and friends, or 'setting' the Other in the context of a deviant set (e.g. family) appear to invoke the likelihood of a deviant base and motivational reservoir being operated from the start.

It seems that an early phase of formulation involves teachers in active processes of *searching* for ground. Teachers then seem to engage in *testing* out *provisional grounds* (perhaps consistent with the notion of the 'elaborative stage' identified by Hargreaves, 1975). Early encounters with pupils will be perceived as episodes to be interpreted as figures in which signs of ground may be sought. In a later phase of typification, however, ground will dominate episodes. There is perhaps a transitional phase where the framework of formulation moves between the *episode* and *trans-episodic* interpretations in searching for appropriate meanings. The formulation frame of reference moves *from* figure *to* ground in the focus of interpretation as the pupil acquires a trans-episodic identity. This may perhaps be the sequence of processes involved in anonymization. A significant emergent point in this sequence was identified by a teacher in School B.[4] It seems for her the boundary in emergence which distinguishes between episodic and trans-episodic forms of deviance is three weeks! In the first three weeks of schooling it seems some forms of deviance may be perceived as merely episodic whereas beyond this point teachers begin to suspect ground as the base for its persistence. The focus of attention then moves from *episodic* (contextual) to *trans-episodic* (personal or dispositional) formulation.

There appear to be two temporal dimensions to pupil careers (at least in the early phase of schooling):

1 Developmental as ground is seen to be moving over time towards or away from a normal-abnormal boundary (as a linear or occasionally a more limited segmental movement).
2 Phasic as ground shifting is perceived (in some pupils) as they go through normal and abnormal phases in their career. This apparent shifting between normal and deviant bases and associated motivational reservoirs seems to be implicit in the apparent *anomic* processes which operate

when, from time to time, the teacher is uncertain *which* ground *is*, or *will* be, in play.

At different times in the processes of emergence there appears to be an *absence of ground* but for apparently different reasons. In early formulation the *groundlessness* seems to rest upon an assumption that ground will emerge in the near future (i.e. temporary anomie or emergent nomos), whereas in later formulation the recognition that there is no stable or predictable ground present for the teacher to discover will lead to anomie *per se* (an apparent meta-deviance in some pupils).

In the case of normal pupils, a feature of groundless formulation which occurs in the early days of relations with pupils is at a point *before* the emergence of any ground at all, but when teachers appear to give most pupils the benefit of any doubt and so presume that a normal ground operates. This is then *tacit ground* — the anticipation of a formulatory ground yet to emerge. This period might be distinguished from the absence of ground during a period of *episodic suspension* (when in later formulation ground is temporarily suspended as an episode is insulated from the enduring trans-episodic identity in the ongoing social construction of reality and interpreted as a free-standing unit of social interaction).

In the early phases of typification, as teachers move away from the episodic, rather than formulating an episode in its own terms, it seems they are operating a more generalized construction of an episode as a member of a more generalized category of equivalent *typical episodes*. It seems to be an apparent mid-position between the earlier episodic and the later ground formulation. It is not trans-episodic but limited in reference to specifiable episodes or particular episodic settings. In the early phase of formulation it might be expected that until a teacher has sampled enough pupil situations to formulate a trans-episodic ground then ground formulation would always be a provisional, tentative and therefore limited interpretation. So the recognition of a restricted range of typical episodic settings appears to be a possible *early and tentative* form of limited ground formulation. It seems that teachers operate first *episodically* and then move towards ground frameworks. In later typification, however, the expression of a *limited* formulation appears to be derived from *ground* and so might be regarded as a *limited* or *segmental* ground formulation. Its essential difference from early typical episodic formulation is its attachment to, and basis in, the underlying motivational reservoir. So *typical episode* often appears in early typification and during *segmental* role formulation in later Other-role construction.

It seems that person formulation proceeds from a general ground base[5] which acknowledges Other's pivotal identity with additional (segmental) and more specific role formulations appended, presenting a problem of observation both to the participant social actors and to the researcher. If a segmental role formulation is identified then the ground on which it is presumed to rest will usually be unknown. It will always be submerged and the nature of its underlying ground will not be readily visible. It seems problematic to discover whether the core is a normal or an abnormal ground since even abnormal pupils may have some normal segments within their Selves. The appearance of a 'normal' segment, then, may hide an underlying abnormal base for an 'abnormal' pupil but indicate continuities with a 'normal' base for a 'normal' pupil. The same 'appearance' may either provide the raw material for a segmental or a core typification in the case of different pupils.

Processes: General

There is apparently a continuing tension between the *episode* (intra-episodic) and the *trans-episodic* in teachers' formulation of pupils. It seems likely that there is a continuing boundary problem in formulation as teachers seek to establish the different elements in the social construction and interpretation of Others perceived to be present in an episode. Those attributable to the underlying personal identity (and so trans-episodic) and those attributable to, and bounded by, the episode (and so episodic). In some cases ground will be imported so as to provide the 'theme' for the episode. *Strategy* will then be related to pivotal ground and its associated motivational reservoir beyond the episode. In other cases the 'theme' will be entirely episodic with interaction perceived to operate as an isolated or insulated unit within its own episodic parameters.

On certain occasions there is, for deviant pupils, an apparent process of 'social structuring of normality'. Teachers attempt to 'structure' the surface appearances for deviant pupils by the pursuit of strategies in the avoidance of deviant outcomes. Although at 'figure' level the interpretation of certain episodes in classroom life may appear 'normal' for some otherwise deviant pupils there may, at a 'deeper' level, still be a continuing deviant ground recognized as an ever-present, though underlying, basis of both Other-formulation and related strategy formulation and its implementation. A deviant potential ground may always operate behind an otherwise apparent normality. Teachers' attempts to negotiate 'normal' outcomes for deviant pupils are in effect a dynamic process involving shifting transactions (or negotiating) between anticipated figures and potential grounds, or between episodic and trans-episodic forms of reality.

It seems the very same event or social action may be seen simultaneously in both *episodic* and *trans-episodic* terms.[6] Different individuals in the same event can be viewed either from episodic or from a trans-episodic framework. Episodic and trans-episodic career lines for different children run concurrently, are juxtaposed within the same episode, and yet may be *insulated* from each other. The perception of any *one* classroom situation may involve the organization and construction of a complex social world through the recognition of both episodic and trans-episodic forms of reality simultaneously. Clearly, active and interpretative processes are found underpinning the social *construction* of reality. The account of reality has indeed to be assembled or accomplished. A stranger to the social world of the classroom will not 'see' the episodic and trans-episodic parameters since these operate at the level of 'deep structure'. These episodic and trans-episodic parameters may operate differently across different interpersonal boundaries at the same moment. *Emergence* is linked to *relativity*; each component of relativity (the differentiation of interpersonal boundaries) has its own temporal or emergent reality. Reality, then, may have continuity with previous forms or not. It is the *perception* and *construction* of present reality as having or not having *continuity* with previous social forms that is critical. In the same incident or event may be perceived a continuity of ground for one pupil or a unique episodic action for another. It can be seen that processes of relativity and emergence are central to the construction of social reality in classroom life.

Another process which is apparent seems to be that of *retyping*, a substantial recategorization of the trans-episodic Other-role, which from the present framework would be regarded as the crossing of a significant boundary in formulation. In effect it takes the form of the crossing of a *motivational* and therefore a *model* boundary — such as in moving from deviant to a normal ground and so moving between their associated motivational reservoirs. A significant boundary crossing would be from a deviant identity, seen as a trans-episodic phenomenon rooted in enduring ground, to the point of its recognition as having been replaced by a framework of formulation in which the occurrence of deviant behaviour is seen as episodic deviation operated by a mere episodic theme bounded within its own contextual parameters. The motivational base for deviance would then be seen to be generated solely by context and so would be operating *within* its own episodic boundaries. This point is critical for figure-ground relations since deviant occurrences may still continue for a formerly categorized deviant pupil but they would now be perceived to rest upon a different pivotal ground and be insulated from it by episodic boundaries.

Processes: Negotiation and Exchange

An identifiable process within ground emergence is that of negotiation and exchange. Exchange of ground seems to depend on the perceived compatibility of data on offer. It has been noted how in some instances the compatibility of formulatory data between 'ground carrier' and teachers (as in the first deviant case) permitted the *addition* of data to construct a fuller picture of Other.

In other instances, however, (as in the second case) the ground exchange on some occasions could not proceed because of *incompatibility* of dissonant data. The transposing of ground data across the interpersonal and spatial boundaries of home and school proved not to be manageable. Aspects of relativity seem to operate at the root of the processes of typification negotiation.

Processes of ground exchange may occur to increase the *contextual range* of its general application. Each party in the exchange presents a contextualized ground from their own sphere of operation and so the contextual range of ground is being extended. In this way knowledge of Other in a different context such as 'at home' or 'at school' is added to each party's construction. Each party in the exchange is getting a firmer, more refined, and more generalizable, view of ground. It seems that it is not just that parents often act as 'typification carriers' but they operate as *ground* carriers — a more critical process since it simultaneously imports a pivotal trans-episodic identity and a motivational base. Although ground will have a defined form to its originator, it can nevertheless be *added* to or *fused* with the ground of a recipient or a carrier. As ground knowledge of Other across new contexts is acquired then the *predictive* value of ground perhaps increases.

The reciprocity of perspectives (Schutz, 1963) is critical or seen to be so by participants. It seems to operate even as a member's own method for constructing accounts of other teachers as formulators of children. Other teachers are recognized at times to be limited role-takers whose view of the 'deep structure' of trans-episodic ground is likely to be problematic. Teachers recognize how different constructions of pupils may arise from different standpoints. It is recognized how the uninformed interpretation of a pupil's figure actions without an appropriate trans-episodic standpoint may lead to a 'misinterpretation' of underlying ground. It is recognized, for example, that new teachers would misformulate Alan, the second case, because they would fail to take account of the *ongoing* ground in the dynamics of its emergence over time. Acknowledging such processes, it is possible to recognize with McHugh (1968) the significance of emergence:

> Emergence makes disparate slices of time continuous enough in their meaning to maintain concerted activity.

From the standpoint of a present teacher, the meaning of 'figure' events in classroom life rests upon knowledge of pupils as biographical Others and of emergence in ground over the course of an ongoing career. To a newcomer or stranger such ground formulation is a critical problem. There can be no immediate access to ground in its *temporal emergence*. Neither the *direction* of movement (towards or away from the normal), the *pace* (rate of movement) or the *distance* covered (within or across critical boundaries) can be known. Nor can the precise nature of ground be known. In consequence, the newcomer to the world of the classroom has only a limited access to motivational reservoir and therefore is denied the appropriate selection from the full range of *ground-based strategies*. The variety of appropriate motivations that may be selected from the underlying reservoir in relation to each context is unknown to newcomers. The in-group world contains knowledge both of *deep structure* (ground) and equally critically its moving or *emergent career*. Both of these are inaccessible directly to outsiders.

Processes: Anonymization

It has been noted in other research that in pupil formulation there are tendencies towards reification in the construction of pupil identities (Sharp and Green, 1975) and to closed or 'stabilized' typifications in the formulation of deviant identities (Hargreaves, 1975). Such views are perhaps over-generalized in apparently not taking account of their ongoing and situated use in the formulation of Others. In the present research it can be seen that the imputation of pupil identity in its ongoing emergence does not always continue in a closed or stabilized form equivalent to the notion of a reification of deviant identity. It has been noted how the 'structuring' of 'normality' for deviant pupils in certain episodes often appears to be an under-reacting form of 'societal reaction' on the part of teachers.

In this research it might be suggested that the reference to ground formulation is equivalent to the notion of a 'reified' or 'stabilized' formulation. They are both, in effect, a form of dismissing Other to a level of *anonymity* in formulation. Yet at the same time there is perhaps some ambiguity since such use of ground construction might also be regarded as an *individualized* form of Other formulation since it is apparently a process of responding to the perceived 'real' or 'deep strcuture' of Other in an individualized construction, rather than to the 'surface' figure manifestations as a stranger would be obliged to do. (Indeed, previous comments have suggested that the in-group knowledge of the deep structure and even of *shifting deep structure* is perhaps an important aspect of Other which outsiders would fail to note.)

The present research began by referring to the work of Schutz in identifying an apparent continuum between individualization and anonymization in Other construction. There is an apparent tension along the supposed continuum between individualized-anonymity forms of Other-construction in the shifting intimacy of relations with Other, as the framework moves from contemporary to consociate relations. Which, then, is to be regarded as the individualized form of constructing Other? The surface (figure) or the deep structure (ground)? Perhaps Schutz's notion of individualized construction presupposes that there is a 'real' Other independent of either 'surface' or 'deep structure'.

The present analysis has suggested three possible categories or degrees of anonymity in Other formulation:

1 episodic (the pupil is generalized as being a certain type for the duration of an episode);
2 trans-episodic (the pupil is generalized as a member of a category across situational and temporal boundaries);
3 trans-personal (the pupil is generalized as a member of a wider type or stereotype).

As the framework of formulation moves from 1 to 3 the construction of Other increases in anonymity. It must be remembered, of course, that even the *episodic* type is a form of anonymization in generalizing Other across an episode as a unit of time. It involves placing a boundary around a temporal unit or an interactional sequence such that the multiple minutiae of the pupil's actions are interpreted as a *whole* and thus as an action or interactional unit either while it is yet emerging or sometimes even after it is complete. If we recognize Type 3 as the most anonymous form of typification then it can be seen that perhaps much of what has been encountered in this research has been moderate in its anonymization. In fact, ground formulation is a middle type (Type 2). This suggests that person formulation is *not* an undifferentiated continuum as it appears in Schutz's account but possibly a framework having identifiable boundaries at points of increasing generalization or anonymity as the focus of construction moves *from* the person or Other-in-general (trans-episodic) *to* persons or Others-in-general (trans-personal).

It should be recognized, of course, that formulation is a *dynamic* process, often involving movement from one form of construction to another. Typifications (whether of 'deviant' or 'normal' pupils) become individualized when used in specific contexts of action. They may perhaps be reified in the course of situations of contemporary relation and perhaps in the third party exchange situations of staffroom life, but they may still be transposed and individualized when transported into the consociality of interaction.

It is important not to oversimplify *reification* or confuse it with *anonymity* (as perhaps Sharp and Green may have done) but to recognize that the use of even reified constructs may have very specific and individualized forms and occasions of use.

However, it has been suggested earlier that there may be a tendency for teachers to differ in the extent to which they appear to use Type 1 or move towards Type 2 in the early days of formulation. This provides a conceptual basis for differentiating teachers; on the one hand those who tend to operate *within* episodic parameters (the episodic formulator) and who show reluctance to move towards categorizing the Other in personal trans-episodic terms, and on the other those who appear readily to move beyond the episodic parameters and see *trans-episodic* or identity implications in relation to events (the trans-episodic formulator). The fromer seems, in effect, to engage in 'societal reaction' contingent largely upon currently perceived phenomena (therefore non-personal or current context-based in formulation — the episodic formulator) while the latter engages in 'societal reaction' to phenomena perceived beyond the episode (person-based formulator). So one teacher may move more quickly into trans-episodic or person formulation after extracting every identifiable episodic variable from the causal analysis of the situation. Another may continually resist the use of person formulation, so retaining a more individualized and episodic view of Other as constructed in the unique consociate relations of each event rather than a more anonymized Other as in the contemporary relations perhaps implied by the construction of ground. However, it can nevertheless be seen that all teachers at times engage in movements between episodic and trans-episodic formulation. It seems to be a fundamental feature of the ongoing processes of classroom life and the construction of pupil careers.

Normality and Deviation

This book has constantly taken issue with some of the more traditional sociological views of deviance and approaches to research into it. In traditional frameworks the deviant episode is seen as critical because it is the *point* of emergence of deviance. It is seen to be the point of boundary crossing. The antecedent processes are rarely introduced as 'natural' elements of the social construction of deviance. There is often a post hoc investigation into the presumed trans-episodic 'factors' as predisposing 'because-of-motives'. Analysis proceeds with little attempt to explore by what processes these antecedent phenomena appear *within* the episode. There is a tendency to see both the episodic and the trans-episodic in terms of the rule-transgression. However, in this research it seems that teachers, in their 'societal reaction', see deviance in both episodic rule-transgression terms and simultaneously in relation to an ongoing trans-episodic framework of personal ground or pupil identity construction. It is the teacher who is the means by which the episodic and the trans-episodic fuse together at the point of 'societal reaction'.

Repeatedly in this research it has been noticeable that the teachers' attention is person-focused in formulation. Of course the research method itself may partly account for this. It approaches formulation through *persons* with an overt interest in a continuing sample of specific pupils rather than through a sampling of deviant incidents or events. Nevertheless, on many occasions when teachers make reference to rule-breaking incidents, the 'real' issue for them in their social construction of reality is usually seen to be more fundamental: rule-breaking against a backcloth of *ongoing person formulation*. Episodic deviance when committed by normal pupils seems to be immediately related to a person formulation context, which often diffuses the episodic rule-breaking and puts into *sharper* focus its trans-episodic features of relativity and exposes a more fundamental inter-personal boundary between the normal and the abnormal and their associated motivational reservoirs.

The apparent tendency for teachers to operate with a recognition of the implications of labelling suggests that the issue for the sociology of deviance is not the matter of mere rule-breaking and the societal reactions to it but a more complex process of interpreting the *nature* of the interpersonal boundaries. Labelling accounts have often tended to treat 'reactions' to rule-breaking as a process of victim creation. However, teachers in the present research seem to show a re-markably measured sense of boundary differentiation which can be seen in their recognition of the long-term implications for enduring Other-role identity beyond the immediate figure of rule-breaking. It seems they often attempt to deliberately manage their reactions to figure-based rule-breaking (surface re-actions) recognizing simultaneously the possible implications for ground-based person formulation (deep structure reactions).

Another indication of the greater complexity of processes beyond those often suggested within the Labelling tradition is the frequently recurring phe-nomenon of teachers focusing their attention upon the *pupil's reaction* to the deviant incident as a reference point for typification. This is perhaps equivalent to the 'societal reaction' of labelling theory but is seen in effect to focus upon the *episodic reaction* of the deviant pupil under scrutiny and not as is more usual the onlooker's reaction. Therefore any account of 'reaction', whether of the deviant or the onlooker, should take an *episodic* frame of reference and so adopt a dynamic or process view of the entire episodic unit of the event over the course of its emergence.

The present research suggests episodic observation occurs in relation to the processes of figure-ground already outlined. Ultimately, of course, the 'societal reaction' is to be found within the onlooker's perception of pupil reaction to deviance. Whether the pupil's response is seen as episodic (in figure terms) or trans-episodic (drawing upon deviant ground) will in turn indicate whether its motivational base is seen to lie inside or outside the episodic parameters. The perceived *ground* may at times be more important than the current *figure* in the formulation of an episode. The trans-episodic ground phenomena may be seen to be manifest beyond an episodic figure and so may be taken as the more fun-damental underlying theme derived from a trans-episodic reality.

The present investigation suggests that the complex processes of interaction in the construction of pupil careers involve inter-relations and tensions be-tween figure-ground, surface and deep structure, episodic and trans-episodic, individualization-anonymity, and consociate-contemporary interpretations of reality. However, most central of all has been the attempt to explore the signi-ficance of processes of *relativity* and *emergence*. The ongoing account has given prominence to the *trans-episodic* parameters of emergence over the first four years of early schooling. There has also been an attempt to recognize *intra-episodic* processes of emergence, as perceived events are seen to become episodes and their parameters defined or constructed as teachers impose temporal and spatial bound-aries around, between and beyond them in their ongoing accomplishment of the social construction of reality.

Notes

1 It has become apparent in this study that the critical issue is the nature of the *trans-episodic* role or game which is in play.

2 In a maths activity, for example, what is 'seen' may not be an academic Other but a deviant Other who on this occasion happens to be engaging in maths activities. The entry point for the construction may be the figure appearances of the academic setting, but in the construction of reality this may be quickly displaced by the underlying trans-episodic reality of ongoing ground phenomena.

3 Lofland has called instances of this sort episodic deviance.

4 In School B Mrs. Strang talks of the deviant pupil Alan's extreme shyness:

> I think that getting into the third week in school if he's still that shy then we're going to have to be quite concerned about him. *I'm* concerned about him anyway.

The teacher sees its persistence beyond three weeks in school as a sign that it cannot be treated as mere episodic deviance. This would have disappeared in three weeks, so an underlying deviant identity begins to be suspected.

5 This process provides a pivotal category (Lofland, 1969) and equivalent to the notion of core typification (Hargreaves, 1977).

6 It is particularly important for researchers to recognize this simultaneity. Research which adopts a rule-based framework in the interpretation of deviance often starts with the deviant event as the entry point for analysis and source episode which is assumed to generate the likely societal reaction. But the teacher's own entry point in the construction of reality may not be the immediate event but can be founded upon an ongoing trans-episodic frame of reference.

Chapter 12

Normal Careers

So far there has been an attempt to generate a theoretical representation of processes of person formulation in classroom life. Several models have been proposed to account for the parameters within which teachers construct pupils. A theory of the dynamics of formulation has also been suggested and illustrated through the analysis of two critical cases as exemplars of pupils who at times appear to be beyond the outer boundaries of these parameters.

Since teachers appear to operate an abnormal/normal boundary as a significant reference point in the construction of classroom reality, it has been appropriate to present case data for pupils on either side of this boundary. So far attention has been focused upon one pupil (as a deviant case) in each school who occupied a position beyond this significant boundary of the normal world. A somewhat detailed emergent and ongoing analysis of each has been attempted so as to explore some of the processes by which such pupils are 'manoeuvred' into, or across, the fundamental boundary of normality in classroom life and by which their occupation of such a position is maintained, continued, or discontinued over a longitudinal time-scale. So as to give proper attention to the ongoing moment-by-moment processes of emergence as they occur within each case, over a full four-year period of schooling, it is necessary to limit the examination of the cases across the sample of over fifty pupils. Instead, I will focus upon an in-depth analysis of within-career profiles of certain critical cases.

Having already examined critical cases of deviant pupils, attention can now be directed to the analysis of processes that underpin the maintenance of 'normal' pupil careers across the critical boundary in the 'normal' sector of the social world of the classroom. Two cases from each school have been selected as exemplars of 'normal' careers. The selection of cases for analysis was on this occasion made more problematic by there being any number of 'normal' cases available for consideration as exemplars since most pupils in the sample occupied 'normal' positions. However, since in the phenomenological world of classroom life teachers seemed to treat certain pupils as though they occupied significant normal positions, even as apparent personifications of the 'normal' category of pupil, it seemed appropriate to select these cases for more detailed analysis.[1]

It is not an intention of the present research to provide a fully developed account of the emergence and maintenance of the full variety of normal career patterns but to identify the parameters of pupil formulation in primary class-rooms and to illustrate these as dynamic frameworks underpinning pupil careers in critical cases. Since teachers seem to differentiate some pupils as personifying 'normality' then it seems appropriate to explore these cases for an indication of formulation processes as they occur in pupils whose status as 'normals' is quite overtly and unproblematically acknowledged by the teachers over much of the four-year time scale. It will be left for future work to examine more fully the possible variety of normal career patterns.

The analysis now continues with an account of 'normal' career emergence in two selected cases in each school. In School A, the cases of James and Louise will be examined, while in School B the cases of Sally and Dawn. The four cases will be examined in order to illustrate the formulation processes which are apparent in the teacher's attempts to get to know, and maintain classroom relations with, these pupils in the ongoing stream of classroom life. The earlier account of two deviant cases has led to the suggestion of a theoretical framework recognizing distinctions between:

— normal and abnormal,
— figure and ground,
— episodic and trans-episodic,

in the social construction of classroom reality.

It has already been seen how these distinctions are manifest or constructed by teachers in their dealings with abnormal or deviant pupils. The focus of analysis now turns to examining how teachers encounter and construct normal pupils and by what processes of emergence and maintenance such careers are sustained over a four-year period. In order to consider these issues, the four normal cases will each be examined in turn.

The four cases have for research purposes been subjected to detailed analysis with the data for each pupil being examined in each successive interview over the whole of the four-year time-scale. There is inevitably a mass of data which could be presented here (even though throughout the research there has been very much less talk arising in interviews about the normal pupils as compared with the deviant pupils). Nevertheless, within the space available here it would still not be possible to present a full account of these four cases as they evolve over the four years. It would also be a rather tedious account which would appear repetitious to the reader when similar patterns among the four cases began to be duplicated from one case to another and even within each of the cases year after year. It should be recognized, of course, that it is always questionable to make assumptions about the equivalence of seemingly common patterns both *within* and *across* cases. Following the phenomenological framework of this research the unique-ness of individual cases and of individual episodes and settings as they occur for each individual pupil is recognized and allowed for by the research methodology and in the procedures for analysis. Indeed, it is my own view exactly that this tendency to over-generalize across samples, across 'systems' and across 'society' in traditional sociology failed to take account in particular of Schutz's 'postulate of adequacy' and led to doubts about the incongruence of the second order constructions of social scientists with those of the first order interpretations of participant social actors themselves. One is always conscious of running a risk

Figure 12.1: The span of pupil careers

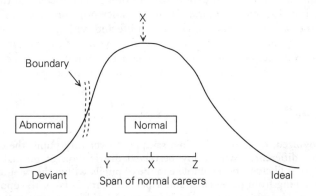

of damaging phenomenological reality, both within and across cases, in attempting to reduce the teacher's ongoing constructions of reality, in relation to four cases of pupil career emergence over a long time-scale, to a mere few pages of commentary. However, the cases are no more than illustrative, being an attempt only to outline and explore the apparent interpersonal boundaries and *frameworks* of formulation within the identified parameters of life in primary school classrooms.

The presentation of the four 'normal' cases has been guided by the principle of theoretical sampling (Glaser and Strauss, 1968). The detailed collection of interview talk and data from a four-year period of continuous research has inevitably generated an extensive mass of data. It has seemed from the analysis so far that a critical phase of formulation is that of the point of *ground emergence*. Consequently, particular attention has been given in this book to the early point of emergence whenever a pupil encounters a new teacher and so when the attempt to construct the underlying pupil identity is perhaps most likely to be taking place. In addition, this research has regarded it as critical to discover parameters within which formulation occurs within the *dynamic processes* of classroom life. This suggests a second principle of selection from the notion of theoretical sampling. It was important to focus particularly upon *situated* formulation — those instances of teacher talk or interview data which were related to the pupil interacting or acting in specific situations, and then to focus upon contextualized talk and so make some attempt to reduce the possible 'third party talk' element (Hargreaves, 1977) that might otherwise artificially limit the research data to highly generalized trans-contextual and so trans-episodic forms of pupil formulation. It was of particular interest to understand the processes of person formulation as they occur within authentic classroom episodes. By giving prominence to the selection of accounts of episodes of classroom action it seemed likely to generate data in which the boundaries between the episodic and the trans-episodic would become an issue for teachers during the research interviews in making sense of the episodes in question.

Consequently, adopting the procedure of theoretical sampling, it is possible to focus on those 'phases' of emergence that appear to offer the most appropriate means for examining the theoretical concerns of this book. Attention will first be given to discovering how 'normal' pupils appear or emerge to teachers in their early encounters and in initial exploratory dealings. The focus will then move on from these initial teacher explorations to consider how processes of formulation operate in the ongoing stream of classroom life and within the continuing school career of each pupil as it evolves over the four years of this research.

The analysis begins with the case of James, a pupil who over much of his career seems to be viewed as a normal pupil by most teachers.

Note

1 It is recognized, of course, that in a sample of over fifty pupils the occurrence of individual differences within any perceived distribution of normal pupils must mean there is likely to be a complete range of pupils within the category of normal cases stretching from the normal/abnormal boundary as far as the upper end of the distribution. An example is shown in Figure 12.1. Although this study has selected (or rather teachers have differentiated) pupils at position X it is nevertheless recognized that pupils along a continuum from Y to Z all experience 'normal' careers and will perhaps do so in a variety of ongoing patterns (over a longitudinal time scale). However, it is intended here to identify only the parameters of pupil formulation and not to offer a complete account of a full range of intra-normal career variations.

Chapter 13

Episodes in the Emergence of a Normal Career: James (School A)

Initial Processes of Emergence

Week One

The earliest interview data indicates James at what seems to be a tentative phase of initial formulation:[1]

> Hardly know he's there. I had to think twice before I realized who he was. Not much to say about James. I don't know him yet.

James in some respects seems to be viewed like Alan, the deviant case from School B who is also seen as 'quiet'. But unlike in the case of Alan there seems to be no deviant base presumed for James in this early formulation.

It can also be seen that there is another similarity with Alan. His teacher can't recall him. Like Alan he may be in some sort of formulatory suspension. He has not yet acquired a trans-episodic identity. However, at this point in his career there was only *one* dimension known about Alan: his deviance! An immediate potential abnormality was recognized in Alan, but for James the formulation seems to assume a normal identity.

As the first interview continues it seems even more evident that a normal category may be in operation. The pupil is now referred to as: 'Bright. "Intelligent." Little thinker'. The previously noticed 'quiet' seems now to be linked to an implicit normal trans-episodic base. Pupil is a 'thinker'. There is no means of knowing exactly what the teacher's underlying meanings are at this point but there is a clear suggestion of conformity to the pupil role as distinct from the disturbing 'quiet' of Alan and its implications of deviation from pupil role. The 'quiet' of James, however, is not the divergent, non-participative 'quiet' that Alan is simultaneously seen to be experiencing in School B.

This seems apparent as the teacher, Miss Bennett, now formulates an episode which could be a figure illustration of the trans-episodic ground formulations now emerging:

> We did some flash cards yesterday. James was picking them ... Little thinker.

The framework for the teacher's formulation has now moved from a trans-episodic base. The earlier formulation was of a trans-episodic kind. Here the focus is episodic. She formulates *from* a trans-episodic *to* an episodic framework. The teacher presents an account of the pupil experiencing a normal classroom episode and so perhaps begins to generate provisional ground straight away.

Nevertheless, although apparently viewing this from a normal base it seems that the teacher could also be operating a potential deviant ground 'search'. But the 'search' it seems is conducted from a quite safe normal base and any deviation accommodated perhaps as mere segmental typification or episodic deviation:

> I know them all. I've got a visual picture of what they've been like over
> the last two days. But the ones that stick and the ones we talk about ...
> the ones obviously that keep cropping up in the staffroom ... and
> they're obviously the ones who're in trouble. James and Mark ... I was
> more concerned about their quietness.

When the teacher says she 'was concerned' it seems to suggest it was already resolved. No strong trans-episodic implications are suggested by the divergence.

In fact it is immediately followed in the interview by what seems to be a neutralizing remark: 'James was just quiet'. The quietness of this pupil, then, is to be regarded not at the outer limits of the boundary of the formulatory framework as might 'the ones ... who're in trouble'; by comparison James was 'just' in a category that seems to cause comparatively less concern. The potential abnormality that might have been recognized is instead immediately neutralized it seems. The neutralization is apparently accomplished by a process of Other matching with more divergent or deviant pupils ('the ones who're in trouble').

Week Two

The headteacher, Mrs. Russell, has less knowledge of the pupil at this time. As yet she has not begun to construct an underlying identity as ground formulation for this pupil: 'I don't know anything about James Ryan at all'. Neither trans-episodic ground nor episodic constructions are offered. Quite clearly at this point Mrs. Russell is using non-formulation — a genuine pre-formulation.

The class teacher, Miss Bennett, however, in the second week now sees the underlying ground of a normal pupil rapidly emerging:

> Yes. I do know him a lot better. A very quiet little boy. Very artistic.
> He's super. He just gets on with whatever you want him to do.

The emergence of a conforming pupil identity is perhaps now well underway: 'he's super' and 'just gets on with whatever you want him to do'.

The previous quietness which caused some moderate concern is already transformed into a thoroughly normal trans-episodic framework:

> He's very shy. But it's not shyness that you would worry about. It's just
> his quiet personality. His mum's the same. I've met his mum. And she's
> very nice as well. They're very quiet. He's just the same.

It seems that quietness can be located by teachers either on the normal or the abnormal side of the critical boundary. The construct 'quiet', perhaps like all teachers' interpretations of children, requires attention to the 'deep structure' of classroom reality in order to appreciate its context of use. Its meaning when used by a teacher seems to depend upon whether it is seen to rest upon a normal or an abnormal base. It is: 'not a shyness that you would worry about.' And: 'it's just his quiet personality'. The teacher seems to be saying that that's *all* it is. Nothing more. The normality in this instance seems to be being formulated with the additional aid of a family equivalent of the 'sibling phenomenon'. (This is also the case with the pupils Dawn and Sally in School B and the other pupil in School A, Louise. It seems to be a common process.) On this occasion it is maternal matching. The teacher seems to see confirmation of ground upon meeting the parent: 'I've met his mum ... They're very quiet. He's just the same'.

Week Five

By this time the conformist identity of a normal pupil is now stable:

'Mixes well with other children';
'Never does anything completely out of the ordinary';
'He responds as you'd expect him to respond to most situations'.

This suggests a normal identity is now recognized for this pupil. There could hardly be a clearer statement of conformity. The pivotal category of normality is seen now to be trans-episodic, as an underlying structure applying to this pupil in most situations.

The normal identity is even more precisely formulated. James is: 'Thoroughly average. Normal'. A clear trans-episodic base for the 'normal' identity as formulatory ground is now recognized.

From this point in the fifth week of his school career a normal baseline of ground is unquestionably seen to be operating and now becomes a continuing framework for Miss Bennett's formulation of this pupil. It seems the teacher has adopted normal ground quite unproblematically for this pupil, apparently beginning with him as an unknown Other and so from a position of pre-formulation moving into episodic and finally trans-episodic constructions, arriving at a point at which ground has emerged. All following accounts of formulation now seem to operate from an established normal ground. Each episode apparently is seen to rest upon a normal framework of ground. From this point the interest of the research is now redirected to examining occasions when this position changes. Consequently, so as to avoid repetition, and with a concern for theoretical sampling, this case illustration will take particular account of those occasions when the pupil is seen to cross a 'boundary' point when the normal framework of

1   episodically within an occasion of episodic deviance (Lofland, 1969) insulated from the normal base;
2   as the pupil is seen to move into an extended period of deviance for a series of episodes (extended episode) or a limited deviant phase;

3 from a qualified or modified normal base when viewing occasional deviation as an indication of either a mere segmental divergence or a limited
situationally specific episodic divergence, so retaining normal ground as
the core of the pupil's identity.

In operating from a normal ground, the teacher's formulations now assume the
pupil is usually operating from within a normal motivational reservoir as the
source of his action. Therefore attention will mainly be given from this point to
those occasions when non-normal motives are sought by the teacher as James's
career now unfolds over the next four years.

Up to this point we have seen the emergence of a normal identity. He is seen
to be quite 'normal' or 'average' and so apparently occupies a position around the
mid-point of the perceived distribution of pupils. It seems the teacher has
adopted normal ground quite unproblematically for this pupil. It is possible now
to examine how, and when, ground appears in the teacher's formulation of the
pupil beyond this point. In the theoretical sampling of critical weeks, attention
now focuses upon the use of underlying normal identity as the ground of
formulation.

The next reference to James in the interviews with Miss Bennett occurs six
weeks later. His omission from the next five interviews reflects both the domi-
nance of the deviant pupil Gavin in this cohort over the same time and the
probable simultaneous submergence[2] of the now perceived normal pupil James.
In the next reference Miss Bennett now makes trans-episodic comparisons between pupils using the ground which has become settled for James:

He's a listener rather than a talker. And he's a thinker rather than a doer.
Just the type he is. No concern. He's that sort of ... That's why Gavin
and he just don't seem to get on together. But it seems to be dwindling a
bit anyhow that relationship.

This is a fortuitous and quite spontaneous relating of the two critical cases from
the present research sample. The teacher is surprised that James and Gavin ever
did have a relationship since she recognized significant differences in them. They
are apparently seen as quite different pupil types. Of course, this is not in itself
evidence that the two pupils are seen as fundamentally different in terms of deep
structure or ground as a normal and a deviant type. Within the context of the
account itself no reference is made to Gavin's deviant ground. Presumably it
would be equally possible for two different normal types to be incompatible and
so not hit it off. However, it does seem to be a probable confirmation at least of
this pupil having a normal career. If the two pupils were operating from very
different ground positions then some incompatibility, or even incongruity, might
be expected in their potential for establishing a relationship. The teacher's interpretation of the relationship is also quite consistent with what may be seen as a
'natural' resolution of the incongruity: 'seems to be dwindling a bit anyhow that
relationship'.

It seems that here is an indication of the possible workings of classroom or
school 'social structure' in the teacher's recognition of the quite different identities occupied by two pupils within the reality of this social world. The ground
constructions are recognized to be in some respects incompatible. The use of

ground here seems to be in operating or defining the 'social structure' of class-room life. The recognition of 'structure' is further demonstrated as the 'deep structure' of ground is used to interpret certain episodes of classroom life.

The Appearance of Ground in the Interpretation of Classroom Episodes

Once ground is settled it seems the teacher may then draw upon it to interpret classroom reality. We have already seen, in examining the deviant cases, how teachers appear to operate a 'surface' and a 'deep structure' notion of reality in which 'surface' appearances become transformed from the merely episodic by the recognition of the 'deep structure' of a trans-episodic reality beyond. For a deviant pupil, of course, the recognition of the trans-episodic can often result in the transformation of an otherwise potentially normal sequence of actions into what is seen to be at root a deviant episode. A significant issue in normal cases seems to be an inversion of this process with the teacher's use of normal ground to neutralize the pupil actions in what might otherwise be perceived in its figure manifestations as a potential deviant episode. This inversion can be examined in the next account. It begins with an interviewing prompt from the researcher's participant observation notes, attempting to discover what the teacher had made of, or even seen in, the previous classroom events:

> [Researcher making reference to observation of James seemingly rather withdrawn and apparently being overwhelmed by his peers while engaged in activities with two other pupils, Andrew and Richard]

> Interviewer: I wondered in fact whether James *was* being sort of led by the other two or ...
> Teacher: Perhaps he just enjoys being led. Maybe he likes taking a back seat. He's an only child and I don't think he's quite used to dominating. He wasn't sort of taking a back seat. He was just a quiet type. And he can lead when he wants to'.

Here, the raising of a potentially ambiguous figure by the researcher to check out whether the teacher had any underlying concerns about the pupil is given a quite normal interpretation. An ambiguity of figure can only be given meaning or be resolved by selecting its underlying motivation. In this case the teacher selects two non-deviant motives and so it seems it is interpreted as operating from a framework of normal ground:

> 'Maybe he likes taking a back seat';
> 'He wasn't sort of taking a back seat'.

The teacher appears to be implying that there is nothing significant to be seen beyond this. She recognized a quite normal situation, which is not to be viewed as indicative of any divergent or deviant trans-episodic reality.

This formulation then opens out into a statement of ground; '... and he can

lead when he wants to'. By relating the episodic with trans-episodic constructions a potential ambiguity is apparently transformed into normality. (Note the
'can' reference. Here the teacher seems to be asserting the absence of pathological
— what Heider refers to as the power dimension. There is no inherent
pathology.)

From this episodic formulation there is a further move into the increasingly
more generalized trans-episodic ground:

> That's why it's not worrying because he does look for other people to
> relate to. He doesn't just isolate himself.

Here, the generalized normal ground is introduced to indicate the underlying base
to the teacher's formulation of the episode and its relation to her chosen strategy:
'That's why it's not worrying'. It seems his teacher has no concern and is
viewing the episode from a trans-episodic ground base of the pupil's prevailing
normal identity.

A new teacher, Mrs. Wardle, takes over the class in the third term. The
pupil's identity again goes through processes of emergence. The new teacher,
however, has previous knowledge of him from an earlier part-time attachment to
the cohort group. In the short time-scale of this term he again seems to arrive at a
fairly normal position within the teacher's framework of formulation:

> He's a nice enough little boy. And he works nicely ... He'll answer
> you. He's not rude or anything. But there's never anything from him.

Some apparent neutralization occurs. A possible ambiguity leads to the interpretation: 'he's not rude or anything'. Although perhaps diverging in his non-
response, he does not operate from a motive beyond the specified episode from a
non-normal base. He is seen, instead, to be restricted in his deviation to a limited
range of episodes and his reputation again receives some neutralization.

Year Two

Initial Processes of Emergence

James moves into his second year in school and on to a new teacher, Mrs. Hope.

Week Three

The new teacher begins with an apparently normal formulation:

> reasons things out well ... Very nice boy. You know. Pleasant. And he
> does his work well.

It seems that a normal identity may be emerging as underlying ground.

Week Seven

A month later the normal ground is well established but with some qualification:

> He'll give a straight answer James. But he doesn't embroider round. You know. Expand it ... A nice enough boy James. He's quite a pleasant child. But ... as I say. Give an answer. But no further. You've to sort of draw it out of him if you want more.

A suggestion that the dominant ground or framework of formulation is that of a normal pupil ('a nice enough boy'). It seems the teacher sees an underlying normality is present, but with some divergence from the 'ideal'.

The Appearance of Ground in the Interpretation of Classroom Episodes

Two weeks later Mrs. Hope encounters a deviant strand in James:

> I've found a streak in James which is a bit uppity. For instance, Andrew was off for one or two days. And his mummy told me he was coming back the next day. I happened to come in the classroom and said Andrew was coming back the next day. And James said: How do you know that? In a sort of tone as though I'd no right to know. How do you know! It was a side of James I hadn't realized.

This account suggests two quite significant points. First, the reference to the deviation as a 'streak' is perhaps a very clear suggestion of a segmental formulation or a mere trait. That the deviation is not indicative of a pivotal identity but may be viewed in segmental rather than core terms. Second, that since a deviant segment is suggested then by implication there must by now be a more fundamental and pivotal category. Since the previously referred to deviance is regarded as segmental, then the implicit identity as fundamental ground seems likely to be that of a normal pupil.

The pupil may have a normal identity but he is certainly not a normal-ideal. Here a segmental ground diverging into deviance is recognized. Whether it is deviance or mere divergence is perhaps not clear. It is nevertheless certainly recognized as having a definite trans-episodic form ('a side of James'). In this way it does not seem to be a threat to the normal base. It is formulated as a non-pivotal category, merely as 'a side' and so appears not to threaten the core typification.

It is important to recognize not only that one segment of Other may be viewed as deviant or divergent even within a normal base but also that it may be emergent over a time-scale. Either its presence may not be permanent or its being revealed may be a matter of emergence over time. This is a case of one term emergence. For one whole term the deviant 'side' has been submerged or hidden.

The same newly discovered deviant segment is seen in another episode:

> There was somebody had dropped something. And I said: I'll have to get somebody to pick these papers up. And he turned round: Well I'm

not going to do it, he said. I thought: Charming!! But he's just started
this. Well, this has just become apparent to me. This side of James.

Again there are signs of an underlying normal base by implication since the
divergence here is both segmental and emergent.

For almost a term this 'normal' pupil has retained a normal career but has
now exposed a deviant segment at this point. Presumably the teacher is left not
knowing whether this is to be regarded as a permanent feature which has been
carefully hidden or just a passing feature. It can remain: episodic (as an extended
episode or phase); restricted episodic (restricted to specific contexts); or become a
new segmental ground. This 'side of James' is a significant figure-ground phenomenon. Movement or emergence is itself a figure-ground phenomenon since
the wider temporal perspective is not known from the mere observation of figure
at a particular point in time.

The normal career continues for the rest of the year with this teacher. There
is an occasional appearance of the divergent segment in specific episodes. However, such deviation is seen to be restricted to:

— segmental role limits
— episodic limits
— intra-episodic limits of within-episode emergence.

Year Three

Initial Processes of Emergence

Week Two

The pupil now moves on to his third year in school and to a new teacher, Mrs.
Bradley. Again the initial processes of normal ground emergence may be viewed.

It seems a normal base is immediately in operation as the new teacher begins
to formulate James as a normal pupil:

He's lovely. He's there and gets on with his work.

The teacher's comment suggests James is settled into a normal pupil role. He is
apparently perceived from a normal baseline straight away. Already the pupil is
formulated within a trans-episodic framework, an instance of quite rapid ground
emergence. It seems he then submerges into the anonymity often experienced by
normal pupils and only 'surfaces' again several months later in the teacher's
recounting of a classroom episode.

The Appearance of Ground in the Interpretation of
Classroom Episodes

This is perhaps a classic indication of normal ground in operation. After the rapid
ground emergence it can be seen that the pupil then experiences the phenomenon

of submergence apparently quite common in an ultra-normal[3] pupil. In the absence of probing in research interviews he 'reappears' five months later in an unprompted reference. Once again it is the abnormal pupil Gavin who dominates the teacher's classroom concerns over this period and the research interview talk too. James is commented upon five months later:

> He does talk sometimes. Normally he's very quiet. You wouldn't hardly know James was there. But there was somebody there having a real good gossip. And when I looked across it was James talking.

This occasion, then, seems to be viewed as a mere episodically limited divergence ('normally he's very quiet') from an otherwise normal baseline of formulation. It can be seen, too, how the framework is perhaps less that of rule-transgression than of the person formulation model (within a quantitative paradigm) of divergence. The pupil's infrequent divergence is seen to be only 'sometimes' against an otherwise dominant conformity. The present divergent incident is seen to be episodically bounded which therefore insulates it from the normal base. His deviance is further neutralized as the account continues: 'Not normally like that. He's human. The same as all the others.' The interpersonal boundaries of the social structure of the classroom itself are restated here to recognize an occasional episodic divergence as 'normal' for everyone!

The deviant behaviour is even further neutralized by recognizing the structurability of the situation:

> You wouldn't [have to] say any more [than once]. You set James his jobs to do and James gets on with them usually.

The teacher strategy in this typical episode is seen to neutralize the potential episodic and infrequent divergence. It draws from a baseline of normality. Clearly the teacher sees the divergence only in 'surface' terms. She is able to see beyond it to a 'deeper structure' which she is able to tap in order to restructure the situation. And so it seems that in formulating this episode, the teacher is simultaneously aware of both the 'surface' and the 'deep structure' features present in the social reality of the setting.

The teacher's reference to only one classroom episode in a research interview during this pupil's third year amply demonstrates how normal ground operates as an ongoing underlying structure to his continuing school career. She sees beyond the immediate episodic figure to a trans-episodic reality of a normal pupil against which the potentially divergent episode, begun here as figure, is replaced by the underlying ground of normal identity. This ends the third year of his career. The pupil's limited appearance in interview data is an indication of pupil ultra-normality and his submergence into anonymity in the phenomenal world of this teacher. By contrast, after almost disappearing in this year, it can be seen how the pupil now swings back into prominence.

Year Four

As the pupil moves into his fourth school year and on to a new teacher, Mr. Lindsay, there is an opportunity once again to examine the emergence of ground.

Initial Processes of Emergence

The teacher begins with a quite tentative and seemingly provisional formulation:

> Seems to be coping. I think he's a bright lad actually. Seems to be able
> to take in what you're saying and act upon it without too much distress.

A quite clear indication of a normal identity as ground then. But it is presented in
an apparent provisional framework of emergence. The present continuous tense
is used: 'coping' and 'taking things in'. It seems the teacher is either being
pedantically cautious in the first interview (as might well be expected in view of
the potentially threatening nature of research interviews!) or is quite clearly
operating a phasic framework in which the construction of Other is recognized to
be very much a provisional one in a situation which is seen to be ongoing or
emergent.

Week Four

A few weeks later, Mr. Lindsay is still fitting together what are seen to be both
normal and divergent facets of James:

> I found it very difficult to work James out. He doesn't give a lot away.
> He doesn't *say* a great deal to me.

So far the pupil shows signs of presenting some resistance to the teacher's
attempt to engage in formulation. Perhaps at most the pupil's reticence is seen to
be just divergence in terms of *frequency* ('not a great deal') rather than *category*.
　　The pupil is also seen as inconsistent. This inconsistency is perhaps a deviation from an assumption that pupils operate from a stable base:

> He's inconsistent. Sometimes he'll say quite a bit about nothing at all.
> But when I *want* him to actually talk to me he won't. I get sort of stinted
> answers. He's a difficult character to read.

The pupil's resistance seems to be noted by the teacher. There is no continuing
abnormality but what may be episodic divergence. This leads to some uncertainty of ground at this point and a suggestion of some divergence: 'He's a difficult
character to read'. There is perhaps some suggestion of deviance, but most
significant of all is the indication that the teacher is still searching for the pupil's
underlying base. It indicates quite clearly that a significant feature of pupil
formulation is the search for an underlying structure or stable framework, and
that in this case the teacher has not yet found one: 'He's inconsistent. . . . He's a
difficult character to read'. There are signs of possible continuing tensions between the normal and divergent elements of this pupil with which the teacher is
presented and which as yet have not been possible to resolve by the formulation
of a stable underlying identity.
　　The next account shows Mr. Lindsay attempting to discover, operate or
resolve the ambiguities of pupil identity in a specific context:

When I saw him looking across I thought: He's sitting there waiting to see what's going to happen to Jason. Thinking is he going to get away with it? Or is he just interested in what's going on around him? It was unlike James. James isn't that sort of boy. He doesn't sort of sit and daydream and look around much. He tends to get on.

It seems the teacher recognizes an ambiguity in the figure formulation of this episode. Its meaning depends upon the motive imputed. Within this episode there are *two* motives introduced by the teacher. One is potentially divergent as though hoping that a deviant incident by another pupil might be overlooked by the teacher ('is he going to get away with it?') and the other is potentially normal ('is he just interested in what's going on around him?'). In the interpretation of this episode, faced with the choice between two motives, the teacher relies on a trans-episodic baseline of normal ground: 'It was unlike James. James isn't that sort of boy'.

Not only is there an apparent confirmation of normal ground for this pupil but also an indication of its use within a particular episode in providing a perceptual base to permit the selection of an appropriate motive from its trans-episodic motivational reservoir. In so doing the episode loses its ambiguity and is transformed into one of underlying normality. An indication that either normal ground is now recognized to be the pupil's underlying pivotal identity, or at least of provisional acceptance in this episode as the appropriate framework to adopt in an attempt to unravel the potential ambiguities on this occasion.

Whether it now becomes the stable or permanent formulation base remains to be seen. On this occasion, however, it demonstrates how the underlying 'structure' of a situation can inform the ambiguities of surface figures.

Week Five

The emergence of normal identity now seems to continue. The pupil's earlier resistance is now seen to be most definitely only temporary since the phase is coming to an end: 'I've been trying to get underneath this veneer. I think I'm getting there'. Mr. Lindsay recounts the incident which indicated the apparent ending of the resistance phase:

I picked him up on a spelling point and pretended to throttle him. I said: You've got it wrong again! And he smiled! We've cracked it. Well, I suppose in terms of James we've cracked it. There was a smile and he gave a little bit. So I think we're beginning to get through the veneer.

This formulation shows how a figure construction may have little meaning without a recognition of the underlying ground. The interpretation of this figure is made in relation to ground. The 'deep structure' of social reality is perhaps an ever present phenomenon in classroom life. Slight changes in figure appearances are given significant meaning by relating to ground:

And he smiled. We've cracked it. Well, I suppose in terms of James we've cracked it.

In the above account can be seen how surface figure always rests upon deeper but often unstated ground. Additionally, it can be seen how the teacher's first order use of the notion of 'veneer' suggests an underlying reality beyond the surface appearance.

Week Nine

It has seemed so far that James is apparently on his way to becoming viewed as a normal pupil. His perceived resistance has merely seemed to delay its appearance. At this point in the fourth year of his career, Mr. Lindsay now seems to recognize that the resistance may be a persisting feature in James:

Teacher: I've accepted that the veneer is there to stay. There's no way we're going to crack it down at all.

Interviewer: What makes you think it's there?

Teacher: Because I've met his dad. And I get the same impression talking to his dad. There's this cool veneer.

So once again, family matching provides the basis for ground verification as it often seems to in this research for both normal and abnormal pupils. The teacher already has provisional or tentative ground well established but it is seemingly given additional assurance by confirmation in family matching.

Mr. Lindsay's account of the parent continues:

But underneath it all he cracks and tells a joke. For two or three seconds he lets it slip and is himself. But then it's back again. And James is exactly like his dad in that respect. And so I've thought: Well, I've seen his dad. Now I know what James is like and it's just one of those things. So that's sorted that one out.

A normalization of potential divergence is seen to be assured on several counts:

1 The potential divergence is seen as a 'veneer'. It is not regarded as a 'real' or permanent phenomenon. The pivotal ground is recognized to be there underneath when 'he lets it slip and is himself'. Once again it can be seen how ground is a crucial element in the construction of reality.

2 James' parent provides a perceptual referent for his divergence to be 'sorted out' and in addition perhaps removes the potential abnormality.

By redefining the pupil as part of his 'family' the ground is extended beyond the individual Other to the family group and so its uniqueness and potential (personal) pathology is lessened. It is important to recognize that the boundaries of ground are apparently constructed not just at the individual level but extend into his family, as is the case with the sibling phenomenon. In this way the family may perhaps be regarded as occupying a significant position[4] within the 'social structure' of society.

At this point in his fourth year the pupil now seems to have arrived at a stable identity. His teacher has accepted that this is how the pupil is. All is seen to be well. The pupil's parent shares his behaviour in some ways so there is nothing to be concerned about. We have arrived at a normal base. (Although it must be noted that with Alan in School B, the parent was also like son yet this is used as confirmation of an enduring pathological phenomenon!)

The Appearance of Ground in the Interpretation of Classroom Episodes

As this pupil was not at the time selected as a normal case for illustrative or exploratory purposes, he was not followed through for more intensive or systematic observation. Consequently he only appears in data when the teacher chooses to make reference to him. His chances of appearing in time-sampling observations of classroom processes or in the researcher's participant observation notes were, as with all pupils, governed by principles of random selection. During this teacher's remaining time in school the pupil does not appear in another contextualized or interactional formulation. The teacher's last interview reveals the continuing but stable normal pivotal identity ground already recognized:

> I can't say a lot about James. Our relationship seems to have peaked. At this stage we seem to have gone as far as we're going to go. The holding back business at the beginning was fair enough. But since then he's opened up a little bit. So I don't think he's holding back.

An emergent or developmental perspective is apparently operated by the teacher. There are possible indications of phenomena consistent with the process of submergence. Of course, some of the anonymity in the formulation of James may be due to his perceived enigmatic 'personality', and his apparently resistant interpersonal strategies, the teacher acknowledges that the pupil has 'opened up a bit'. The fact that the teacher 'can't say a lot about James' is consistent with, if not indicative of, the processes of submergence that often seem to occur with such 'ultra-normal' pupils. He apparently accepts that the interpersonal resistance is to be seen as a ground-related phenomenon since its phasic basis is ended. As it is seen to be not moving further it perhaps becomes increasingly seen as a ground phenomenon.

New Teacher — Term Three

With a new teacher taking over the class, James again seems to experience a normal identity. To avoid unnecessary repetition, much of the data will be omitted. The final interview with this teacher seems to sum up a quite normal pupil identity: 'Just good all round. Even games and things like that'. James seems to be a model or even 'ideal' pupil: 'just good all round'. He is here being formulated as 'ideal' segmentally, at least in an academic role-identity situation. The apparent significance of 'even games' can be seen because it is regarded as a sort of boundary. A significant test. So:

His build doesn't sort of lend itself. But he still tries very hard. He puts even effort into that though it's more difficult for him.

The normal ground is seen to provide a basis for motive imputation *even* in this specified episode where the boundaries of normal motivation might be seen to be stretched to their limits. It is a clear case of normality operating as the dominant framework of formulation.

Perhaps even more significant here is how the underlying structure of this interpretation is *person* formulation, even in this area of academic categorization. The critical matter here is seen not to be how good he is in relation to different 'academic' criteria or categories but how such categorization is apparently regarded as a mere *segmental* formulation founded upon the more critical underlying reality of a personal trans–episodic baseline. It is the *baseline* of pupil motivation which is seen to be critical and so transforms the construction 'good all round' and 'even games' from a mere *surface* academic category, by the recognition of the motivational base upon which such formulation is seen to rest. As with the deviant pupils already examined, there is a clear indication that person formulation of a dominant (normal or abnormal) pivotal identity takes precedence even as a base for academic formulation, which in turn often appears to be treated by teachers merely as a subordinate or segmental element in Other interpretation.

Notes

1 At this point in a career, when the pupil is barely known to the teacher and when the teacher has hardly begun to formulate the pupil as an individual, it may even be more accurate to regard this phase as pre-formulation.
2 See note 9, Chapter 10.
3 Certain pupils are apparently seen to personify the mode position within the 'normal distribution' of a classroom population. In this respect they appear to be regarded by teachers as representative cases of the normal pupil. They are frequently referred to by teachers as 'average' or 'normal' pupils. Their unique modal identity is in this study referred to as 'ultra-normal'.
4 Some writers have recognized in respect of the 'class system', the family and not the individual is more appropriately viewed as the basic 'structural' unit of 'society' (Parkin, 1971).

Chapter 14

Episodes in the Emergence of a Normal Career: Louise (School A)

A second normal case provides another opportunity to examine career emergence and maintenance in a pupil occupying the position of representative 'normal' type in the social world of primary school A. Like James, Louise also at times appears to be viewed as an ultra-normal pupil. Once again, it will not be appropriate to present the complete analysis of this pupil's career. Consequently, where a repetition of processes apparently similar to those already identified in relation to James would arise they have been omitted in the present case. Instead, the different forms of career development and maintenance are highlighted so as to indicate the variety of patterns possible within a 'normal' pupil career.

Year One

Initial Processes of Emergence

Louise is so clearly viewed as a classic normal case that she seems to rapidly become submerged into the classroom 'culture'. Her virtual omission by the teacher from the interviews in the first two months suggests an ultra-normal pupil who is quickly absorbed into an anonymous ground. She does not appear in interview talk until two months into the research.

Week Eight

When Louise does appear, it is only for Miss Bennett to state what seems to be a clear normal ground: 'A pretty average kid. Sort of a norm. She copes with most things'. Miss Bennett's comment represents a clear formulation of a pivotal identity and the emergence of a ground framework.

She also notes a quite modest academic segment to Louise: 'She gets there in the end but she's a bit slower than the others'. Perhaps Louise diverges somewhat from 'the others' in academic terms. At this point it seems the teacher has begun to identify segmental role categories for this pupil. Both in academic and more general aspects of the pupil's role-identity there is normal ground, but perhaps operating respectively at different segmental role positions while remaining firmly within the normal category of the normal distribution of pupils. In respect of the general pupil role, she is the personification of the normal while in an academic role Louise is diverging from the norm.

The Appearance of Ground in the Interpretation of Classroom Episodes

Louise has clearly begun a normal career. From this point onwards she is interpreted from a ground framework of normal identity. Her 'normalcy' is particularly noticeable in the teacher's use of normal base to interpret an ambiguous episode. Since this occurence has already been encountered with James, there is perhaps little to be gained by repeating the similar processes as they occur with Louise.

Term Two

In the pupil's second term there is a quite spontaneous confirmation of this pupil as a similar type to the other normal pupil, James:

> I think she's a bit old-fashioned. Like James in a way. She likes things you wouldn't expect a 5-year-old to like.

A confirmation of some equivalence in the identity of these two pupils but also some uncertainty of teacher's meanings here. The reference to old-fashioned suggests a possible divergence from the norms of 'a 5-year-old', but in what direction? Towards the 'ideal' pupil? Or in deviating divergence? Earlier references suggest the pupil is seen as 'mature' and that perhaps the implied divergence is towards that of an older age group. Indeed, on another occasion the paired pupil, James, is described as 'advanced beyond his years'.

Throughout her second year Louise appears to be viewed in a similar way and from a normal framework. This case illustration now picks up the pupil's career in her third year.

Year Three

Initial Processes of Emergence

Again Louise's 'normal' identity is confirmed:

> Getting on like a house afire. But I wouldn't say there's very much ... really there shouldn't be very much with any of them. Except our friend.

This comment is a formulation in terms of apparent conformity to the pupil's role and so a suggestion of 'normal' identity as the pivotal category ('Getting on like a house afire'). There is also a spontaneous confirmation here of the 'social structure' of this classroom and its socially constructed boundaries. The teacher refers on the one hand to the majority of pupils, apparently occupying the category of normality 'there shouldn't be very much with any of them' — apparently meaning not much to be concerned about and on the other hand the deviant pupil Gavin, whose status within the taken-for-granted world of the school's 'social structure' (including the researcher as no longer a stranger to it) is seen to be so widely recognized that the teacher makes reference to him only in terms of the implicit in-group social category ('our friend'). Louise by implication is included with the rest 'of them' within the boundaries of normality. Up to this point in year three it seems normal ground has been emerging. In the next account can be seen how normal ground operates beyond the point of its emergence.

The Appearance of Ground in the Interpretation of Classroom Episodes

Week Ten

Two months later the pupil is referred to in terms of apparent ultra-normality:

> I find she's fine. She tries very hard. Getting on quite nicely I would think. I wouldn't pick her out in a hurry at all.

It seems Mrs. Bradley is quite clearly viewing Louise as one who is experiencing a normal career: 'She's fine [and] getting on quite nicely'. An implication of submergence is also suggested here: 'I wouldn't pick her out in a hurry at all'. The teacher's meaning is not entirely clear here but it seems to be congruent with the notion of submergence employed in this research. This can be seen more clearly as the account continues and the teacher recounts an episodic figure construction when probed about her observations of Louise that morning:

> Interviewer: This morning?
> Teacher: She didn't stand out at all. I never noticed her. And I think I would've if things had been wrong with her.

This reference strongly supports the classroom processes of 'scanning mechanism' and of 'normal submergence' frequently recognized in this research. In fact, the pupil now submerges for the next six months, not being referred to by her teacher and so disappearing from the interview data. It suggests that perhaps the average or normal pupil may often be constructed or processed in ground terms, perhaps barely impinging upon teacher 'consciousness' in figure terms at all in everyday dealings. This would correspond with the anonymity of typification recognised by Schutz (Schutz and Luckmann, 1974). It is clearly the case that in the formulation of pupils it is not just in the reification of deviant identity that social processes of anonymization are found (as was apparently claimed by Sharp and Green, 1975). A continuing feature of formulation suggested in this research is that anonymization is a process frequently and perhaps even more likely to occur to 'normal' pupils.

Year Four

Initial Processes of Emergence

Again, the pupil appears to be viewed as one who conforms to the social world of the classroom in much the same way as she has previously. Once again there is data which seems to confirm processes of submergence, as can be seen in the next account.

The Appearance of Ground in the Interpretation of Classroom Episodes

Week Seven

As the process of random selection throws up Louise as a pupil as the focus of a time-sampling observation the teacher, Mr. Lindsay, is required to take note of the pupil at a randomly selected moment during the morning:

> I didn't see her at all, I'm afraid. I didn't see her at all. She was there this morning. Yes, I just didn't see her come out from the games lesson.

This teacher's response to the time-sampled moment is again quite congruent with, though not in itself evidence of, the processes of submergence frequently noted in relation to the social construction of normal pupils. Even though the teacher was alerted to look out for this pupil for a research observation Louise was still quite unnoticeable, in spite of the fact that the time sampling method on this occasion might be expected to encourage an increased selective attention to this pupil.

The same indication of submergence is seen as the teacher continues:

> Louise is one of ... No ... No ... I'm getting her muddled with Melanie. I've got two girls in my group. Louise and Melanie, and I muddle them all the time. I even wrote the wrong name on the maths book this morning.

This account suggests a perceptual confusion of mistaken identity rather than of interactional submergence. Nevertheless, the pupil appears to experience some anonymization in formulation. Another instance occurs later.

Week Fifteen

The next account confirms once again the position of Louise as an ultra-normal:

> She's sort of Miss Average. The sort of girl who just gets on with it. Chatters quite a bit. But nothing really outstanding.

It also suggests something of the processes of person formulation occurring with normal pupils. The comments that the pupil 'just gets on with it' and 'nothing really outstanding' suggest that processes of submergence may be operating. She is perhaps being viewed with some anonymity, as the teacher experiences Louise within contemporary relations as one who is known to be located not only within the parameters of normality but even as a representative type of ultra-normal pupil at the modal position of the pupil distribution.

The processes of submergence are further revealed as the account continues:

> Unlike Clare there's no sort of distinguishing features about her. I mean, when you look round and see their faces, her face is one that you would just pass. I quite often confuse her with another girl. With Melanie. Because she's another Miss Average.

This indicates the apparent submergence of pupil into the anonymity of contemporary typification. It also suggests that the earlier notion of a 'scanning mechanism' or 'scanning process' may indeed be an authentic classroom process and not merely a hypothetical speculation of early theorization. In this account, then, the teacher seems to suggest some personal anonymity for this pupil in her appearance. It would be too easy to assume the teacher's meaning corresponds with the present developing notion of submergence as a process experienced by ultra-normal pupils. It is not inconsistent with it, of course, but there can be an alternative interpretation. The submergence may be a largely visual phenomenon of *perceptual* anonymity rather than *personal* or *formulation* anonymity. The earlier reference to Melanie being seen as an average pupil as well, suggests that the unremarkable disappearance, or submergence, may frequently be a feature of life in classrooms for 'average' pupils.

Term Three, New Teacher: Initial Processes of Emergence

Week Twenty-eight

As a new teacher, Mrs. Craven, takes over the cohort group in the final term there is again a continuing difficulty of recognition:

> I keep getting her mixed up with another girl. I mix her up with a girl called Melanie. Facially they look alike. And I don't really know her. She hasn't made a great deal of impression on me so far.

At this point in emergence it perhaps is inappropriate to consider this as an instance of submergence. That the teacher 'doesn't really know her' may be quite consistent with the anonymity of one who would later submerge into the mid-point category of pupil parameters (as one who does not make an 'impression'). But it is perhaps important to distinguish the initial anonymity experienced by such a pupil in early processes of emergence from the later submergence.

The Appearance of Ground in the Interpretation of Classroom Episodes

Week Thirty-two

As the year comes to a close there is an indication of the teacher operating the normal ground and its motivational base to interpret the pupil within a videotaped observation of a slice of classroom life. The normal base is used to interpret an episode in which the pupil is caught taking time out from the work assigned to the group, and therefore when the episode might be thought to have perhaps ambiguous and even possible divergent implications:

> Louise seems to have just had a break. I don't think there's anything. Children all have sort of breaks in concentration. She's not one who wastes a lot of time. She will just sort of turn back into it.

The figure appearance of this episode, then, is potentially ambiguous. It could perhaps be seen divergently but the teacher offers immediate trans-episodic neutralization by:

— interpersonal normal bracketing ('children all have sort of breaks in concentration');
— normal motivational reservoir selection ('she's not one who wastes a lot of time').

and even draws further from the normal motivational reservoir to predict a typical normal outcome: 'She will just sort of turn back into it'.

The pupil is being viewed from within the framework of normal ground as the teacher imports into the interpretation of this episode the trans-episodic framework of normal pupil identity and its associated motivational reservoir, from which meanings can be selected to impute into 'surface' appearances of pupil actions the 'deep structure' of their underlying base. This final instance of normal ground in operation ends this brief scrutiny of significant processes, and their points within a longitudinal time-scale, in the emergence and continuity of a second pupil in School A who experiences a 'normal' career.

Chapter 15

Episodes in the Emergence of a Normal Career: Sally (School B)

Next, two normal cases from School B are considered: the pupils Sally and Dawn. The inclusion of these additional pupils from the cohort allows a broadening of the empirical base upon which this illustration of normal pupils rests and so goes some way in reducing the untypicality of data that would otherwise occur in theorizing from one school as a single case. It also permits an intra-school comparison of the present two normal cases with the previously considered deviant case in School B: Alan.

Year One

Initial Processes of Emergence

Week One

As the pupil begins her school career it is possible to examine the processes of emergence in early formulation. It seems that formulation begins immediately from a potentially normal ground:

> She's a fairly confident little girl. She went round the other classes. She hasn't realized which group is which. Which most of them haven't. Which I think is good.

This suggests a pupil who is categorized as part of a general (and by implication normal) pupil cohort. She is included in the interpersonal set 'most of them', suggesting perhaps at the moment that the teacher sees the cohort as a rather undifferentiated group who are as yet not formulated in differentiated ground terms.

In fact, Sally is seen to be unexpectedly normal. In the formulation of this pupil the teacher approaches with a ground framework derived from previous knowledge of her family. When compared with the pupil's parent this ultra-conformity is surprising to the headteacher, Mrs. Strang:

> Mrs. Hopkinson had always been a rather unusual woman. She's certainly a one-off. And Sally in fact from starting school seems to me to be *so* ordinary.

The pupil is provisionally regarded as ultra-normal: '*so* ordinary'. Here the sibling or family rule is apparently being operated. It proves to be incongruent, which is an indication that teachers operate expectations of equivalence in family and sibling relations. This early provisional ground is already expressed in terms of the family as referent.

The retrospectively constructed ground certainly indicates signs of a generally conforming pupil:

> ... would sit and enjoy everything and smile about things. And really accept everything in such a pleasant way. She'd be able to sing or dance or something very confidently. And do it in *such* a conforming way that it is almost as if she's a reaction against her mother's. As if she's trying very hard to be just normal. And just sitting there as being a conforming member of the group. *Too* conforming really when she first started. For a 4-year-old.

The conformity of the pupil here leaves little doubt that teachers recognize the general ground of motivation for this pupil. This is not just a normal pupil but one who is trying to be ultra-normal — a quite overt pupil strategy! At this point it seems the pupil's strategy is at odds with what is expected by the teachers. It has been noted how 'In the early years of infant school, the boundaries between school and home are softened to ease transition' (Woods, 1980, p. 12). Yet this pupil is seen to be adopting strategies more compatible with those of older pupil groups.

Here then, in addition to the appearance of what seems to be normal ground, the teacher recognizes this pupil may even be engaged in 'taking the role of Other' with some sophistication in the fitting of a normal performance. It is interesting, of course, how teachers are already looking beyond 'appearances' to deeper realities and not merely focusing upon just what the pupil is seen at present to be actually doing, but upon the motives and general interactional baseline upon which it is presumed to rest.

It seems up to this point a normal ground is more than just provisionally established. It can be seen, as the interview proceeds further, how Sally's teacher now draws upon a normal motivational reservoir in the interpretation of classroom episodes.

The Appearance of Ground in the Interpretation of Classroom Episodes

In the same interview Mrs. Strang recounts an episode in which a normal framework is adopted to make sense of mother-pupil-school interaction:

> Mother'd taken her down [to the dentist] before school this morning to get an emergency extraction so that she could have her in school for nine o'clock. And come really obviously not well enough to come to school.

Here is an instance of drawing upon the trans-episodic normal base to impute a motive to this episode. Considered from surface appearances there is a potential ambiguity or tension within this account because of competing motives. The teacher's interpretation of the episode ('to have her in school for nine o'clock') seems to elevate this motive as dominant over a potentially divergent motive that otherwise might be seen within the episode itself ('obviously not well enough to come to school'). The teacher's interpretation of the meaning seems to come from the implied normal ground. As there are two competing episodic motives here, one normal and one divergent, and since the first can also be seen to have a trans-episodic base then this seems to take precedence.

Week Four

Two weeks later a further example of normal ground now apparently in operation can be seen:

> I never see Sally. She's so capable. I don't know if it's capable. But she's involved in all her own activities.

Signs of possible submergence are to be seen here: 'I never see Sally' — A phenomenon which is congruent with, and empirically appears to be frequently experienced with, the ultra-normal pupils in this research.

In this episode a normal or even ideal identity is at first suggested ('she's so capable') and then discarded. However, in continuing a further search for the appropriate motive the class teacher, Mrs. Thompson, still selects from the same baseline of conformity and its normal motivational reservoir ('she's involved'). After one motive is selected and discarded the teacher then selects an alternative but from the same motivational reservoir. This suggests a normal baseline is in operation.

As the class teacher continues her account the submergence of this ultra-conforming pupil is further elaborated:

> I hardly see her at all. If you didn't make an effort to look out for her and see what she's doing you wouldn't know she was there.

This comment indicates once again the quite common occurrence of submergence into ground formulation and anonymity of identity frequently noticeable in the case of an ultra-normal pupil.

The same point is again made by Mrs. Thompson but this time making reference to the more complex parameters of formulation within a vertical group setting:

> She spends [her time] with the other children. Reading or something. And she'll sit in a table with I3s and join in their activity quite happily. She fits in so well ... it's like into the classroom. Unless you do look you don't notice her. She doesn't ever stand out.

This account is a clear description of the process of submergence! The teacher makes an overt reference to the phenomenon of submergence: 'Sally fits in so well ... like into the classroom'. There is also an indication of the 'scanning mechanism' which has been suggested earlier (as though in looking around the classroom the teacher's perceptual set was 'programmed' to look out only for striking phenomena, or that which might 'stand out').

Here, the teacher makes reference to an older age-group within this vertical group as Sally, an I1, naturalistically interacts with, and provides a comparative referent from the teacher in relation to, the older pupils in I3. What is not so clear, of course, is what norms are operating for teachers as they engage in pupil formulation in such vertical group situations. Are they age or cohort-related or do teachers recognize a cross-group combined-age vertical group norm?

As the interview continued there was an attempt to test this out in the next interview probe:

Interviewer: You don't think of her as an I1 then?
Teacher: I don't *think* of her very much at all.

The teacher's reply confirms the total submergence of a normal pupil within vertical group parameters.

Week Five

The following week there is an indication of the quite unique formulation framework that seems to operate in vertical group contexts.

So far in this research, processes of submergence have seemed to operate for normal pupils. Pupils are seen to be so convergent within the social structure of the classroom that they seem to blend into a background of some anonymity, as though located at the modal position within a normal distribution. However, in a vertical group context taking in three separate cohorts, the normal parameters might be expected to be more complex as there will be two age cohorts 'older' than the younger children who are the new entrant cohort. The formulatory position of ultra-normal pupils within vertical group arrangements may then be in the form of one of the following categories:

1   Perhaps as her or his conformity as a pupil reaches ultra-normality she or he either has to diverge more towards the 'ideal' of her or his own cohort so as to fit the more moderate vertical group mode position; or
2   Maybe such a pupil is seen to be interactionally more sophisticated in recognizing the complexity of teacher expectations and so deliberately adopts a modal, in preference to an 'ideal', position within a recognized broader range of parameters; or
3   Teachers are so pressured by a wide spread of pupils that it is easier for pupils to get lost or to submerge.

The teacher's account in this case suggests the first approach as the pupil is seen to diverge towards the I2s and I3s:

She refers to her 'drawer' and her 'writing book' and 'reading the book' and things. The same vocabulary as the older children are using. So her sentences don't pick her out immediately as an I1. You tend to accept her more as a school child rather than another I1.

Here, the pupil seems to merge in as a 'normal' pupil within the vertical group parameters and possibly even as an 'ideal' within the I1 cohort parameters. In a vertical group context, as might be expected, teachers are likely to incorporate an entire vertical group's developmental range of pupils within the parameters of the social world of the classroom group life. But the problem here is to know whether the pupil merges or submerges as an 'ideal' or as a 'normal'. An age-range ideal presumably is not likely to submerge but would be prominent or outstanding. By implication any submergence would suggest a 'normal' framework of formulation. The pupil's apparent submergence here suggests the teacher is operating a 'normal' category and so within a vertical group rather than cohort parameters. Is it possible that teachers of vertical groups switch between the different parameters of the vertical and the cohort group?

This interview, as it continues, indicates how a normal pupil is seen to encounter what for the school is a significant point in a pupil's school career — that of starting school dinners:

At dinnertime, she's just started this week, and we haven't had any bother at all with her.... [Started] on Monday. Settled straight in. Just no bother at all. Her mother's been asking for a few weeks. We've said: Wait. And fortunately she was one of the mothers that's accepted it.

It seems here that both pupil and parents are regarded as part of a conforming family — a normal set. The teacher seems to be dipping into a normal motivational reservoir to interpret the pupil's settling in as 'no bother at all' and the mother's 'accepted it'.

Week Eight

At this time, as normal ground is seen to be in operation, it can be seen how two recurring aspects of the ultra-normal pupil appear.

First is the recognition of the category 'sensible':

Sally is proving to be quite a good worker and a good little girl. And she's very sensible.

This category becomes elaborated later.

Second is the use of ground in the recognition of a normal deep structure beyond certain ground elements which might otherwise present ambiguity: 'She's so quiet. But she makes sure she's in everything'. It can be seen how the potential divergence of being 'quiet' is for Louise neutralised by a normal motivational base: 'makes sure she's in everything' (how different the formulatory base to Alan's 'quiet' was in the same school at this time!).

New Teacher: Term Two

Initial Processes of Emergence

As a new teacher takes over the class some of the processes of emergence can again be examined.

> *Week One*

The new teacher, Mrs. Gill, begins with an exploratory attempt at formulation of Sally:

> Very, very quiet. She's hardly spoken to me. Whether it's shyness or she just doesn't like the upset from another teacher ... she's having to adapt again and finding a difficulty. Don't know. It might be me. I've not given her enough time. I might not have sat with her enough and encouraged her to talk to me.

A new teacher who is faced with quietness in a child ('very, very quiet') in order to interpret its meaning inevitably explores both aspects of ground and features of episode. Here she postulates a possible ground: 'whether it's shyness'. Then as alternatives, two episodic themes are constructed: 'the upset from another teacher' or 'it might be me'. Obviously, Mrs. Gill has no means yet for deciding. This is the first week. All three are at this point plausible reasons.

Towards the end of the term there are indications of both normality of pivotal ground and submergence:

> She's not a problem child. She's very difficult to talk about because she's so conscientious in all the work she does. And her approach in school. I've never had any problems with her since I came.

A statement of apparent normality by indicating which side of the critical boundary she is on: Sally 'is no problem'. Also there are signs of submergence as perhaps the pupil is viewed as a member of the ultra-normal category: 'She's very difficult to talk about'.

The Appearance of Pivotal Identity as Ground in the Interpretation of Classroom Episodes

At this point, as the interview continues, it can be seen how Sally is viewed in submergent terms, a recurring feature of classroom life for an ultra-normal pupil. Also, as several teachers express similar formulations it can be seen how ultra-normality seems to be a widely shared category, part of the apparently taken-for-granted world of staffroom culture.

The first teacher to express it is Mrs. Williams, a member of the team working with another vertical group in the same 'open' area:

I cannot say a great deal about her. She joins in. She responds. And she conforms. She's got smiling eyes. But I can't say that she's outstanding really. She's outstanding in the fact that she's not outstanding I suppose.

The submergence and apparent anonymity of ground also seems to be confirmed by Mrs. Charles:

She's got nothing very special about her at all. The only thing is that she *does* always look happy.

Here is an indication of how 'average' or ultra-normal pupils are perhaps perceived by other teachers who themselves are not attached to the pupil's own cohort group — in terms which suggest even greater anonymization. What a contrast with the position of such deviant pupils as Alan in the same school, or Gavin in School A, who so dominate staffroom conversation and its 'taken-for-granted' world that their public reputations are widely recognized within school culture (including teachers, parents, dinner staff, caretaker and pupils).

The class teacher, Mrs. Gill, continues, elaborating her own view of the pupil's anonymity:

She's sort of a model child really. If you could have a model child! She's my idea of a model child. She's got the enthusiasm but she's not pushy. She's not too quiet. She's just average at everything. I mean she's not brilliantly clever. And she's not terribly poor. She's my ideal model child really. If I could build a model child.

Year Two

Unusually for this school, in operating vertical grouping, and continuing contact with the same base teacher, the sample cohort of pupils now get another teacher, Mrs. Byrne; the previous term's teacher was only temporary. Again it is possible to examine how formulation proceeds as a new teacher attempts to get to know this pupil.

Initial Processes of Emergence

Again it seems that the teacher is immediately operating a tentative normal identity as ground in the formulation of Sally:

There's nothing outstanding about her. She's quite normal. In a way nothing.... Not like Alan, you know his moods. They're quite interesting. It depends what mood he's in. But Sally's always bright and ready to work.

Quite fortuitously the deviant case is again invoked as a comparative referent: 'not like Alan'. Her normal motives can be regarded as operating from a predictable base: 'always bright and ready to work'. At this point it seems evident that

Mrs. Byrne has recognized a normal identity as pivotal ground for this pupil and it can perhaps be assumed to be already in operation.

The Appearance of Ground in the Interpretation of Classroom Episodes

As the same account continues it can be seen that the teacher is using the recognized conformity of a normal identity as an interpretative framework:

> Doesn't really object. She'll do it if she's told to. If she's wanting to do something else she won't do it straight away. But she will do it because she's been told to.

This reference to the pupil's reluctance suggests a divergent tendency is formulated within a recognized intra-episodic framework: 'she will do it'. As such it is viewed as a predictable event of limited duration and no more than a temporary divergence. The formulatory base of normal identity can presumably be invoked to give it meaning during the intra-episodic delay when the surface appearance otherwise suggests divergence.

Week Five

The next account probes the teacher's reference earlier in the interview to the pupil being 'nice'. It introduces again a suggestion of the scanning process (earlier hypothesized as a possible teacher formulatory strategy) and the submergence that seems to occur frequently, or perhaps even continually, with pupils who are perceived to be in the ultra-normal category:

> Interviewer: Nice?
>
> Teacher: Pleasant girl. When you're looking round the room she's always a smiling face. Like ... Lisa's the same. Whereas if you compared them like ... Alan's the one who was sitting. He'll be slumped and: Ooh, What's she going to do with us now? ... kind of. Whereas Sally's eager and waiting. And smiling.

Here there are a number of significant points. First, a suggested 'scanning process'. It seems that the teacher regards the scanning as a significant enough element of classroom life to make reference to it in interviews. Second, it is an ongoing process that allows the scanning of significant interpersonal boundaries apparently perceived in the types of response exemplified by Sally and Alan. It also spontaneously and quite fortuitously provides a comparative referent in the form of Alan, the deviant case in School B, who once again is confirmed to be beyond a significant boundary. Finally, Sally is seen to be in some respects perhaps as an 'ideal' pupil, and certainly is viewed from a conforming pupil identity

Week Fifteen

The next account indicates the teacher recognizing the underlying normal trans-episodic base which is seen to provide a motivational explanation of how Sally has succeeded in coping at a time of special difficulty:

> Sally lost a lot of school time last term. But it doesn't seem to have particularly bothered her. She had to move into a different house because their house was badly burnt. So she wasn't in school. But that hasn't unduly troubled her. She mixes in again.

Although she has a family setback her secure normal identity maintains normality throughout the phase of domestic and personal difficulty.

As the year continues she appears again to submerge into anonymity, only featuring in interview talk when prompted and in consequence merely confirming the continuing normal base of formulation for this pupil.

Year Three

The pupil moves on to her third year in school and on to another class teacher, Mrs. Wilson. Once again this is a quite unusual occurrence for children in a vertical group. But, as in the previous year, the class teacher moves. On this occasion it is a change of role within the school, moving into the nursery. Later in the pupil's third year, Mrs. Prentiss, who was with the sample cohort as a part-time teacher in the first year of the research takes over the class.

Week Twenty-eight

Her teacher adopts a developmental framework in formulating the pupil over an emergent time-scale:

> I don't think Sally's got on quite as well as I would've expected her to. Perhaps because of the circumstances of that particular group. I think that's a lot of it.

It seems, however, that the pupil's divergence is largely neutralized by invoking the 'circumstances of that particular group' and so leaving the pupil's own (personal) normal base intact. The divergence is perhaps seen largely as episodic (within its temporal or maybe its contextual parameters so long as the circumstances are seen to persist). It seems that the teacher's perception of the pupil's personal base is not affected at all. The normal base is seen to persist through this extended episode.

The teacher then refers to the specific impact of changing teachers on Sally's developing academic ground:

> I think her work's been on a plateau for so long. And now they're just beginning to go forward again really.

In Sally's case the teacher sees 'a plateau'. She formulates the pupil's academic career in developmental or emergent ground terms. This is then probed further:

Interviewer: Why should it have affected Sally?
Teacher: Just perhaps because she hasn't been stretched enough.

This account suggests the teacher is operating a trans-episodic developmental model of how such a pupil might be expected to develop. The teacher is recognizing an aspect of the pupil which was seen to underlie the pupil's present actions and performance and which was not being brought out. This is now probed further:

Interviewer: Are you saying that perhaps Sally's the sort of child who would be missed?
Teacher: Well, she may be in that she's getting on quite nicely anyway. She wouldn't be a lot of bother in the classroom. And she wouldn't demand a lot of teacher's attention. And as her work is at a reasonable level it wouldn't cause anyone a lot of worry. And so it would be allowed to sort of flatten onto a plateau I would think.

This analysis is not only a confirmation of what seems to be submergence but it becomes a feature of the teacher's own accounting system — an explanation for this pupil's suspension 'at a reasonable level . . . and so it would be allowed to sort of flatten onto a plateau'. The probing here comes close to being a leading question. The answer, which is so elaborately developed, may, of course, be no more than a teacher giving a researcher what is apparently the unstated agenda. But the depth of the teacher's reply seems to be far more than might be expected if this were merely the case. The account is taken far beyond such an interpretation.

The pupil finishes the year with a clear recognition of normal ground. So her career in the infant school finishes with Other-role formulation indicating normality.

Week Thirty

Sally would get on all right anywhere I would think.

This same framework of apparent ultra-normality seems to underlie the teacher's comment in the next account, a month later.

Week Thirty-six

Mrs. Prentiss is asked to give a summarizing view of Sally at the end of her time in the infant school:

She's sensible. And reliable. That she's enthusiastic about doing her work. Can certainly be trusted to get on. That she's reached a satisfactory level in all her work.

What could be a clearer statement of normal ground to end her infant career! Additionally, it is made by a teacher whose knowledge of the pupil extends back to her first year and so perhaps is operating from an underlying 'deep structure' of identity extending over three years. This may perhaps be an additional validation of the assumption in this research that for much of her school career Sally was viewed as an ultra-normal or 'average' pupil.

Year Four

The pupil and her cohort group now move into the next phase of schooling: 'the juniors'. There is an amalgamation of junior and infant schools to produce an all-through primary at the very point of this cohort's transfer. 'Spatially' and 'organizationally' the children remain in the same classroom area or workbase which most of them have occupied for the last three years. They are given a new teacher, Miss Tait, who is new both to the school and the profession.

Initial Processes of Emergence

The year begins with Miss Tait perceiving Sally as a normal pupil in much the same way as previously noted with other teachers. Consequently, the details are omitted here so as to avoid repetition for the reader. Sally is first identified as a conforming pupil, contrasted against Alan the deviant pupil, and even identified as 'about the middle' in the rate at which she 'sits up straight' when the class is requested to do so.

As the teacher is questioned about the pupil being 'in the middle' at 'sitting up straight' there are indications of both divergence and normality. There is apparently a continuing ambiguity or figure-ground tension:

Interviewer: About the middle?
Teacher: She sort of drifted along a bit. It's usually 'cause she's talking. I don't think she hears necessarily the first time. She will do it.

There seems to be a possible neutralization by invoking a non-deviant episodic motive: 'it's usually 'cause I don't think she hears necessarily the first time'. So normal ground is seen to underlie her apparent divergence. Additionally, there is an intra-episodic recognition of normality within the episode — a phenomenon likely to emerge before it is through: 'she will do it'. Normality can be relied upon to emerge within the episode. It seems that the teacher operates an intra-episodic emergent framework of normality.

The Appearance of Ground in the Interpretation of Classroom Episodes

Week Four

The next account is an academic formulation. It seems the pupil is being interpreted within a normal framework as the teacher indicates Sally's allocation to an activity group:

> In Green group. She could be in Blue group more or less. So I'll probably move her. Because I wasn't sure about her at first 'cause I didn't think I knew her well enough. Although she's quite capable of writing she didn't seem to do a great deal ...

This seems very significant. The academic formulation here suggests the pupil may be viewed as a possible 'ideal' in terms of 'capability' but in behavioural output she is less than 'ideal'. So the person formulation seems to be quite critical at this point. It is what the teacher bases classroom grouping on: not upon segmental academic identity which might be above average but on the more moderate underlying normal motivational reservoir!

It seems Sally is viewed within a normal framework:
'Sally is Green drifting into Blue. She's sort of going turquoise at the moment'. This normal formulation is used to interpret the grouping system with some 'intelligent' flexibility:

> I've also given Sally [the odd exercise] as well [as the Blue group]. Not the other Greens. Just Sally at the moment. Partly because she tends to work with Michelle who is Blue group. And she's put a spurt on. So it seems appropriate for her to do that really. And she's managed it.

Sally is seen as perhaps 'average' but oriented towards the 'ideal'. She is differentiated from the other more average Greens by the teacher and attached to the Blues. In certain respects Sally is perhaps seen to be diverging positively in the direction of the ideal 'tail' of the normal distribution of pupils.

The next observation is in response to a video tape allowing entry into some 'live' classroom episodes. An incident interpreted by Miss Tait seems to be one of some divergence:

> She'd been carrying on a conversation as to the effect of: You get here ... there ... and everywhere!

The apparent motivational base operated by the teacher in the interpretation of this episode is task and pupil-role related and therefore any potential divergence is possibly neutralized. The teacher is able to supply a motive from a normal identity as ground and introduce it as a likely interpretation of the episode (in which it was not possible, because of the position of the microphone, to hear what the pupil said). The ground, then, provides the teacher with a base from which to fill in the likely meanings of a classroom episode.

As the video action sequence continues, Sally is next seen to embark upon a deviant episode:

> There's Sally having a quick sulk. I hoiked her out of the line for making too much noise. That was her voice. Yes, always shouting. That was a quick flounce. But soon over. She doesn't bear a grudge. She bounces straight back!! I don't think she can control it. But it doesn't stop you, every so often having to take measures.

Here is an episodic instance of segmental divergence of Sally having a quick sulk. The teacher reacts to it with a segmental ground-based strategy: 'I hoiked her out of the line for making too much noise'. She obviously sees it as no more than a typical episodic deviation. It seems that the deviance here is viewed as an instance of rule-breaking. The pupil has overstepped the line (too much noise), and the teacher brings to the situation, as a basis for formulating her strategy, the knowledge of the pupil's trans-episodic Other-role. For the teacher the incident is interpreted from an enduring segmental deviant ground:[1] 'always shouting'. It has trans-episodic connections or continuities or continuities then.

However, the broader trans-episodic base also provides some neutralization of the incident. The motivational reservoir which the teacher draws upon is that of the normal pupil: 'she doesn't bear a grudge'. This is seen to produce a typical intra-episodic sequence: 'she comes back' and 'but soon over'. The normal ground and its motivational reservoir provide predictive and explanatory accounts of intra-episodic sequences of actions.

Week Nine

Here normal ground is being used in a time-sampled observation to interpret an episode of some surprise to Miss Tait:

> When I looked up Sally had gone. So Sally had gone with Michelle who she's been playing with. Unusual that she would go without telling me. They mention going anywhere.

This seems to be viewed as an episodic divergence of a quite moderate kind, resting upon normal ground. It is perhaps an implicit element of the teacher's account here that she regards the fact that 'they mention going anywhere' as a 'normal' (i.e. routine) rather than deviant phenomenon.

Miss Tait continues the account:

> I was quite surprised actually. I was amazed!! Usually Sally will come and announce: Oh I'm just going to so-and-so. And if you say: No you're not! Then she doesn't go.

The teacher has apparently restated the normal (i.e. conformist pupil role) ground.

The incident is further elaborated:

I think she'd interpreted the situation as being: Well, I'm playing a game
so ... She's obviously not in one of these moods where you have to sort
of sit down and ask, sort of thing. This is perhaps typical of her. She
didn't expect that I would be cross. Because of the way she answered
me. With a big grin on her face.

The teacher here seems to suggest she is relying on episodic cues (as figure) to
interpret the situation ('big grin'). It would have been possible, in interpreting the
pupil's action, to have related to either a deviant ground or a normal ground!
Of course, here it is interpreted from a normal baseline. The teacher assumes that
her pupil had interpreted the situation as routine: 'didn't expect that I would be
cross'.

Week Thirty-four

The expected segmental divergence is again remarked on in a video playback
session. It seems the teacher approaches the situation with segmental divergent
ground as an interpretative base for formulation. Consequently, the mismatch
is remarked on as an otherwise 'normal' episode appears when a 'divergent' one
was expected: 'There's Sally. She's not talking then. And Katie seems to be
talking to her'. The expected segmental divergence is anticipated from a
framework of ground and so causes the teacher some episodic surprise once again
when it does not occur.

In fact the teacher switches immediately from the formulation of the taped
episode to reaffirm the very trans-episodic segmental ground which she sees
beyond the 'figure' appearances of it:

Oh, still as noisy as ever!! She's changed very little. It's usually her that
has to be reminded to pipe down a bit or to get on. She still enjoys
working. She's very enthusiastic about everything.

The segmental ground is still retained. And the normal base or ground as pivotal
identity is also reaffirmed as the predominant provider of underlying meanings:
'still enjoys working' and 'very enthusiastic about everything'.

In the final account, the class teacher, through her knowledge of school
records, and in addition to (or perhaps as a consequence of) her access to
school 'culture' (and therefore to the pupil's 'official' status) over her time in this
school, sees the normal core ground plus segmental deviant ground as a continuing base to the pupil's identity:

What I remember she's always been similar. Enthusiastic. Lively. Talker!! Interested in what she's doing. Keen to work. Keen to get on.

In this final summing up by the fourth-year teacher, Miss Tait, and in the last
formulation for Sally, the segmental divergence can again be seen to be dominated by a continuing and predominant Other-role of normality which has accompanied her over her school career.

Note

1 The deviance here is not conventionally episodic since the motive is not entirely drawn from within the boundaries of the episode. It is derived partly from ground even though it is a highly specific segmental formulation. This is segmental rather than episodic deviance. It can be seen that there is a hierarchy of typification. The dominant, core or pivotal category is *normal*. It supersedes the deviance in providing a motivational explanation for the whole episode: its beginning and more especially its ending.

Chapter 16

Episodes in the Emergence of a Normal Career: Dawn (School B)

A second example of a normal pupil in School B is now considered. However, once again it is recognized that many processes appear similar to those already presented for other pupils. Consequently, this case study of a four-year career will be highly selective while still attempting to reflect the longitudinal and emergent character of the pupil career.

Year One

Initial Processes of Emergence

Week Three

The pupil appears to be viewed straightaway as one who is conforming to the framework of classroom expectations:

> She likes singing. She's asked if she can sing in front of the group. And she's always smiling. She's very happy looking. And today she was sitting with her reading book. Quite a difficult reading book. Next to an I3 pretending that she was reading. With her marker. Moving the marker along. I haven't seen the other I1s doing that.

In addition to signs of conformity is the suggestion that Mrs. Thompson, the class teacher, is here operating a framework for formulation within parameters extending across the vertical group. It is possible, as was indicated in the case of Sally, who was also in a vertical group setting, that the parameters of formulation in vertical group situations extend beyond the pupil's own cohort to that of the entire pupil population of the vertical group.

The Appearance of Ground in the Interpretation of Classroom Episodes

It can be seen from this point how a pivotal ground for the pupil is now regarded as established. The following extract from the same interview suggests that the emergent ground, and its associated motivational reservoir, now plays its part in decisions about starting children on reading schemes:

> I'd say Dawn is more or less now [ready to start reading]. But I like to give them as much pre-reading as possible. Lesley is more forward. She wants to perhaps a little more than Dawn. Maybe it's just that Dawn is quieter. But she's pressurizing me. Dawn hasn't, and yet she's able to match certain things. But she hasn't got quite the same pushiness as Lesley has for it just yet. Dawn has [shown signs]. She's shown an interest. But she's still very worried about making a mistake.

It can be seen here how person formulation is used as a basis for teacher decision-making. In terms of 'readiness' it seems Lesley is more positively diverging towards the 'ideal' tail of teacher's construction of pupil distribution. Dawn is perhaps in a more middle position: 'Lesley is more forward ... she wants to perhaps a little more than Dawn.' It is possible that here, when it comes to what seems to be merely an 'academic' categorization, the teacher may actually be reacting to more deep-seated underlying motivational formulations such as 'wants to' rather than to mere narrow 'academic' categories. So it is not just a cognitive formulation of the pupil in question but a *total* person formulation which seems to guide the teacher's actions.

In terms of temperament, too, it seems Dawn displays some of the interaction strategies associated with the submergence of a mid-position normal pupil: 'Dawn's quieter ... she hasn't got quite the same pushiness yet'. It seems the teacher formulated this within a continuing emergent framework: 'She's shown an interest. But she's still very worried about making a mistake'.

It can be seen that the teacher's view of this as a continuing or developing phenomenon ('yet' and 'still' indicate processes of emergence) becomes the basis of her present strategy:

> This is one reason why I wouldn't put her on as well yet because I would hate there to be any failure for her yet. Because I don't think she's able to take that. She's still finding her feet a lot.

Teacher strategy appears to rest upon, and take account of, the framework of person formulation, and especially of its dynamic and emergent processes. It takes particular account of formulating a *total* person and attempts to transpose this by taking the role of the pupil as Other into a future situation in order to predict how the pupil might react to the reading scheme ('I don't think she's able to take that')

Week Twenty-two

After going through the first two terms with an apparently stable, normal identity as pivotal ground, the teacher, Mrs. Gill, now notices some change in the pupil:

> I would say that she has withdrawn quite a lot recently. She doesn't work with other children like she used to then. She tends to be very much on her own.

Faced with apparent changes in the pupil's 'surface' or figure actions the teacher presumably recognizes certain incompatibilities or incongruency with the present established pivotal identity as base. As the teacher continues, it seems that there is now an attempt to explain the divergence in merely episodic terms:

> Her mother a few weeks ago came in and said had I noticed any change in Mary [her sister]. That she was much more aggressive than she was at home towards Dawn. So that could have something to do with it of course. And she's keeping out of her way and keeping out of others'.

The teacher here seems to be making use of typification exchange between herself and the parent to explore the causal structure of what seems to be a mere episodic form of divergence. First, then, the predisposing 'because-of motive' is offered. Her sister's aggression 'could have something to do with it'. Then the pupil's interpersonal response to this is suggested: 'she's keeping out of her way'. It seems the teacher may be making a distinction between the perceived 'structural' parameters of the situation and the perceived *personal* or interpersonal parameters of the phase or episode. Her accounting succeeds in provisionally restoring the normal ground as a deep structure which is temporally disguised (for the duration) by the divergence which proves to be episodic or is seen likely to be: 'could have something to do with it'.

Several other times in her career Dawn is seen to experience a potentially divergent phase. It seems, however, that the stable ground is usually resistant to revision. In each case the divergent phase is suspended or insulated from the normal pivotal ground by recognizing its own separate phasic structure and causal framework.

For example, as the second year begins:

> She's always been a bit of a wanderer. And wandering around. But at the moment she's just coming round into any little corner she can to be by herself. And she hasn't got any confidence at all in her work at the moment. And she did have before.

The teacher's recognition of its phasic framework can be seen in her attempt to explain it and construct a phasically contingent set of strategies:

> I think I'm going to have to give her extra attention. I think it's possibly because of me. We've been very tied up with this Space project this half term. And I think that reflecting on it I probably let her slip through. And she needs a lot of attention. And her sister has gone up into the juniors. So this may be a lot to do with it. That she does need this extra attention.

Here, it seems that the teacher, Mrs. Byrne, sees two elements of causal 'structure' that may account for this divergence and so justify her treatment of it as an episodic phenomenon:

1   the Space project 'probably let her slip through',
2   the pupil's sister having 'gone up into the juniors'.

The teacher's strategy seems to be linked more to the episode's perceived causal 'structure' than to the underlying dispositional ground of the pupil. So for the duration of the phase, the teacher intends to 'give her extra attention'.

Later on in year two another episodic divergence is noted:

The last week or so ... well the last few days, has been very uppity. Highly excitable and could be to do with moving house. She's possibly a little bit uncertain in her new surroundings. It's a flat she's moved into. Perhaps her mother's often saying not to make too much noise. I don't know. But she is certainly an awful lot noisier than she ever was.

The teacher sees the pupil's moving house as apparently providing a causal framework which generates a divergent episode. Obviously, she is seeing it as temporally situated within 'the last few days'. It seems that the teacher's operation of a normal trans-episodic base throughout this episode results in her seeking its causal structure within its own episodic parameters. It is seen to relate to the 'moving house'. This gives it both *causal* and *temporal* structure together, seemingly viewed as potentially unthreatening to the established normal ground.

After the divergent phase occurring as the second year of Dawn's career opens, when her sister moves up into the juniors, it seems the phase can be seen to have now come to an end as Mrs. Byrne indicates once again a pupil conforming to the classroom world:

She stands out because she's so quiet. And she's so satisfied with her own company. And yet at the same time she is well-liked by other children. And she gets on well with other children herself.

The teacher sees the pupil as 'so quiet', a phenomenon which, if viewed from the deviant base of Alan, would no doubt be seen as abnormality and a cause for concern. But a striking point here is the power of the normal ground to provide a normal base to this formulation of Dawn. It transforms it. The motivational base is seen to be quite normal:

'she's so satisfied with her own company',
'she's well-liked',
'gets on with other children'.

It seems all is seen to be quite normal. There is now nothing to cause concern to the teacher.

Week Twenty

Later in year two the pupil experiences a deviant incident. Mrs. Byrne recounts an episode which occurred that morning:

Something happened today. I've never noticed her do anything like this before. She'd had her milk in the morning. And I happened to walk past. And I saw her starting another bottle. And I said: I thought you'd

had your milk this morning? And she said: Yes. I have ... and put it
down. But there was no attempt to cover up anything. Straightaway she
admitted. And I really appreciate that in her. She loves milk. She loves
food.

The teacher on this occasion was faced with a potentially deviant incident here as
Dawn engages in an act of rule-breaking. Although the teacher's account indicates it is viewed as a rule-breaking incident there is still a suggestion of the
presence of an underlying normal identity as dispositional ground. It seems to be
implicit as the teacher attempts to neutralize the incident: 'I've never noticed her
do anything like this before.' This appears to set a framework of normal trans-
episodic identity as ground against which the incident is to be interpreted. It
perhaps proves to be an insignificant incident when viewed against a prevailing
backcloth of normal ground.

More important, however, is how the incident is seen to unfold within the
emergent *intra*-episodic framework. The teacher sees normal ground (and its
motivational reservoir) underlying the *manner* in which the pupil responds to the
investigation of the incident:

'There was no attempt to cover anything up',
'Straightaway she admitted',
'I really appreciate that in her'.

It seems that the teacher sees normal ground operating beneath all this. She is not
perceiving the event as a mere surface *figure* but is apparently recognizing a more
dominant underlying phenomenon of *ground*. Then almost as an afterthought
adds a further neutralizing element: 'She loves milk. She loves food.' It seems
again that Dawn's teacher is recognizing an absence of malicious motives (that
would apparently operate in the case of deviant abnormal ground) in the episode
and suggesting instead what may perhaps be viewed as a 'normal' framework of
motives.

On those rare occasions when Dawn encounters a deviant incident the
normal ground is used to interpret her actions and to provide a normal baseline
upon which to construct a motivational framework. This can be seen again in her
fourth year:

She got into trouble this morning. Not off me either. She's working
quite well. As usual. There's her and a couple of her little buddies had
gone over this area here to work. Now I can't see them from where I am
if they go over there. But being three Red Group that I would normally
have thought: Well fair enough.

Again, it seems the deviation is episodic only, since the teacher appears to
present the normal trans-episodic ground here as a framework against which the
divergent episode is to be viewed. Apparently treating it as a merely episodic
figure and as though the more significant reality to take account of was the
trans-episodic ground. The incident is further elaborated:

Apparently, one of them, who's a bit silly at times, has been encouraging everybody to have a little look around. So they got told off. So she's going to have to do a little bit of work for me this afternoon. I wouldn't imagine that she was actually doing a lot to contribute towards it. But she's been sitting having a good laugh at it. And she'd have got involved with the other two!

The deviant incident here is seen to have a causal structure in which another pupil is seen to have been a likely influence: 'one of them, who's a bit silly at times, had been encouraging everybody to have a little look around'. The role of Dawn in the divergent episode is seen to have been marginal.[1] This is perhaps a process of neutralization by recognizing Other as occupying a role of episodic marginality.

Here, in the recounting of this episode, the account has jumped forward to examine another instance of deviance which could be viewed as having equivalence with the earlier one in year two. We now return to the proper temporal sequence of the pupil's career.

The longitudinal account is now picked up again in the third year.

Week Ten

Dawn on a number of occasions is selected by Mrs. Wilson as a 'sensible' pupil for certain classroom purposes. It seems to be a further indication of normal ground in use and especially of an ultra-normal position within the pupil distribution:

Interviewer: I wondered why you'd picked on Dawn
Teacher: Because I thought that she would be able to be ... she'd be sensible enough.

Here is a recurrence of the term 'sensible' which has often appeared in relation to the pivotal ground of the normal, and especially ultra-normal, pupil. It suggests that the pupil is continuing to be viewed as a typical normal. More significantly it actually becomes the basis of the teacher's method for selecting a pupil in this episode as one who would be 'sensible enough'.

However, the outcome is somewhat divergent:

But she wasn't. She was putting the hoops over. The idea is for her just to hold the hoop so that there's something red. But she copied other children. Now that is unusual for her. She often isn't affected by outside influences. I don't know. She must've been quite giddy and off balance.

Clearly, the divergence here is given an episodic interpretation: 'must've been quite giddy and off balance'. So the teacher preserves a normal ground as pivotal identity. Instead, she hypothesizes an episodic theme to account for the divergence.

This method of interpretation is further probed as the interview continues to explore the basis of the teacher's selecting the pupil. It reveals an underlying relationship with ground structure:

> Interviewer: You chose her because you thought she'd be sensible?
>
> Teacher: Yes. Not sensible. But I thought she wouldn't be playing around with them and jumping in and out of them. That she'd hold it and children go to her. I was surprised by that ... [she was influenced by] the atmosphere as well. If you remember I said that the children were *very* high that day. And I think it was just an atmosphere that she tuned into.

Again, it seems that the teacher adopts a normal ground in operation as the basis of the selection of this pupil. Therefore there is surprise at the resulting divergence. However, she affirms very strongly the episodic theme rather than the dispositional ground as the underlying structure of the event:

> The children were *very* high that day. And I think it was just an atmosphere she tuned into.

The parameters of the situation (as episode) are invoked to interpret and account for the course of this event. The pupil's personal normal identity as ground is apparently preserved.

On this occasion the pupil appears to have been selected at least in part as a 'sensible' pupil but the episode proved to be divergent. On a later occasion, in year four, a similar selection occurs quite independently by a different teacher, Miss Tait, but on this occasion it results in a more predictable and ground-congruent episode:

> She's been doing jobs all morning. Because she's *reasonably* sensible. So she's been sort of going to places like upstairs in the library. And putting books back that we were finding.

The teacher's action towards the pupil (teacher strategy) is based upon a normal ground of 'reasonably sensible'. It is not clear, of course, how the teacher's use of 'sensible' corresponds with the category of 'normal' pupil in general or with ultra-normal category in particular. There is, perhaps, an implication that the term 'sensible' might apply to all pupils diverging positively within the pupil distribution towards the 'ideal'. If so, then the ultra-normal would perhaps be a critical boundary as it would be the first position to which the term 'sensible' could be applied in moving from the deviant to the ideal or positive tail of the distribution. This definition is apparent as the teacher, Miss Tait, next identifies the critical boundary or border line between the 'sensible' and the 'non-sensible':

> With some of them, if you send them on a job, and they realize when they get there they've either forgotten, or they're not sure what to do, they'll just plonk the thing down and walk off. Whereas Dawn would ask somebody around. She wouldn't just leave it and wander back to me. So she's sensible in that way.

Here is the boundary between the 'sensible' type' who 'would ask somebody around' (normal-ideal motive) while the non-sensible type would 'just plonk it down' (divergent motive).

Having moved into the fourth year to illustrate a second occasion in which the use of the category 'sensible' was apparent, it is appropriate now to return to the longitudinal presentation of this pupil's career and follow the year four processes of emergence and maintenance over their course.

Year Four

Initial Processes of Emergence

Week One

In the first week the new teacher, Miss Tait, appears to have adopted normal ground for this pupil. The following account is of a 'normal' pupil who can be relied upon to operate within normal role-identity parameters:

> Dawn's about a middle sort of person. I think she could work in a reasonably sort of average group of about five ... six children. She'd be all right.

The teacher seems to be forming a view of Dawn as a 'middle' category of pupil. The formulation here is quite tentative:

> 'about a middle sort',
> 'I think she could work in a reasonably sort of average group ...'

This tentativeness is quite consistent with the early exploratory work of teachers in constructing provisional formulations of pupils.

The reference to pupil as a 'middle' or 'average' person is then probed:

Interviewer: Average? Middle sort of person?
Teacher: They're the children who're coping more or less with the work I would expect from that age level. They seem to be coping quite easily with what I call sort of mid ... You always get a middle sort of level in your class. And then you get them rising above and dropping below. And they're about there. They're sort of children who you work steadily with and improve steadily with.

— a clear account of a normal pupil. In this case it suggests the teacher's notion of interpersonal relativity in a pupil distribution. It also recognizes a 'level' of work, a pace of work ('work steadily') and a developmental dimension of Other role ('improve steadily'). This is quite a clear and sophisticated account of the many facets of Other role implicit in the teacher's apparent use of 'normal' ground in the formulation of pupils.

The Appearance of Ground in the Interpretation of Classroom Episodes

As the account continues there is once again an indication of the fusion of academic and dispositional ground. The interview attempts to probe the basis of the teacher's allocation of Dawn to a pupil group:

> Interviewer: A middle sort of person? Does this mean that you had some difficulty in deciding whether she should be a Red or a Green?
>
> Teacher: Yes. I did at first. I think I was expecting more of her than she's capable of doing. Once I found out what level she was on ... she's quite capable of doing the work at her level. I think I was pushing too high at first.

The inter-dependence of academic and personal ground is then indicated:

> I think she definitely needs to be in Red group. Because of her attitude. I know that I can't leave her as much ... as I would.... And I've found now that talking to her a little bit more she's coming on quite nicely. So she's not doing too badly.

It seems that it is 'attitude' rather than academic 'ability' which places the pupil in her group (a reminder then of how 'academic' and 'personal' decisions are often dependent on pivotal ground as base). The teacher is perhaps here indicating the motives presumed to operate as a trans-episodic pupil ground: 'I know that I can't leave her as much ... as I would.' It seems that the teacher has evolved a strategy for maintaining what she perhaps regards as acceptable ('not doing too badly') development: 'I've found now that taking her to one side she's coming on quite nicely'.

Additionally, in both these formulations of motive and strategy, there is a *temporal* and *emergent* dimension. The teacher has come to a realization, after some exploration or testing of the pupil in context, and now discovers an appropriate strategy and its base: 'I know now' and 'I've found now' The social construction of Dawn seems to be a matter of *emerging* ground over time.

Week Sixteen

In the second term of the fourth year there are signs of the submergence that has continued to appear with such ultra-normal pupils as Dawn:

> Dawn seems to be running true to form. Getting on quite nicely. She's about what I would consider.... Doing quite well really. I don't worry too much about her. She's OK.

This comment is an indication of a submergent ultra-normal pupil: 'I don't worry too much about her'. The same view is extended as the account continues:

She always seems fairly quiet to me. She doesn't really stand out. Because you know she's not extrovert in any way. You don't seem to notice her very much somehow. She sort of fades into the background because ... you know there's nothing peculiar about her. Or nothing absolutely brilliant about her. She seems very ordinary in a way. Normal.

There perhaps could hardly be a more spontaneous and unsolicited 'validation' of the concept 'submergence'. The teacher actually uses the concept of 'background': 'She sort of fades into the background'.

The pupil is obviously to be recognized as an ultra-normal type. There is 'nothing absolutely brilliant about her'. The teacher's final summing up refers to the pupil as 'very ordinary' and 'normal'.

Week Thirty-five

As the year comes to a close the headteacher, Mrs. Strang, who has known the pupil over the four-year period, reviews her career:

Dawn is a quiet girl. I think there would be many instances for her to recede into the background.

This statement is an account, perhaps, of a teacher's own recognition of possible processes of submergence. Yet this may of course be a reference to some notion of 'personality' rather than a recognition of the processes of anonymity submergence that have often featured in this analysis.

As Mrs. Strang continues she relates this formulation of pupil to notions of types of school 'organization':

I think if Dawn had gone into a sort of organization where there was a formal timetable and work was structured, and at certain times she'd been expected to do maths, and at another time had been given a title that she had to write about, I think she would have found that difficult. But she's able to offer talents in a variety of ways.

The headteacher is claiming that a school organization and culture that focuses on *individualized* person perception, curriculum organization and pedagogy allows Dawn to present 'talents in a variety of ways'. The ground-based formulations that may encourage pupils to 'recede into the background' are discouraged by *this* school's organization and ideology. To present this account, the teacher must be relying upon a *base* and its motivational reservoir, the baseline of a normal pupil. In a more traditional school it would have led to excessive submergence. Perhaps the headteacher is presuming that the ultra-normal pupil in a 'traditional' organization would never have achieved the individualization of identity so highly valued in her own version of school ideology, a school ideology that is seen to allow Dawn to 'offer talents in a variety of ways' even as an ultra-normal and 'quiet' pupil.

Mrs. Strang concludes the formulation:

She's creative and is able to support certain activities with the other things that she's good at. And I think that at the end of it comes out making a contribution that makes her noticed.

Mrs. Strang seems to be using an overt teacher strategy to avoid *anonymity*, in this case either in respect of being an ultra-normal or even as a 'quiet' pupil. Certainly there is nothing in this final formulation to indicate a concern for a 'quiet' pupil, only of 'making her noticed.' The teacher is clearly formulating against a presumed normal ground that is recognized to be likely to generate anonymity of identity. In effect, the pupil is perhaps recognized to be a critical case for the particular 'ideology' and 'culture' of the school. The ultra-normal pupil perhaps always presents a continuing ideological challenge to child-centred schools. The headteacher's final comment suggests a strategy oriented to the avoidance of pupil anonymity with a form of social organization which will allow her to make 'a contribution that makes her noticed'.

Additionally, of course, the ongoing formulatory time-scale can be seen in the teacher's operating a developmental framework. A temporal or emergent framework is used in making reference to a school organization that will allow pupil identity to *emerge* over *time* and so 'at the end of it' to come out 'making a contribution'. This is the final summing up, in fact, of the highly *participatory* school 'culture', the very 'culture' from which an extreme divergence in the deviant case of the pupil Alan, causes the school such concern.

Note

1 Dawn's marginal role is perhaps equivalent to the phenomenon of 'drift' (Matza, 1964). It also illustrates common sense theories of 'contagion' and of situational 'triggers' in teacher thinking.

Chapter 17

Social Processes in Primary Schools:
Normality and Deviation

This research has sought to identify the parameters which operate in the course of teachers' formulation of pupils, particularly over the early years of schooling. The present investigation has suggested that teachers operate a form of pupil differentiation which might be represented diagrammatically as a 'normal distribution' or Gaussian curve extending from a 'deviant' negative pole to an 'ideal' positive pole and with the majority of pupils occupying the main section of the curve around a mode point of normality. Certain pupils are apparently seen to personify the *mode* position and are referred to overtly by teachers in the course of interviews as 'average' or 'normal' pupils. In the present research their unique modal position has been referred to in using the concept 'ultra-normal'. The 'norm' position occupied by such pupils seems to operate as a significant reference point in relation to which teachers locate and formulate all other pupils in a comparative process — a strategy that might for simplicity be termed Norm-matching, apparently a different framework to the process of formulation suggested by Becker (1952). Indeed, whereas the teachers studied by Becker seemed to operate an 'ideal' pupil as the yardstick of classroom life, rather than the average, it seems in the present research settings that the average pupil occupies a position which is viewed as the 'model' pupil of classroom life. The view was expressed by a teacher in referring to Sally, one of the 'normal' pupils from School B:

> She's sort of a model child really. If you could have a model child! She's my idea of a model child. She's got the enthusiasm but she's not pushy. She's not too quiet. She's just average at everything. I mean she's not brilliantly clever. And she's not terribly poor. She's my ideal model child really. If I could build a model child!!

This view suggests almost a relocation of the goals of classroom life away from the positively divergent 'ideal' pupil, as though, perhaps, to the more attainable mid-position 'normal' or 'average' pupil as the 'model'. (A similar view is suggested by Baudelot and Establet, 1977, but arguing that the 'middle class' child is the yardstick).

In qualitative research of this sort, although it is not the intention to produce 'findings' generalizable to other cases, the problem of within-case generalization nevertheless becomes an issue. In the case of the two deviant pupils selected as critical cases for scrutiny in this research there was never any reason to doubt their correspondence to the sociological categories of 'deviance'. The disruption they presented to teachers and their disturbance to classroom life in general was empirical verification of their status as deviants. Although the nature of deviation from each of the social settings was different in each of the two cases, the extreme concern shown for each pupil as a problematic case and the reputation of each pupil throughout the entire school 'community' was sufficient evidence of a 'societal reaction' to deviation. Their position within the 'taken-for-granted' of the school was treated as an empirical justification for regarding these pupils as deviant cases. They were recognized as such in 'what everyone knows'. Their deviant reputations seemed to extend out even beyond the 'community' of teachers to others in the social world of the school setting — to school ancillary staff, to the pupils, and (in one of the cases) to many of the parents.

In the case of the 'normal' pupils, the extent to which it has been valid to regard the 'normal' or 'average' pupils as representing a shared set of underlying meanings is perhaps more problematical. It cannot be assumed that there was a common set of meanings operated by teachers across the two schools, or even by different teachers within the same school in their use of such formulation categories as 'normal' or 'average'. It was not the concern of this research to unravel the meanings of such terms within the educational world but merely to explore their situated use by teachers within the particular social settings in which they occurred. Indeed, the account presented here examines each case not only as an embedded set of meanings within the social setting of a particular school, but also within its situated temporal context, recognizing that such meanings are not necessarily constant over time but may have an emergent and perhaps continually evolving usage over the course of a pupil's career. However, the frequent occurrence within the careers of the normal cases of successive teachers using terms such as 'average' or 'normal' in reference to the same pupil, does increase grounds for suspecting a set of common meanings within the same inter-subjective world of school 'culture'.

The category 'sensible' has often been applied by teachers to the 'normal' pupils in this sample. This use suggests that normal pupils might, in general, be being viewed as 'sensible', perhaps a polar opposite type to that of deviant pupils. Although the term 'sensible' is sometimes also applied to pupils not categorized as 'average' it seems to occur more frequently and more consistently in making reference to those children referred to, and seen clearly to be, 'normal'. One interpretation of this might be that the 'ultra-normal' in conforming to many of the teachers' expectations of classroom life (as a 'model' child) is viewed as 'sensible' in not being prone to either the negative or positive divergent extremes of action typical of the 'deviant' or even the 'ideal' pupil of Becker's (1952) teachers. Another interpretation may be that in a continuous distribution, the ultra-normal or mode pupil is the first point along a continuum extending from 'deviant' to 'sensible' in which the ultra-normal is the boundary point beyond which all pupils are seen as 'sensible'. The first point perhaps at which the category 'sensible' begins to apply across the positive pole of the distribution.

This book set out to uncover some of the basic social processes of primary classrooms. It has been found that there are fundamental distinctions operating between '*normal*' and '*abnormal*' pupils and, in respect of the *ongoing* processes of classroom life, a distinction between the *episodic* and the *trans-episodic* dimensions of their interpretation. A distinction was suggested earlier between two categories of deviance as evident in the postulated *pathological* and *divergent* models for formulating pupils. However, in the examination of cases as the analysis proceeded it has become apparent that the divergent category of deviance has no long-term career implications for pupils. Such forms of negative divergence can be experienced by both 'normal' and 'deviant' pupils. These divergent occurrences are usually perceived in themselves as short-lived, temporary and without a trans-episodic ground base. Such divergence is equally congruent with a 'normal' as with a 'deviant' career and the trans-episodic baseline associated with either identity. The critical boundary of formulation is that which invokes the pathological model and its trans-episodic base. It can 'operate' as formulatory ground beneath an episode of perceived deviance, perceived divergence or even of perceived normality. The interpretation of acts at both 'deep' and 'surface' levels is critical. This interpretive work and its practical 'accomplishment' by teachers is a fundamental process of classroom life. It is the interpretation of *present* episodes as representing surface (or figure) elements of reality and the recognition of their *continuities* or *discontinuities* with ongoing trans-episodic (or ground) forms that seems to provide a 'mechanism' by which pupil careers are constructed — a process indeed of 'accomplishment'! It is the teachers' *active* interpretation of the 'surface' reality and what is seen to be its relationship with a 'deeper' structure that is the critical process.

This investigation reveals that in teachers' interpretation of classroom reality two opposing social processes are perceived. The processes of convergence towards, and of divergence away from, conformity to classroom norms.[1] Since the 'normal' or 'average' pupil seems to be a critical reference point in the construction of classroom reality then the social processes of convergence and divergence may perhaps themselves operate directly in relation to the normal pupil, as the significant reference point in the social construction of identities for children in primary schools. Pupils appear to be constructed as though their actions may be interpreted as positively or negatively oriented in relation to a notional 'norm'. In this way the construct 'normal' or 'average' is not a mere descriptive category within something akin to a normal distribution but it becomes a critical point for teachers' construction of reality and classroom dealings. A significant boundary or yardstick — the very notion of sociological norm which conveys not only the notion of patterns of behaviour commonly occurring within a given population but also the prescriptive implications conveyed in traditional notions of 'norm' as socially 'required' conduct (Durkheim, 1933, p. 4). As the classroom action or behaviour of a pupil is oriented towards the sociological norm it can be regarded as *convergent*, while its negative divergence from the 'norm' can be termed *divergent*. The use of 'norm' in this way operates as a *process* rather than as the *structural* phenomenon to be found in earlier usage in the literature of sociology (Parsons, 1966, p. 18). Durkheim's own discussion of norms has quite properly given greater emphasis to norms as social processes (pp. 102–3). In this research, the major structural elements are apparent in the notion of 'surface' and 'deep' structure, when episodic actions are seen as in continuity or discontinuity with trans-episodic ground.

It has become clear in this investigation that an additional social process is in operation with those pupils who occupy a mode position as 'average' or 'normal' types. It seems that pupils whose convergence reaches a point of ultra-conformity with classroom 'norms', experience processes of extreme anonymity that are here termed '*submergence*'. Conformity to either such a degree, or to such a continued extent, seems to result in processes of anonymization in which the pupil is experienced largely in trans-episodic and highly anonymized ground terms. Recognizing the two significant classroom processes already referred to as divergence and convergence, then, submergence may perhaps be regarded as a process of further convergence. So, as pupil actions or behaviours become convergent to the extent of ultra-conformity then the perception or formulation by teachers appears to move into the ultra-anonymity of type-construction in submergence. Such processes of submergence appear to be unique to those pupils occupying the position of ultra-normal or 'average' pupils.

This investigation has distinguished a number of *critical boundaries* operating in classroom life:

1 between deviant and normal pupils,
2 between episodic and trans-episodic constructions of reality,
3 between figure and ground,
4 between 'deep' and 'surface' structure.

Additionally, it has recognized *fundamental processes* of:

1 divergence
2 convergence
3 submergence

The 'average' or 'ultra-normal' pupils might then be viewed as an additional critical boundary point as they appear to personify both the sociological 'norm' of classroom life and the point at which convergence becomes accelerated or transformed into submergence.

This book has sought to make a contribution to the field of sociology of education by developing a framework for understanding the processes by which pupils are formulated by teachers in the ongoing processes of classroom life. The attempt to explore this issue has generated three sets of concerns which might be followed by future researchers and which have been examined here in the particular social setting of two primary schools as the pupil careers of a specific cohort of children in each school began to emerge.

1 It has attempted to explore a framework for understanding Other formulation as a *holistic* process in classroom life rather than offering a separate account of either 'deviant' typification (Hargreaves, 1975) or of 'academic' typification which is implicit in the literature of self-fulfilling prophecies and teacher expectations (Rosenthal and Jacobson, 1968; Brophy and Good, 1974) and in many case study accounts of secondary schooling (Keddie, 1971; Woods, 1979; Ball, 1981). It seeks to examine Other-formulation in its totality and so to consider processes by which both 'academic' and 'deviant' typification proceed as a constituent element in a more dominant process of total person formulation. It therefore attempts to relocate sociological interest in the fields of both

'academic' and 'deviant' typification within a more appropriate framework of Self-Other interaction and person formulation.

2 This exploration of processes of formulation has suggested that the phenomenon of deviance in primary schools at least may be more appropriately viewed from a framework of Other-formulation and especially in a recognition of, and acknowledgment of distinctions between, episodic and trans-episodic Other-roles. That is by formulating a social actor within a framework of *role* rather than the framework of *rule* (and rule-transgression) more widely used in sociological research. It suggests that (at least perhaps in primary schools) rule-transgression takes inadequate phenomenological account of the interpretative standpoint adopted by teachers themselves as they continue their ongoing relations with pupils in school and classroom contexts.

3 Finally, this investigation has sought to take proper account of emergent properties in the temporality of teacher-pupil interaction by examining a range of temporal processes. It has focused upon:
—longitudinal monitoring of pupils over a time-scale which takes account of the long-term nature of teacher-pupil relationships (more usually found in primary schools);
— the ongoing dynamics of pupil formulation, by examining these interpersonal processes as they are constructed and revealed in ongoing moments of emergence and continuity in classroom life, and so attempts to recognize 'the evolutionary and developmental nature of teacher-pupil relations in the classroom setting' (Ball, 1980, p. 143) rather than adopting the traditional frameworks which have tended 'to treat and portray classroom relationships as fixed and static patterns of interaction' even when used by researchers within the ethnographic paradigm.

Ironically, the adoption of a phenomenological standpoint in conducting this research has uncovered a perspective on classrooms not dissimilar from some earlier sociological accounts of education that the newer perspectives helped to displace. The pre-eminence of social 'norms' in the social world of schools and classrooms is clear in this ethnographic account of some of the significant social processes to be found in primary schools. It seems that a normative view of the social world persists in teachers' construction of reality.

Note

1 This convergence and divergence is widely recognized as a recurring or fundamental feature of all forms of social organization (Erikson, 1966). Early theories of sociology have taken it for granted. It emerges 'naturalistically' at a micro-level as a classroom concern of the teachers in this study. However, the norm is personified in *personal* rather than *rule* terms. The norm is statable in terms of the typical actions of a normal pupil. A similar view of norms is found in the work of Baudelot and Establet (1977).

References

BALL, S.J. (1978) *Processes of Comprehensive Schools*, Unpublished PhD thesis, University of Sussex.

BALL, S.J. (1980) 'Initial encounters in the classroom and the process of establishment', in WOODS, P., *Pupil Strategies*, Beckenham, Croom Helm.

BALL, S.J. (1981) *Beachside Comprehensive*, Cambridge, England, Cambridge University Press.

BARKER-LUNN, J.C. (1970) *Streaming in the Primary School*, Windsor, NFER.

BARTON, L. and MEIGHAN, R. (1978) *Sociological Interpretations of Schooling and Classrooms*, Driffield, Nafferton.

BARTON, L. and MEIGHAN, R. (1979) *Schools, Pupils and Deviance*, Driffield, Nafferton.

BARTON, L. and WALKER, S. (1981) *Schools, Teachers and Teaching*, London, Falmer Press.

BAUDELOT, C. and ESTABLET, R. (1977) 'What is a normal pupil?' in GLEESON, D. (Ed.) *Identity and Structure*, Driffield, Nafferton.

BECKER, H.S. (1952) 'Social class variations in pupil-teacher relationships', *Journal of Educational Sociology*, **25**, pp. 451–65.

BECKER, H.S. (1963) *Outsiders: Studies in the Sociology of Deviance*, New York, Free Press.

BENNETT, S.N. (1976) *Teaching Styles and Pupil Progress*, London, Open Books.

BERKOWITZ, L. (Ed.) (1965) *Advances in Experimental Social Psychology*, **2**, New York, Academic Press.

BERGER, P. and LUCKMANN, T. (1971) *The Social Construction of Reality*, Harmondsworth, Penguin.

BERLAK, H. and BERLAK, A. (1981) *Dilemmas of Schooling: Teaching and Social Change*, London, Methuen.

BERNSTEIN, B. (1971) *Class, Codes and Control, Vol. 1: Theoretical Studies Towards a Sociology of Language*, London, Routledge and Kegan Paul.

BIRD, C. (1980) 'Deviant labelling in school: The pupil's perspective' in WOODS, P. (1980) *Pupil Strategies*, Beckenham, Croom Helm.

BLUM, A. and McHUGH, P. (1971) 'The social ascription of motives', *American Sociological Review*, **36**, pp. 98–109.

BLUMER, H. (1962) 'Society as symbolic interaction', in ROSE, A.M. (Ed.) *Human Behaviour and Social Processes*, London, Routledge and Kegan Paul.

BLUMER, H. (1965) 'Sociological implications of the thought of George Herbert Mead', in COSIN, B. (1971) *School and Society*, London, Routledge and Kegan Paul.

BROPHY, J.E. and GOOD, T.L. (1974) *Teacher-Student Relationships*, London, Holt, Rinehart and Winston.

BURGESS, R.G. (1982) *Field Research: A Sourcebook and Field Manual*, London, George Allan and Unwin.
BURGESS, R.G. (1983) *Experiencing Comprehensive Education*, London, Methuen.
BURGESS, R.G. (Ed.) (1985) *Field Methods in the Study of Education*, London, Falmer Press.
CHOMSKY, N. (1957) *Syntactic Structures*, The Hague, Mouton and Co.
CHOMSKY, N. (1968) *Language and Mind*, New York, Harcourt Brace Jovanovich.
CICOUREL, A.V. (1964) *Method and Measurement in Sociology*, Oxford, Free Press.
CICOUREL, A.V. (1972) 'Basic and normative rules in the negotiation of status and role', in SUDNOW, D. *Studies in Social Interaction*, New York, Free Press.
CICOUREL, A.V. (Ed.) (1974) *Language Use and School Performance*, New York, Academic Press.
CICOUREL, A.V. and KITSUSE, J.I. (1963) *The Educational Decision-Makers*, Indianapolis, Bobbs-Merrill.
CLARRICOATES, K. (1980) 'The importance of being Ernest ... Emma ... Tom ... Jane: The perception and categorisation of gender conformity and gender deviation in primary schools', in DEEM, R. *Schooling for Women's Work*, London, Routledge and Kegan Paul.
COSIN, B. (1971) *School and Society*, London, Routledge and Kegan Paul.
COULSON, M. (1972) 'Role: A redundant concept in sociology?' in JACKSON, J.A. (Ed.) *Role: Sociological Studies No. 4*, Cambridge, England, Cambridge University Press.
CRAFT, M., RAYNOR, J. and COHEN, L. (1980) *Linking Home and School*, London, Harper and Row.
DAVIE, R., BUTLER, N.R. and GOLDSTEIN, H. (1972) *From Birth to Seven*, London, Longman.
DAVIES, L., (1984) *Pupil Power: Deviance and Gender in School*, London, Falmer Press.
DEEM, R. (1980) *Schooling for Women's Work*, London, Routledge and Kegan Paul.
DELAMONT, S. (1976) *Interaction in the Classroom*, London, Methuen.
DELAMONT, S. (1978) 'Sociology and the classroom', in BARTON, L. and MEIGHAN, R., *Sociological Interpretations of Schooling and Classrooms*, Driffield, Nafferton.
DENZIN, N.K. (1970) *The Research Act in Sociology*, London, Butterworth.
DOUGLAS, J.D. (1971) 'Understanding everyday life', in DOUGLAS, J.D. (Ed.) *'Understanding Everyday Life*, London, Routledge and Kegan Paul.
DOUGLAS, J.D. (Ed.) (1971) *Understanding Everyday Life*, London, Routledge and Kegan Paul.
DOUGLAS, J.W.B. (1964) *The Home and the School*, London, MacGibbon and Kee.
DOUGLAS, J.W.B., ROSS, J.M. and SIMPSON, H.R. (1968) *All Our Future*, London, Peter Davies.
DOWNES, D. and ROCK, P. (Eds) (1979) *Deviant Interpretations*, Oxford, Martin Robertson.
DURKHEIM, E. (1933) *The Division of Labour in Society*, London, Collier-Macmillan.
DURKHEIM, E. (1953) *Society and Philosophy*, London, Cohen and West.
EDWARDS, A.D. (1980) 'Patterns of power and authority in classroom talk', in WOODS, P. *Teacher Strategies*, Beckenham, Croom Helm.
ERIKSON, K.T. (1966) *Wayward Puritans*, New York, Wiley.
ESLAND, G.M. (1971) 'Teaching and learning as the organization of knowledge', in YOUNG, M.F.D. (Ed.) *Knowledge and Control*, London, Collier-Macmillan.
EVANS, J. (1985) *Teaching in Transition*, Milton Keynes, Open University Press.
FESTINGER, L. (1957) *A Theory of Cognitive Dissonance*, Evanston, Row Peterson and Co.
FILMER, P. *et al.* (1972) *New Directions in Sociological Theory*, London, Collier-Macmillan.

FLOUD, J., HALSEY, A.H. and MARTIN, F.M. (1956) *Social Class and Educational Opportunity*, London, Heinemann.

FRANKENBURG, R. (1963) 'Taking the blame or passing the buck'. Paper presented to the British Association, 4 September 1963 (quoted in Lacey, 1970).

GALTON, M., SIMON, B. and CROLL, P. (1980) *Inside the Primary Classroom*, London, Routledge and Kegan Paul.

GARFINKEL, H. (1967) 'Studies in the routine grounds of everyday activities', in GARFINKEL, H. *Studies in Ethnomethodology*, New Jersey, Prentice-Hall.

GEER, B. (1971) 'Teaching', in COSIN, B. (1971) *School and Society*, London, Routledge and Kegan Paul.

GIBBS, J. (1966) 'Conceptions of deviant behaviour: The old and the new', *Pacific Sociological Review*, **9**, pp. 9–14.

GLASER, B. and STRAUSS, A. (1968) *The Discovery of Grounded Theory*, London, Weidenfeld and Nicolson.

GLEESON, D. (Ed.) *Identity and Structure*, Driffield, Nafferton.

GOFFMAN, E. (1961) *Encounters*, Indianapolis, Bobbs-Merrill.

GOFFMAN, E. (1968) *Asylums*, Harmondsworth, Penguin.

GOFFMAN, E. (1971) *The Presentation of Self in Everyday Life*. Harmondsworth, Penguin.

GOOD, T.L. and BROPHY, J.E. (1978) *Looking in Classrooms*, New York, Harper and Row.

GOODACRE, E. (1968) *Teachers and their Pupils' Home Background*, Slough, NFER.

HALSEY, A.H., FLOUD, J. and ANDERSON, C.A. (Eds) (1961) *Education, Economy and Society*, New York, Free Press.

HALSEY, A.H., HEATH, A.F. and RIDGE, J.M. (1980) *Origins and Destinations*, Oxford, Clarendon Press.

HAMMERSLEY, M. (1980) *A Peculiar World?: Teaching and Learning in an Inner City School*, Unpublished Ph.D. thesis, University of Manchester.

HAMMERSLEY, M. (1984) 'Staffroom news', in HARGREAVES, A. and WOODS, P. *Classrooms and Staffrooms*, Milton Keynes, Open University Press.

HARGREAVES, D.H. (1967) *Social Relations in a Secondary School*, London, Routledge and Kegan Paul.

HARGREAVES, D.H. (1972) *Interpersonal Relations and Education*, London, Routledge and Kegan Paul.

HARGREAVES, D.H. (1977) 'The process of typification in classroom interaction: models and methods', *British Journal of Educational Psychology*, **47**, pp. 274–84.

HARGREAVES, D.H., HESTER, S. and MELLOR, F. (1975) *Deviance in Classrooms*, London, Routledge and Kegan Paul.

HARRE, R. and SECORD, P.F. (1972) *The Explanation of Social Behaviour*, Oxford, Blackwell.

HARTLEY, D. (1980) 'Sex differences in the Infant school: Definitions and "theories"', *British Journal of Sociology of Education*, **1**, 1, pp. 93–105.

HARTLEY, D. (1985) *Understanding the Primary School*, Beckenham, Croom Helm.

HARTLEY, D. (1987) 'The time of their lives: Bureaucracy and the nursery school', in POLLARD, A. (1987) *Children and their Primary Schools*, London, Falmer Press.

HEIDER, F. (1958) *The Psychology of Interpersonal Relations*, New York, Wiley.

HOROWITZ, I. and STRONG, M.S. (Eds) (1971) *Sociological Realities: A Guide to the Study of Society*, New York, Harper and Row.

HUGHES, E.C. (1937) 'Institutional office and the person', *American Journal of Sociology*, **43**, pp. 404–13.

HUGHES, E.C. (1945) 'Dilemmas and contradictions of status', *American Journal of Sociology*, **50**, pp. 353–9.

HURN, C.J. (1978) *The Limits and Possibilities of Schooling*, Boston, Allyn and Bacon.

JACKSON, P.W. (1968) *Life in Classrooms*, New York, Holt, Rinehart and Winston.

JONES, E.E. and DAVIS, K.E. (1965) 'From acts to dispositions: the attribution process in person perception', in BERKOWITZ, L. (Ed.) *Advances in Experimental Social Psychology*, **2**, New York, Academic Press.

KECSKEMETI, P. (Ed.) *Essays on the Sociology of Knowledge*, Oxford, Oxford University Press.

KEDDIE, N.G. (1971) 'The social basis of classroom knowledge', in YOUNG, M.F.D. *Knowledge and Control*, London, Collier-Macmillan.

KELLY, G.A. (1955) *The Psychology of Personal Constructs*, London, Norton.

KING, R. (1978) *All Things Bright and Beautiful*, Chichester, Wiley.

KLAPP, O. (1962) 'Dynamics of self typing', in RUBINGTON, E. and WEINBERG, M.S., *Deviance: The Interactionist Perspective*, New York, Macmillan.

KOUNIN, J.S. (1970) *Discipline and Group Management in Classrooms*, New York, Holt Rinehart and Winston.

LACEY, C. (1970) *Hightown Grammar*, Manchester, Manchester University Press.

LEITER, K.C.W. (1974) 'Ad hocing in the schools: A study of placement practices in the kindergarten of two schools', in CICOUREL, A.V. (Ed.) *Language Use and School Performance*, New York, Academic Press.

LEMERT, E. (1967) *Human Deviance, Social Problems and Social Control*, New Jersey, Prentice-Hall.

LITTLE, A. and WESTERGAARD, J. (1964) 'The Trend of Class Differentials in England and Wales', *British Journal of Sociology*, **15**, (3), pp. 311–14.

LOFLAND, J. (1969) *Deviance and Identity*, New Jersey, Prentice-Hall.

LOFLAND, J. (1971) *Analysing Social Settings*, Belmont, Wadsworth.

LOFLAND, J. (1976) *Doing Social Life*, New York, Wiley.

LUNDGREN, U.P. (1977) *Model Analysis of Pedagogical Processes*, Stockholm, Stockholm University Press.

MACBEATH, J., MEARNS, D. and SMITH, M. (1986) *Home From School*, Glasgow, Jordanhill College of Education.

MANIS, J.G. and MELTZER, B.N. (1972) *Symbolic Interaction: A Reader in Social Psychology*, Boston, Allyn and Bacon.

MANNHEIM, K. (1952) 'On the interpretation of Weltanschaung' in KECSKEMETI, P. (Ed.) *Essays on the Sociology of Knowledge*, Oxford, Oxford University Press.

MATZA, D. (1964) *Delinquency and Drift*, New York, Wiley.

MARDLE, G. and WALKER, M. (1980) 'Strategies and structure: Some critical notes on teacher socialisation', in WOODS, P. *Teacher Strategies*, Beckenham, Croom Helm.

MCCALL, G.J. and SIMMONS, J.L. (1966) *Identities and Interactions*, New York, Free Press.

MCCALL, G.L. and SIMMONS, J.L. (1969) *Issues in Participant Observation*, Reading, Addison-Wesley.

MCHUGH, P. (1968) *Defining the Situation*, Indianapolis, Bobbs-Merrill.

MCINTYRE, D., MORRISON, A. and SUTHERLAND, J. (1966) 'Social and educational variables relating to teachers' assessments of primary school pupils', *British Journal of Educational Psychology*, **36**, pp. 272–9.

MCNAMARA, D.R. (1980) 'The outsider's arrogance: The failure of participant observers to understand classroom events', *British Educational Research Journal*, **6**, (2).

MEAD, G.H. (1934) *Mind, Self and Society*, University of Chicago Press.

MEAD, G.H. (1959) *The Philosophy of the Present*, Illinois Open Court.

MELTZER, B.N., PETRAS, J.W. and REYNOLDS, L.T. (1975) *Symbolic Interactionism: Genesis, Varieties and Criticism*, London, Routledge and Kegan Paul.

MERTON, R.K. (1957) *Social Theory and Social Structure*, New York, Free Press.

MILLS, C.W. (1940) 'Situated actions and vocabularies of motive', *American Sociological Review*, **5** (Dec 1940), pp. 904–13. Reprinted in COSIN, B. (1971) *School and Society*, London, Routledge and Kegan Paul.

MORTIMORE, P. (1988) *Better Schools*, London, Open Books.

References

Nash, R. (1973) *Classrooms Observed*, London, Routledge and Kegan Paul.
Natanson, M. (Ed.) (1962) *Alfred Schutz: Collected Papers 1: The Problem of Social Reality*, The Hague, Martinus Nijhoff.
Natanson, M. (1963) *Philosophy of the Social Sciences*, New York, Random House.
Nias, J. (1984) 'The definition and maintenance of Self in primary teaching', *British Journal of Sociology of Education*, **5**, (3), pp. 267–80.
Parkin, F. (1971) *Class, Inequality and Political Order*, St Albans, Paladin.
Parsons, T. (1966) *Societies: Evolutionary and Comparative Perspectives*, New Jersey, Prentice-Hall.
Pidgeon, D. (1970) *Expectations and Pupil Performance*, Slough, NFER.
Plowden Report (1967) *Children and their Primary Schools*, Report of Central Advisory Council (England) for Education, London, HMSO.
Plummer, K. (1979) 'Misunderstanding labelling perspectives', in Downes, D. and Rock, P. (Eds) *Deviant Interpretations*, Oxford, Martin Robertson.
Pollard, A. (1980) 'Survival threat in primary school classrooms', in Woods, P. (1980) *Teacher Strategies*, Beckenham, Croom Helm.
Pollard, A. (1985) *The Social World of the Primary School*, London, Holt, Rinehart and Winston.
Pollard, A. (1988) *Children and their Primary Schools*, London, Falmer Press.
Reynolds, D. and Sullivan, M. (1979) 'Bringing schools back in', in Barton, L. and Meighan, R. (1979) *Schools, Pupils and Deviance*, Driffield, Nafferton.
Reynolds, D. and Sullivan, M. (1987) *The Comprehensive Experiment*, London, Falmer Press.
Rist, R.C. (1970) 'Student social class and teacher expectations: The self-fulfilling prophecy in ghetto education', *Harvard Educational Review*, **40**, pp. 411–51.
Rogers, C. (1982) *A Social Psychology of Schooling*, London, Routledge and Kegan Paul.
Rose, A.M. (Ed.) (1962) *Human Behaviour and Social Processes*, London, Routledge and Kegan Paul.
Rosenthal, R. and Jacobson, L. (1968) *Pygmalion in the Classroom*, New York, Holt, Rinehart and Winston.
Roth, J.A. (1963) 'The study of career timetables' in Cosin, B. *et al.* (Eds) (1971) *School and Society*, London, Routledge and Kegan Paul.
Rubington, E. and Weinberg, M. (1973; 1987) *Deviance: The Interactionist Perspective*, New York, Macmillan.
Ryle, G. (1949) *The Concept of Mind*, London, Hutchinson.
Schatzman, L. and Strauss, A. (1973) *Field Research*, New York, Prentice-Hall.
Schur, E.M. (1971) *Labeling Deviant Behaviour: Its Sociological Implications*, New York, Random House.
Schutz, A. (1962) 'Concept and theory formation in the social sciences', in Natanson. M. (Ed.) *Alfred Schutz: Collected Papers I: The Problem of Social Reality*, The Hague, Martinus Nijhoff.
Schutz, A. (1963) 'Common-sense and scientific interpretation of human action', in Natanson, M., *Philosophy of the Social Sciences*, New York, Random House.
Schutz, A. (1967) *The Phenomenology of the Social World*, London, Heinemann.
Schutz, A. (1971) 'The stranger: An essay in social psychology', in Cosin, B. *School and Society*, London, Routledge and Kegan Paul.
Schutz, A. and Luckmann, T. (1974) *The Structures of the Life-World*, London, Heinemann.
Scott, M.B. and Lyman, M. (1968) 'Accounts', in Manis, J.G. and Meltzer, B.N. (1972) *Symbolic Interaction: A Reader in Social Psychology*, Boston, Allyn and Bacon.
Sharp, R. and Green, A. (1975) *Education and Social Control*, London, Routledge and Kegan Paul.

SMITH, D.E. (1978) 'K is mentally ill: The anatomy of a factual account', *Sociology*, **12**, 1, pp. 23–53.

STEBBINS, R.A. (1969) 'Studying the definition of the situation: Theory and field research strategies', *Canadian Review of Sociology and Anthropology*, **6**, (4) reprinted in MANIS, J.G. and MELTZER, B.N. (1972) *Symbolic Interaction: A Reader in Social Psychology*, Boston, Allyn and Bacon, pp. 337–55.

STRAUSS, A.L. (1959) *Mirrors and Masks*, New York, Free Press.

STUBBS, M. and DELAMONT, S. (1976) (Eds) *Explorations in Classroom Observation*, Chichester, Wiley.

SUDNOW, D. (1971) 'Dead on arrival', in HOROWITZ, I. and STRONG, M.S. (Eds) *Sociological Realities: A Guide to the Study of Society*, New York, Harper and Row.

SUDNOW, D. (1972) Studies in Social Interaction, New York, Free Press.

SYKES, G.M. and MATZA, D. (1957) 'Techniques of neutralization: A theory of delinquency', *American Sociological Review*, **22**.

THOMAS, W.I. (1928) *The Child in America*, Knopf.

THOMAS, W.I. (1931) 'The definition of the situation', in MANIS, J.G. and MELTZER, B.N. (1972) *Symbolic Interaction: A Reader in Social Psychology*, Boston, Allyn and Bacon.

TOMLINSON, S. (1982) *Educational Subnormality: A Study in Decision-Making*, London, Routledge and Kegan Paul.

TROYNA, B. (1987) (Eds) *Racial Inequality in Education*, London, Tavistock.

TURNER, R.H. (1962) 'Role-taking: Process versus conformity', in ROSE, A.M. (Ed.) *Human Behaviour and Social Processes* London, Routledge and Kegan Paul.

VERMA, G.K. and BAGLEY, C. (1982) *Self-Concept, Achievement and Multi-Cultural Education*, London, Macmillan.

WALLER, W. (1932) *The Sociology of Teaching*, New York, Wiley.

WARR, P.B. and KNAPPER, C. (1968) *The Perception of People and Events*, London, Wiley.

WERTHMAN, C. (1963) 'Delinquents in schools: A test for the legitimacy of authority' in COSIN, B. *et al.* (1971) *School and Society*, London, Routledge and Kegan Paul.

WHITTY, G. (1977) *School Knowledge and Social Control*, Milton Keynes, Open University.

WILLIS, P. (1977) *Learning to Labour*, Farnborough, Saxon.

WOODS, P. (1979) *The Divided School*, London, Routledge and Kegan Paul.

WOODS, P. (1980) *Pupil Strategies*, Beckenham, Croom Helm.

WOODS, P. (1980) *Teacher Strategies: Explorations in the Sociology of the School*, Beckenham, Croom Helm.

WOODS, P. (1983) *Sociology and the School*, London, Routledge and Kegan Paul.

WOODS, P. (1985) 'Ethnography and Theory Construction in the Study of Education', in BURGESS, R.G. (Ed.) *Field Methods in the Study of Education*, London, Falmer Press.

WOODS, P. (1986) *Inside Schools*, London, Routledge and Kegan Paul.

WRIGHT, C. (1987) 'Black students — white teachers', in TROYNA, B. *Racial Inequality in Education*, London, Tavistock.

YOUNG, M.F.D. (1971) *Knowledge and Control*, London, Collier-Macmillan.

Index